Your Garden Homestead

Books by Thomas and Betty Powell

THE AVANT GARDENER
A HANDBOOK AND SOURCEBOOK OF
ALL THAT'S NEW AND USEFUL IN GARDENING

YOUR GARDEN HOMESTEAD
ON INCHES, YARDS, OR ACRES

Your Garden Homestead

On Inches, Yards, or Acres

Thomas and Betty Powell

Illustrated with Photographs

Houghton Mifflin Company
Boston 1977

Library of Congress Cataloging in Publication Data

Powell, Thomas, date
  Your garden homestead on inches, yards, or acres.

  Bibliography: p.
  Includes index.
    1. Vegetable gardening. I. Powell, Betty, date
joint author. II. Title.
SB321.P66   635'.0973   77-672
ISBN 0-395-25404-3
ISBN 0-395-25403-5 (pbk.)

Printed in the United States of America

A   10 9 8 7 6 5 4 3 2 1

Dedicated to Robert Rodale,
who has called for "a new declaration of
individual independence, with gardening
as the basic act of liberation."

❧ Acknowledgments ❧

Many people over many years have contributed to this book — not only information but especially inspiration. We owe thanks to countless plantsmen, seedsmen, researchers and information specialists in horticultural institutions, government and industry who are developing the new plants, techniques and energy systems so greatly needed today.

Our deepest appreciation to Lee Goldman, Managing Editor of *Organic Gardening and Farming,* for much assistance and pleasure in his company; Sophie Powell, who inspired a lifelong interest in food of wholesome quality; Richard B. Farnham, in the top rank of horticulturist-teacher-communicators; Vincent Gisoldi, an Old World gardener who knows so much that should be in the books but isn't; Cholly Wong, for unfailing confidence and support; and most especially to our editor, Frances Tenenbaum, one of the most patient and perspicacious in the business.

❧ Contents ❧

❧ Introduction ❧

Our first vegetable garden was one of the great experiences of our lives, and it reinforced an idea we had long believed in: that one should do for oneself everything that one can. Growing even a small part of our own food has tremendous implications — physical, psychological, even political.

Grow-your-own isn't exactly a new concept in the modern urbanized world. People have been doing it for a long time in the towns and cities of Europe, particularly in France and Germany where the backyard vegetable plot is virtually a hallmark of solid citizenship. China is going much further, building a whole new agrarian society that will enable its vast numbers of people to live off the land should industrialization fail or energy sources be exhausted.

What is happening here only partially resembles the European experience, and is in one major respect the opposite of the trend in China. In America the new garden-homestead movement is totally unmanaged, undirected by any group and without formal structure. It is a quiet revolution, a peaceful one that originates with the individual. People all over the country are seeking a new kind of security based on personal autonomy. They start by growing as much of their own food as possible. Often they go on to build improved forms of shelter, test new energy systems, develop home businesses and work cooperatively with their neighbors. To the greatest extent they can, they provide for their own needs with their own hands, becoming producers instead of consumers, and in so doing find great satisfaction and personal growth.

There are many who believe that this course can give a new and positive direction to our national life, as it has already to the lives of those who are following it. This is not an unreasonable conclusion, for the new movement promotes a quality of life rather than a standard of living and so works against a great many economic and environmental ills.

This book is intended as an aid to those who want to move toward independence through self-sufficiency, to show how food gardening can be a means to the good life and a good living. We have stressed organic methods not only because pure food is a vital concern but also because these methods produce high-quality vegetables and fruits cheaply and safely. Our twice-monthly newsletter, *The Avant Gardener*, which we began publishing in 1968, covers all the newest developments in horticulture without emphasis on any particular "school" of gardening, but it is our personal feeling that the organic or natural method is the best for the home gardener and garden-homesteader. *The Avant Gardener*, incidentally, is an example of a cottage industry, for the two of us handle every phase of its production, promotion and mailing (except printing — there just isn't room for a press in our apartment!).

Gardening has been called a superb entrance into a different way of existence. We've found it so, and hope that you will too.

— Thomas and Betty Powell

Your Garden Homestead

⚔ 1 ⚔

Stake Your Claim!

AMERICANS ARE GOING BACK to the land — wherever they find it. Tomatoes and blueberries are being raised on high-rise balconies, countless suburban yards have their corn and soybean patches, and all-year indoor-outdoor production of vegetables and fruits is being practiced on a host of new garden-homesteads.

Even people who don't have land for gardens are gardening, through the tremendously popular community garden movement. Vacant land in cities and towns across the country is being divided into plots which are rented for nominal fees to anyone who wants to grow vegetables. Garden clubs, companies, churches, youth and senior citizen groups, block associations, landlords, tenant groups and others sponsor these "neighborhood farms" and "inflation gardens," and a nonprofit organization, Gardens For All (Charlotte, VT 05445), serves as a clearinghouse for information.

Along with all this has come a major revolution in techniques, products and plants. Growing-your-own has become much easier and more satisfying. There are new watering systems that keep a constant just-right supply of moisture in the soil, yet use less water than conventional methods. Little cubes of peat that swell up when moistened provide a super-easy, clean means of sowing seed to give crops a head start. Natural gardening methods produce free fertilizer from kitchen wastes, leaves, all sorts of readily available materials. Soil improvement has been made vastly easier by new lightweight tillers. Mulching has taken the hoeing out of gardening, and new plastics make it possible to grow crops while Jack Frost holds sway.

Seed companies and nurseries are producing a great array of crops tailored to the needs of the home gardener. More high-yield-

Growing their own and selling it at a roadside stand has given this couple the best kind of social security. (*U.S. Department of Agriculture*)

ing varieties of superior flavor have been bred in the past few years than in several previous decades. Characteristics of special value to the limited-space gardener have also received much attention. There are bush cucumbers, even bush watermelons that produce fruit in less space than a tomato vine, and 'Tiny Tim' tomatoes and the dwarf 'Bonanza' peach can be grown in containers anywhere. Earliness is being emphasized, too, not only to please the gardener who wants to be the first on the block to pick a ripe tomato, but also to enable him to "double-crop" his land by planting a second crop as soon as the first is harvested.

Many Happy Returns

What's behind this sudden surge of interest in gardening, this great new vitality in an art that — let's face it — has never been as highly regarded and devotedly practiced here as it has been in Europe? After all, gardening must compete with a multitude of other recreational activities, and yet it is more than holding its own.

The recent recession, of course, gave gardening much of its new impetus. With reduced incomes, and forced by the oil crisis to stay close to home, people turned to improving their own properties. And they discovered they could save quite a bit of money by growing their own food. More lawns and flower beds were torn up and converted into vegetable plots in the mid-1970s than in the Victory Garden years of the '40s.

Every $1 spent on seed and supplies, they found, returned at least $4 worth of food. A 15' x 25' vegetable plot could save the family budget $250 or more and provide fresh vegetables from spring through summer and frozen, canned or stored produce for the winter. The right-out-of-the-garden freshness and flavor of their crops was a bonus. And the exercise involved in planting, cultivating and harvesting them — actually creative exercise, since it produced a worthwhile product — proved to be both enjoyable and healthful.

But these were not the only rewards these gardeners reaped. They enjoyed a better diet. Their home-grown produce replaced much of the devitalized processed supermarket food that is low in nutritional value and high in calories and additives which do the body no good and may actually harm it.

Mass production and mass marketing, we're beginning to realize, have resulted in "food pollution" that is as potentially dangerous as air pollution. As Bess Myerson said while commissioner of New York City's Department of Consumer Affairs, "No reasonable person would knowingly drink a glass full of the chemicals he unwittingly consumes in his daily diet."

The economics of producing and getting a food product to the

A love of the land is one reason why Mr.
Jimmy Carter of Plains, Georgia, is
America's most prominent citizen! (*Charles
M. Rafshoon*)

market and making it more attractive than the competitor's product have made appearance, convenience and long shelf life the watchwords. Several thousand additives are currently used in achieving these objectives, from preservatives and artificial flavors and colors to softeners, hardeners, thickeners, texturizers, emulsifiers, alkalizers, stabilizers, bleaches, buffers, and so on. Some of these have already been banned because they have been proved dangerous to human health.

Another form of food pollution the grow-your-own consumer seeks to avoid is pesticide contamination. DDT was banned when the evidence of its accumulation in the human body became too strong to ignore, and several other persistent pesticides have since been phased out. But a great many powerful poisons are still used by farmers and fruit growers with virtually nothing known of the hazards to the human body their residues may cause.

Though allowable residues are very small, parts per million or parts per billion, there is the possibility that some of these chemicals even in tiny amounts may cause genetic changes, or that they may build up in the body to concentrations that will eventually be toxic to certain tissues. Another danger is the synergistic effect: two or more of these substances, each perhaps harmless alone, may interact to produce a third that is harmful. This applies to food additives as well as to agricultural chemicals — the Food and Drug Administration tests additives for toxicity singly, and so has no information on the combined effects of several consumed at one time.

Fruits and vegetables you grow yourself are not only free of this contamination, but they're also far more wholesome. The most startling health statistic of recent years is found in the latest Federal diet survey: more than 50% of Americans — and this includes

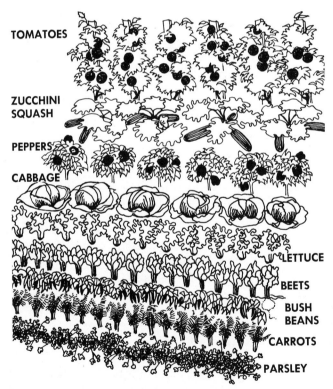

Less than $5 worth of seed will produce $100 worth of vegetables on a 10′ x 15′ plot.
(*National Garden Bureau*)

many middle- and upper-income families as well as the poor — do not have an adequate diet. Nutritionists are warning that the vast amount of processing to which our food is subjected greatly reduces its nutritional value, removing vitamins and minerals, altering proteins, and leaving empty calories. They link this decline in nutritional quality to the rising incidence of many diseases, most notably hypertension, heart disease, diabetes and certain types of cancer. "Hidden hunger," they say, may be a major causative factor in the majority of degenerative diseases.

The grow-your-own movement is at least in part a reaction to this. People are becoming health conscious and reversing the trend toward increased consumption of snack and convenience foods and decreased consumption of vegetables and fruits. The latter, by the way, are rich in non-nutritive fiber, the "bulk" that very recently has been found to be tremendously important for the health and proper functioning of the digestive tract.

Food choices and eating habits are changing. People are seeking food that is closer to its natural state, and the only way to be sure of getting it at its peak of flavor, freshness and nutritional value is to grow it themselves.

People Are Powerful

We should mention that growing it yourself has good effects beyond your own family. Our present system of agriculture and food marketing is energy-intensive: it takes 10 to 15 units of energy from fossil fuels to produce 1 unit of food energy on the table.

The fuel that runs all the machines used in growing food and transporting it to the consumer is only one aspect of this. Vast amounts of fuel are also expended in the production of agricultural chemicals, and even greater amounts in food processing. The Center for Science in the Public Interest reports it takes less than half the energy to grow potatoes at home that it takes to bring commercially grown potatoes to the market; home-grown apples take one-sixth the energy of farm-grown ones.

By substituting the family's labor and growing crops right where they are to be used, the food gardener is helping to reduce this vast expenditure of energy. Multiplied by millions of gardeners, the energy saved makes an impressive contribution toward avoiding future energy shortages.

The home gardener is also a champion recycler. While the farmer has not yet learned that it is practical and even profitable to renew the soil with organic wastes, the gardener routinely returns all plant residues to the soil. This greatly reduces the need to purchase fertilizers, and puts to use materials that would otherwise be wasted, or even disposed of in ways that pollute the environment.

Children won't choose junk foods when they
can have fruits and vegetables they've had a
hand in growing themselves! (*U.S.
Department of Agriculture*)

Soul-Building

There are all solid, practical reasons for the new popularity of gardening. But they are far from the only ones.

Working with the soil and plants satisfies a very basic need in people. This idea is emerging from a research study, called the People-Plant Program, being conducted by the American Horticultural Society (Mount Vernon, VA 22121). Plants not only beautify man's surroundings, but they also "add beauty and serenity to the 'landscape' of the human spirit," reports the Coordinator of the Program, Charles A. Lewis, Horticulturist at the Morton Arboretum (Lisle, IL 60532).

Studying stress situations, Mr. Lewis found that gardening has great therapeutic value. In the urban ghetto, mental hospital, physical rehabilitation center and prison,

> an intimate association with plants stimulates important social and behavioral responses . . . It has been responsible for reduced vandalism, cleaned streets, painted and repaired buildings, new neighborliness, and improved patient response . . .
>
> Plants are alive and communicate life qualities to those who tend them. Since no living thing is static but is always changing, plants speak of a dynamic stability through continuous change. The phases of growth from seedling to mature flowering plant follow a stable and orderly progression, not erratic and bizarre. They differ from life patterns in our technological society which respond rapidly to fads and other distractions and are subject to threats by new man-made terrors. The stability of plant growth indicates sustaining patterns in life . . .
>
> The feel of soil between fingers is something very basic, connecting one with all earth, even from a 25th floor apartment, hospital ward, or concrete-asphalt world . . . Plants provide a sense of natural place in non-natural surroundings. They tell us in an infinite variety of ways that beauty has not gone out of the world . . .

People appear to be "genetically programmed" to require plants in their immediate environment, says Dr. Hugh Iltis of the Univer-

Every Cleveland public school pupil learns the real values of working with nature in grow-your-own classes from kindergarten through high school. (*Cleveland Public Schools*)

sity of Wisconsin, who is investigating this concept for the American Association of Nurserymen. Everett Conklin, one of the most well known and respected interior landscape designers, comments that "research in human behavior seems to indicate a symbiotic relationship" between people and plants, and quotes a doctor as saying that "not only do plants need man's care to develop best, but man also requires direct contact with plants to develop and retain a mental wholeness."

In the 1975 B. Y. Morrison Memorial Lecture (sponsored annually by the Agricultural Research Service), Nash Castro of the National Park Service said:

> The movement today in society is away from the false, the shoddy, the ersatz, and toward the last things we touched that smacked of quality and life — soil, sun, air and water. It is as though we were seeking to touch base again, to reassure ourselves that we do indeed belong here . . . We fulfill ourselves by shaping nature, in response to nature's shaping us. We are most at ease in systems that bespeak the harmony that such man-and-nature can express.

Gardening, it seems, is more than just a marvelous antidote to the pressures and tensions of modern life. Green and growing things are a necessity to sustain the human spirit. A person tending a garden is not conscious of being old or young or beset by problems, but only of being a part of surging, growing life.

A whole new sense of values appears when you cultivate your own bit of earth, whether it is a few plants in containers or several acres. The frustration, confusion, uneasiness and disillusion that mark so much of American life are in great measure the result of our separation from nature.

Social Security

One aspect of the people-plant relationship that has barely been explored is a very special need we have today — the need to have some control over the production of our basic necessities. We're surrounded by impersonal agencies, by a philosophy of specialization that says only the expert knows anything, by a multitude of economic and social problems the individual cannot influence or often even understand. "Bigness" overwhelms us — big business, big labor, big government — and opportunities for accomplishment, creativity and decision-making are limited and restricted on all sides.

Growing at least some of your own food counteracts this as nothing else can. It promotes that wonderful feeling of independence and self-sufficiency that has been very nearly lost in modern life. It replaces a sense of powerlessness with a sense of security.

This security can be tangible as well as emotional. In *Small Is Beautiful: Economics As If People Mattered* (Harper & Row; $3.75) — one of the most important books of this decade — Dr. E. F. Schumacher proposes returning production to the people. Dr. Schumacher, who is not only one of England's most respected economists but also president of the Soil Association, Britain's oldest organic gardening and farming organization, envisions a whole new lifestyle built around production by the masses instead of mass production.

Big agriculture and big industry are resource-wasteful, squandering both the natural capital of the earth and man's substance. "Human-scale technology," on the other hand, does violence to neither the environment nor people. Dr. Schumacher, who is head of Intermediate Technology Development Groups, Ltd., a nonprofit London organization that researches and develops low-cost, low-

Projects such as the Community
Environmental Council's La Mesa in Santa
Barbara, California, integrate intensive food
growing with other new homestead
technology to develop "urban villages."
(*Community Environmental Council*)

energy tools and techniques, sees salvation in increasing people's ability to be self-sufficient. He calls for more cottage industries and more home growing of food by "methods which are biologically sound, build up soil fertility, and produce health, beauty, and permanence." A small factory can be as productive as an assembly-line plant, and a one-acre garden-homestead can be as efficient as a mechanized farm several hundred times its size.

This idea of building small, of decentralizing the production of food and goods, is receiving favorable attention even in the industrial and agribusiness sectors of the economy. But its greatest support is coming from people in all walks of life who have instinctively reached the same conclusions and are working to simplify their lives and stand more on their own feet. They're fighting as free individuals against a blight of synthetics, pollution and joyless occupations that stultify the human personality and that very possibly may eventually destroy human life.

They're doing this by creating "microenvironments" of beauty and productivity with plants wherever they live — and some of them are going much farther than that.

A Place to Grow

There's a great "reverse migration" from the cities, the U.S. Department of Agriculture reports. For 75 years, people left the farms in great numbers and went to the burgeoning urban centers. But now they're fleeing the central cities, many going to the suburbs but an even greater number going to the exurbs, the more rural small communities at the edge of the suburbs and beyond.

Ohio State University reports that 13 urban counties in Ohio lost population from 1970 to 1975, while 15 rural counties gained. In 1976, Pennsylvania had 1000 more farmers and 108,000 more acres in cultivation than it did in 1975. The Department of Agriculture's Population Studies Group says that four rural areas now lead the United States in population growth: the Ozarks from Oklahoma into Texas, the upper Great Lakes region, the Rocky Mountain area and the southern Appalachians. And recently the magazine *American Vegetable Grower* saluted a new wave across the nation of modern small-acreage garden-homestead-farmers who grow high-quality produce for themselves and for extra income.

This trend is continuing and increasing. A Gallup poll indicates that 68% of city dwellers would prefer to live in a suburban area, small town or rural area, or on a farm. A "sizable piece of land up to one acre" is regarded by 66% of all Americans as an important criterion for the selection of a new home, and a majority consider the opportunity to grow their own vegetables and fruits one of the most important reasons for owning a home.

The new back-to-the-land idea is attracting all groups, from youth and blue-collar workers to executives and retirees. People are making a conscious decision to find more real satisfactions by living closer to the earth and achieving independence and security through growing much or all of their own food. They back up this decision with intelligent planning and sufficient financing, they're prepared to learn the craft of food-growing in all its aspects, and they're taking advantage of and even developing a whole new technology of "free energy."

It will be a long time before solar energy will be harnessed on the large scale required by great cities, but already homes and private and commercial greenhouses are successfully using solar heating. The equipment presently available, though still primitive, is simple to install, moderate in cost and pays for itself quickly in fuel savings. Producing electricity economically from solar power is reportedly a decade or more away, but in many areas improved types of windmills can generate electricity efficiently on the scale needed for home use. Domestic wastes, instead of being wasted into the seas and rivers, are increasingly being converted into gas energy and fertilizers by means of methane digesters.

This new "soft" technology is being developed and disseminated by a number of research centers such as the New Alchemy Insti-

Two acres with a large garden, greenhouse and solar-heated home give a Connecticut family a fine measure of self-sufficiency. (*Thomas Powell*)

tute in Massachusetts, the School of Engineering of Stanford University in California, and the Organic Experimental Farm in Pennsylvania. These and others are also examining specialized food-producing techniques like aquaculture — high-yielding home culture of fish, shellfish, and algae — and devising smaller, less-energy-consuming machinery for the food gardener.

Some old tools and appliances are being revived and improved, too, such as the wood-burning stove, fruit press and stone grain mill. New forms of homes and plant-growing structures that are simple, permanent, energy-efficient, and respect the fragile fabric of the environment are coming from architects like Ken Kern and Malcolm B. Wells.

The subsistence arts can be learned from a wealth of new books or from the homesteading schools that are springing up from coast to coast. You can learn to build your own home or any other structure, for instance, from the Shelter Institute in Bath, Maine, or the Rural Skills Workshop in Seattle, Washington. For cash income, not only surplus crops but also an almost unlimited range of plant-related, craft, service, retailing and even small manufacturing businesses offer opportunities. Most modern homesteaders still work full- or part-time in factories and offices to which they commute — and this is being made easier by the exodus of industry from the cities — but the trend is toward developing home-based sources of income that confer a higher degree of independence.

One of the best things about the new garden-homesteads is that they entail far fewer sacrifices than were required of homesteaders in the past. The telephone and television are everywhere to supply instant communication; good roads and transportation insure freedom of movement, and an ever-growing number of mail-order companies provide easy access to almost any necessity or luxury.

——————— Gardening by Inches, Yards, or Acres ———————

How far one can or wants to go on the road to self-sufficiency is a matter of individual circumstances and abilities. Total subsistence farming, even with all the new plants, tools and methods that ease its labor and increase the chance of success, certainly is not for everyone. Limits of land, money, and time — not to mention temperament and capacities — put this beyond the reach or inclination of most people.

But in almost every situation, the grow-your-own features of the homestead can be applied to great benefit. The city dweller can have a tiny indoor, balcony or rooftop "farm," or share land in a vacant lot with neighbors in a community garden arrangement. The suburbanite with a third of an acre has ample room for a sizable garden and orchard. With a full acre, it's possible almost anywhere in the United States to provide a family of four with all the vegetables and fruits they can consume, plus meat, milk and eggs.

Maximizing food production on your land, however, does not mean turning it into a farm. As we will show later, many food plants are beautiful and provide shade, screening, color and other landscape values as well as bountiful crops. Vegetables from asparagus to zucchini are superb "edible ornamentals." Dwarf fruit trees are handsome and have magnificent bloom, and many nut trees supply as fine shade as any maple or elm. Many of our favorite flowers, from violets to daylilies, have edible blooms, leaves or roots that make them valuable dual-purpose plants.

The backyard, it's been said, is America's most neglected natural resource. It can produce lavishly; it can give the gardener exercise, fun, and control over what goes into the bodies of all who live on and from it. Making the home property an oasis of beauty and productivity improves the quality of the family's life — and the quality of life in the community.

Going "back to the land" is not really going back, it's going forward. In whatever degree it's practiced, it's moving toward a way of life that is more physically and emotionally satisfying, and that gives a measure of freedom from dependence on faraway economic powers and costly, precarious energy sources.

Its aim, as the renowned architect-planner-philosopher Lewis Mumford has said, is the good life instead of the "goods life." The latter has brought us pollution, shortages, worsening health and a joy-deadening loss of contact with the natural world. The good life, based on grow-your-own, promises — and delivers — just the opposite.

So get ready to stake your claim, So get ready to stake your claim! it.

⚡ 2 ⚡

An Eden of Edibles

WHEN THE GARDENER looks at edible plants in a new way, seeing their beauty as well as their utility, it soon becomes apparent that vegetables don't have to be grown in a vegetable plot, fruit and nut trees in orchard plantings, berries in a berry patch. Some vegetables are fine ornamentals for the front yard, and it's just as easy to have shade where you want it from a tree that produces a crop of fruit or nuts as from one that is merely decorative.

Many of our common crop plants have excellent landscaping value. But in addition to these, there are thousands of less well known plants that are both productive and ornamental. They range from grasses and groundcovers through flowers and bulbs to trees of all kinds and sizes. Those that don't produce food for people supply food and shelter for birds and small animals who help the gardener by keeping pests in check, or are valuable as "companion plants" for direct control of insects and diseases.

―――――――――――― Mixed Vegetables ――――――――――――

Vegetables offer forms, colors and textures found in no other plants, and a good gardener can develop real artistry in combining them with each other and with other plants.

Study illustrated seed catalogs and you'll see a great many possibilities. Chives, parsley, lettuce in many colors, beets, and carrots are excellent as edgings. New Zealand spinach and curly kale make fine small-area groundcovers. Parsley and lettuce can be interplanted among spring bulbs. Flowering cabbage and kale provide magnificent colors late in the season.

The vivid green leaves and red stalks of rhubarb chard are spectacular combined with white alyssum or sweet william in flower

The bright curly leaves of kale add unusual beauty to the garden in autumn. (*Organic Gardening and Farming*)

beds. The many kinds of peppers and eggplants lend an exotic touch to flower plantings, too — try them as background for pink or scarlet petunias. Brussels sprouts are tropical-looking. Radishes may be tucked in wherever there are spare inches. 'Royalty' purple-pod beans and purple-headed cauliflower add unusual color, while texture is provided by the lacy leaves of endive, curly-leaved mustard, and corn salad's pretty rosette of rounded leaves.

Okra is very useful with its hibiscus-like foliage and flowers, celeriac makes a handsome 36″ accent plant, and even low-growing bushy tomatoes like the 18″ 'Dwarf Champion' and 'Stakeless' are good border subjects. For feathery foliage on a 30″ plant, there is Florence fennel or finocchio. Garlic has long grassy leaves. Bush-type squashes have decorative bright green foliage, and zucchini hybrids and the new yellow 'Seneca' squash have beautiful blooms and foliage.

Don't neglect the unusual vegetables — the ground cherry or husk tomato, for example, is a pretty much-branched plant with yellow flowers and fruit in an inflated calyx, and Spanish peanuts bear orange blooms on clover-like plants. Salsify has grassy leaves and daisy flowers. Globe artichoke is dramatic, with spiny foliage and thistle flowers.

Corn is one of the very few plants not suited to mixing with many other plants — for proper pollination, it should be grown in a patch. But even corn can be improved in appearance by planting two vines of climbing beans, Indian style, to grow up each stalk.

Herbs have unusual beauty and thrive in
poor soil with virtually no maintenance.
(*Hertha Benjamin*)

This works well with other tall-stalked plants, like Jerusalem artichoke and sunflowers. Actually, any crop that will climb should not be allowed to waste ground space by crawling. Many cucumbers, squashes and melons, as well as pole beans, scarlet runner beans, climbing tomatoes and Malabar spinach can "beautify" a fence, stone wall, dead tree, trellis, building wall, even the compost heap. An unusually handsome climber is the chayote or vegetable pear, a fast grower with big lobed leaves and furrowed green fruits.

Remember that root and leaf crops can tolerate a little shade, which enhances their design usefulness. In spacing plants, keep in mind their size at maturity. Be wary of competing tree and shrub roots.

And don't forget that many vegetables — not only salad crops, but also tomatoes, eggplant, even squash and melons — can be grown in containers. Ground, wall and window boxes, or more unusual containers like hanging baskets, pillow paks and moss walls, are all suitable and make productive and decorative use of otherwise unplantable space (see Chapter 4 for more about these).

Permanent Producers

The backbone of any edible ornamental garden should, of course, be perennial plants — those that produce harvests year after year with little maintenance. The few perennial vegetables, fortunately, are highly decorative. Rhubarb's big shining heart-shaped leaves and red stems make it a fine accent for shrubbery, the edge of the patio or in flower borders. The ferny foliage of asparagus provides a fine background for flowers all summer. Jerusalem artichoke, whose underground tubers have more food value than potatoes, grows 6' to 10' tall and is an excellent screen or background plant that bears yellow flowers. Several species of bamboo, particularly of the genus *Phyllostachys*, are not only valued for screening but also produce crisp shoots in spring, delicious parboiled and sautéed or used raw in salads and Oriental dishes. And for a bold specimen plant, there is comfrey, with handsome deep green, broad sword leaves, rich in food value and useful in salads or like spinach.

And there's always room for herbs, since only a few plants will supply ample seasonings, teas and medicinal aids. Many, both annual and perennial, offer colors and textures that suggest their planting in numerous areas of the garden. Green- or purple-leaved basil is invaluable for bold edging effects . . . rosemary has beautiful gray-green needle foliage . . . fennel and dill are outstanding for feathery foliage, tansy is ferny . . . rue, with delicate blue-green leaves, yellow-green flowers and red-brown seedpods, makes an unusually attractive specimen or low hedge . . . two especially fine mints for the border are curly spearmint and woolly apple mint . . . borage is a rapid grower and bears purest blue flowers . . . 3″ lemon thyme and 6″ common thyme are great edgers or groundcovers for hot spots.

Consider herbs for container as well as ground planting, and remember that while most herbs need full sun, a few — lovage, chervil, mints, sweet cicely, costmary — stand some shade.

Floral Delicacies

Most gardeners know that nasturtium flowers and leaves impart delightful flavor and color to sandwiches, salads and soups. But there are dozens of other "flower edibles." Oriental cooks prize daylily buds and flowers, boiling or sautéing them and adding them to soups, vegetable and meat dishes. Young leafy shoots of *Chrysanthemum coronarium,* called chopsuey greens, are used like spinach, and chrysanthemum petals enhance the flavor of numerous Chinese dishes.

Dried marigold petals give rich color and flavor to sauces, puddings, soups. Yucca flowers have an asparagus flavor and are used raw, creamed, boiled, fried and in soups. Violet leaves and flowers are rich in vitamins A and C and may be shredded into salads or omelets. Pansy, tulip and gladiolus flowers are edible, carnations have a spicy flavor, teas are made of hollyhock, lavender, marigold and honeysuckle blooms; and roses are candied, made into wine, and used in everything from syrups and puddings to omelets, pancakes and crab salad.

Not all flowers are safe to eat, so check a source such as *The Forgotten Art of Flower Cookery*, by Leona Woodring Smith (Harper & Row).

Feast of Fruit

Today almost any fruit tree or shrub on the market makes a wonderful edible ornamental for any garden. There's been a revolution in garden fruits, with a tremendous increase in easy-to-grow, climatically adapted dwarf and semi-dwarf trees and high-yielding berry plants.

A dozen or more dwarf trees will fit into the space required by one standard tree. The gardener can have apples, peaches, pears, plums, cherries, apricots and nectarines bordering a path or fence, in shrub borders, even in foundation plantings. These mini-trees will produce lavish spring flower displays plus fruit as large as standard trees, in return for simple care. A selection of varieties can give a continuous and varied harvest from early summer to late fall.

Dwarf trees can be made even dwarfer by growing them in tubs and pruning the roots as well as the tops. Or you can grow the new very small but highly productive genetic (natural) dwarfs, such as 'Bonanza' and 'Golden Treasure' peaches, 'Nectarina' nectarine and 'North Star' cherry, ideal for container culture.

There are some old-new training methods for in-the-ground plants, too, that make it possible to grow fruit in extremely confined space. The time-honored art of espalier, or making plants grow in a flat plane, is one of the best of these. Besides espaliering plants against a wall, you can make free-standing espaliers, trained on wires stretched between posts, for garden dividers, screens, path liners and enclosures (espalier methods and plants are described in the catalog of the specialist Henry Leuthardt Nurseries, East Moriches, NY 11940; 25¢). These "fruiting fences" are so high-yielding that commercial orchardists have adopted the method, calling it "trellising." Less of an architecturally handsome feature but equally productive is the hedgerow system — the trees are planted 6' apart and pruned to make a dense hedge.

Some less well known fruits are decorative assets grown almost anywhere on the home grounds. Figs are striking plants, and can be grown much farther north than most people realize. The native pawpaw or "hardy banana," which bears clusters of delicious 4" to 5" fruits, is a showy small tree with lustrous tropical-looking foliage and fragrant purplish flowers. Another very pretty small tree is the Chinese jujube, with shining light green leaves and sweet round fruits that look and taste like dates.

The new natural dwarfs produce full-size fruit on very small pretty trees. (*Armstrong Nurseries*)

The beautiful foliage, flowers and fruits of
blueberries make them an asset in
foundation plantings or anywhere else in the
garden. (*Organic Gardening and Farming*)

Few gardeners know the American persimmon, but it is much
hardier than the Oriental persimmon grown in the South, and
many consider its fruit more flavorful. This handsome 50′ tree
thrives as far north as the Great Lakes. A smaller but equally fine
ornamental is the 25′ quince tree — now also available in a 10′ to
15′ dwarf form — which has marvelous spring bloom and bears
large golden fruit.

Three beautiful round-headed trees that give excellent shade as
well as fruit are the white, black and red mulberries. Certain flowering crabapples, besides giving spectacular spring bloom, produce
extra-large and flavorful fruits for eating raw and making jelly,
apple butter and cider. There's even an edible-fruited dogwood,
called the Cornelian cherry, a small tree or shrubby hedge plant
that bears yellow flowers and abundant red "plums" good for
sauces, jellies and preserves. Some other popular trees which
have species that bear good edible fruits are hawthorn, mountain
ash, hackberry and shadblow.

If you'd like something really unusual in fruit trees, here are two
worthy subjects, one very old and one very new. The medlar dates
back to ancient times but is still highly regarded by connoisseurs
for its delectable clingstone fruits. The Chinese che, which bears

red-fleshed fruit of unique flavor, is so new it's still being studied and tested for hardiness and cultural needs, but it promises to be one of the finest new edible ornamentals. (See Chapter 7 for details on these.)

The bush fruits also present exciting landscaping possibilities. Blueberries are beautiful plants in every season, and as specimen plants or hedges rival almost any nonfruiting plant. Blackberries and red, yellow, black and purple raspberries make attractive high-yielding hedgerows, or they can be trained on horizontal wires. In the South, the same can be done with loganberries, boysenberries, youngberries and dewberries. Currants bear flowers and fruit profusely on 4' to 8' shrubs and are especially valuable because they will stand some shade. Some American and European gooseberries yield fruits near the size of eggs, and the bushes are handsome in almost any garden situation.

Gardening's new popularity is spurring improvement in a number of fruit-bearing shrubs that lack orcharding potential but are ideal for the home grower. Improved varieties of the beautiful white-flowered elderberry, a fine specimen, hedge or screen plant, have larger berries of superior flavor for pies, jelly and wine. Some of the new varieties of viburnum, particularly of the species known as the American highbush cranberry, yield extra-large crops of red berries. Selections are also being made of the autumn olive to produce a handsome tall shrub that yields great quantities of fruit.

Handsome foliage and colorful fruit make grapevines a landscape asset when trained on trellises or arbors. (*Organic Gardening and Farming*)

'Cardinal' autumn olive has beautiful silvery
leaves and yellow flowers, and bears big
crops of berries. (*Soil Conservation Service*)

The bush cherries are valuable garden fruits, and their new hybrids with plums, called cherryplums, should be even more useful.
More well known, at least in coastal areas, is the beach plum,
which has showy white blooms and purple fruits and which will do
as well inland as on the dunes. There are even roses, certain of
**the long-blooming and pest-free shrub types, that produce great
crops of "hips," which are extremely high in vitamin C.**
Finally, nut trees are among the best ornamental food resources.
In just about any part of the country, you can find at least one
species or variety that will bear dependably. There are nut trees
small enough for hedges and foundation plantings (filberts, hazels,
filazels), quite a few in the 20′ to 35′ range for lawn plantings
(almonds, Chinese chestnuts, chinkapins), and towering giants
(pecans and walnuts). All the nut trees are wonderful minimum-
maintenance ornamentals that return big dividends in flavorful,
nutritious food.

────── Stop, Look, Listen — Then Landscape ──────

Unless you have almost unlimited acreage, your biggest problem
will be how to grow as many of these plants as possible without

creating a cluttered, piecemeal or jungle effect — in other words, how to design your plantings for maximum productivity and maximum beauty, without sacrificing one for the other.

This means planning, and taking time to learn about your land so the planning will be intelligent. The new homeowner who thoughtlessly hastens to alter the landscape runs the risk of disrupting its vital ecological systems, thereby destroying the very values for which the land was purchased. So before making any drastic changes, get to know your property at all hours, in all seasons and all weather.

Study first its macroclimate — the way the sun crosses it, the direction of prevailing winds, any problems of runoff from or onto the property in heavy rains. Then make what landscape architects call a site survey, a simple plan to scale on graph paper that shows existing structures, the driveway, paths and plants.

The last two of these may be left largely as they are, but usually they will be subjected to what horticulturist Alan D. Cook calls the "RRAM" principle: Removal, Replacement, Addition and Movement. Some plants and paths may be removed completely for bet-

The new dwarf varieties of American elderberry have beautiful flowers and foliage, and grow only 5' to 6' tall. (*New York State Agricultural Experiment Station*)

The carefree rugosa roses bloom all summer,
then produce hips that are very rich in
vitamin C. (*Soil Conservation Service*)

ter traffic flow through the garden or to make room for such necessities as a utility area where the compost heap, tool shed and
other garden work items are grouped. Many plants will probably
need replacement by better species or varieties — don't cringe at
digging out a plant that's inferior in quality, disease-prone or unproductive. You'll likely be adding a great many permanent
plants, but also consider which of the existing plants might be
transplanted to locations where they will grow better, look better or
contribute shade, screening or other amenities.

For wind, snow and/or noise control, and perhaps for privacy,
you'll want some "living screens." Small trees and large shrubs on
the windward side of your property will reduce wintry blasts that
raise heating bills and hot summer winds that stunt plant growth
(a 20 mph wind, England's National Vegetable Research Station
reports, reduces the weight of lettuce by 60%). Plants, says William Flemer III of Princeton Nurseries, are much more effective
than solid walls: wind striking a solid barrier is forced upward,
causing considerable turbulence on the lee side, but some wind
will pass through a plant barrier to create what is known in aero-
dynamics as spoiling currents, which dampen turbulence.

Some good ornamental edibles for cutting wind, trapping snow
and absorbing noise are filberts, elderberries, highbush cranberry,

buffalo berry and autumn olive. It's a good practice in areas of severe winter winds to choose plants that are hardy farther north than your location, since wind increases the chilling. All plants in windbreaks and shelterbelts should be planted sufficiently close together to insure that their outer branches will interlace.

Also helpful in conserving energy are deciduous trees on the south and west side of the house. In summer they shade the home to keep it cool, in winter their leafless branches block very little of the warming sun.

How much lawn is essential to you? A lawn requires mowing, feeding and watering, taking time you may need for more productive plants. Groundcovers and mulches can make equally attractive "groundscapes." But no matter how large or small a turfgrass area you decide on, make it as low-maintenance as possible by giving it a good foundation. Mix in organic matter liberally to 6″ depth when preparing the seedbed (or grow a green manure crop

Many a front lawn these days is being converted to vegetable production, with results pleasing to both the eye and palate. (*National Garden Bureau*)

for one or two seasons) to make a rich, healthy soil, and use high-quality seed.

You can plant the best locally recommended grass — usually an improved Kentucky bluegrass or a bluegrass-fescue-ryegrass mixture in the North, bermudagrass in the South — or use a special minimum-maintenance grass. Centipede grass is being grown increasingly in the South, making a low, dense turf on poor soil with little fertilizing. In northern states, red fescues produce a fine-textured, easy-care sod. There are varieties of zoysia for almost every state, and in most areas this grass needs mowing only every three or four weeks, but remember that this is strictly a hot-weather grass — it is a glorious bright green all summer, but from fall through midspring it looks like a close-cut field of straw. Don't look on white clover, by the way, as a pest in the lawn, for it is a legume that takes nitrogen from the air and feeds it to the other grasses, making less fertilizing necessary.

A poor lawn can be made into a fine one without digging if you're patient. Simply mow the grass very close — actually scalping it — after a good spring rain. Then apply seed and organic fertilizer at the rate directed for making new lawns. Sprinkle lightly and often to encourage sprouting. Through the summer and autumn, mow the grass no lower than 3″. Repeat this process each year until the increasingly vigorous new grasses completely crowd out the ragged and weedy old growth.

In making all these decisions, look at your property with a completely open mind. Don't be influenced by your neighbors' gardens, but consider only what is suitable for your land and you. Just as there are no longer any conventions or rigid standards in dress — the idea is to look natural and comfortable — so should your garden suit you, rather than conforming to any locally popular style or a particular school of landscape architecture. It's what you have to live with and work with, so it should be what you want and like.

Knowing a few principles of landscape design, however, can be very helpful. Every plant should be evaluated in terms of four characteristics — size (at maturity), form, texture and color. These determine how well plants will blend or contrast with each other, and influence every landscape objective. To achieve a feeling of distance and spaciousness, for example, use the size of plants to advantage: plant progressively smaller trees and shrubs in the distance . . . or form: contrast rounded plants with tall columnar ones . . . or texture: plant bold large-leaved plants in the foreground and compact small-leaved ones farther away . . . or color: closely knit masses of a single color draw the eye farther afield than mixed colors.

A garden should be peaceful as well as productive. A feeling of serenity results from keeping the design simple and unified, avoiding all fussy effects and jarring notes. Long smooth curves are better than undulating ones. The color white will blend many design elements that otherwise would clash. So will a groundcover, or any large massing of plants of one or two species or varieties.

Landscaping can be a complex subject, and if you really get into it you'll find yourself using terms such as balance, scale, sequence and emphasis, thinking of plants as space articulators and mood delineators, and using techniques like pooling and enclavement. All of this is fascinating but not at all necessary to achieving your twin goals of beauty and productivity. Remember that nature is the best guide, and you won't go wrong if you look at each area of your garden as well as the garden as a whole as a smaller but enhanced version of nature's fields and woods, hills and valleys.

Window boxes, a window greenhouse and raised beds all contribute to the beauty and productivity of a city garden. (*Hertha Benjamin*)

Many gardeners seem to realize this instinctively, for the new vogue in landscaping is the naturalistic garden. It has much to recommend it — minimal maintenance, often unusual beauty, and a feeling of "ecological fitness."

In its simplest aspects, it means avoiding straight lines and unnatural shearing of plants. Sweeping lines and flowing shapes are more pleasing than squared or angular beds, borders and paths. The exception, of course, is row crops, but even here varying the lengths of rows or growing in clumps and beds helps to avoid a shooting-gallery effect.

Mixed plantings, in fact, are the key to naturalistic landscaping. A mingling of trees, shrubs and groundcover plants is practiced wherever feasible. Foundation plantings, for example, are no longer the monotonous parade of upright evergreens alternated with spreading ones — all soon outgrowing the space assigned to them — that have been commonplace for so long. Instead, curved beds of low shrubs of varying forms, textures and tones are used, interplanted with flowers and even low-growing vegetables.

At the house corners, taller shrubs are added, and perhaps a small tree if the house is big and imposing. For good proportion, the largest plant is placed out from the corner at a 45° angle. Extend the plantings well beyond the corner if you want to make a small house look longer; sweep them forward more into the front yard to shorten a long house.

Hedges should be informal, and blueberries, beach plum, rugosa roses and others serve beautifully. Many of these plants also blend well into mixed borders, combined with all sorts of lower-growing and taller plants. If a border of this kind is not needed or wanted, there's almost always room for a miniature woodland in a corner of the garden. A medium-sized tree or one or two small ones, with an "understory" of shrubs and a carpeting of low herbaceous plants, provides a carefree planting that is attractive in all seasons and, like hedges and shrub borders, provides food and homes for helpful wildlife.

A fascinating feature for a slightly to much larger garden is a cultivated meadow. Sometimes called an alpine lawn, it is composed of grasses, clover and wildflowers, and requires only clipping every four to six weeks when it reaches a height of 4″ to 8″. It need not be extensive in area, for even a small meadow is always interesting because it changes from day to day as the various plants grow, bloom and go to seed. In the Midwest, a popular variation is the prairie lawn. A sod of buffalo grass, sideoats gramma and blue gramma needs cutting only two or three times a year and makes a beautiful tight carpet on the poorest soils without watering. A specialist in these grasses is Wilson Seed Farms (Polk, NE 68653).

A wild section of the garden improved by
thinning and planting will produce food for
wildlife and even for the gardener.
(*Clarendon Gardens*)

If you have fairly extensive acreage, consider leaving part of it in
its wild state except for some thinning and selective replacement
of plants. Such an area will supply wild fruits, nuts and many
weeds that make good eating with virtually no work on your part
once it is established in the form you want it, and will also support
a great variety of birds and small animals that hold down crop
pests. Many states supply plants at very nominal cost through
their departments of conservation, forestry or environmental protection (secure addresses from the State House in the capital).
Connecticut, for instance, offers a "Wildlife Buffer Bunch" of 50
tree, shrub and vine seedlings for $6, and in Ohio every Soil Con-
servation District provides "Wildlife Packets" at $5.75, containing
45 tree or 40 shrub seedlings. Several nurseries are also valuable
sources, particularly Dutch Mountain Nursery (Augusta, MI
49012), a specialist in wildlife plants.

An "improved wild" landscape is both self-sustaining and productive. These advantages can be gained in a more cultivated garden landscape, too, by two simple tactics: grow as many native
plants as possible, and give every plant you grow the right site.

Plants that are native to your area are well adapted to its climate
and have natural resistance to disease. They establish quickly and
need minimum care. They are almost always far more beautiful in
the garden, where they have better soil and less competition from

other plants, than they are in the woods or field. Many of them are fine edible ornamentals, such as the wild cherries and plums, or the delightful woodland strawberries that do so well when transplanted into the shade of acid-loving plants like rhododendron and laurel.

In transplanting shrubs from the wild, a horticulturist advises cutting them back to the ground but carefully lifting as much of the root system as possible. The sprouts that come up from these roots will have better form and color than the original top growth. There are also nurseries that specialize in native plants, such as the Dutch Mountain Nursery mentioned previously, Valley Nursery (Box 845, Helena, MT 59601), and The Shop in the Sierra (Midpines, CA 95345; catalog 50¢). Two sources of seed are J. L. Hudson, Seedsman (Box 1058, Redwood City, CA 94064; catalog 50¢) and F. W. Schumacher Co. (Sandwich, MA 02563). To give seedlings a good start, it usually pays to establish a small nursery bed where they will not be subjected to competition from larger plants.

Investment Planning

Before buying any plant, learn all you can about it so you'll give it the proper microclimate — a location where soil, moisture, sun and wind are right for it. Siting a plant in a hospitable microclimate where its ecological requirements are met lets it develop its full potential without coddling by the gardener. Many plants adapt to a wide range of growing conditions, but others have special needs such as wet or acid soil, shade, or protection from wind, and not paying attention to these will result in disappointment.

Much of this information can be gleaned from books, but it's an even better idea to get to know your local nurseryman and your county agricultural agent or the horticultural specialist at your County Extension Service Office. The extension office also has many helpful publications. When traveling, visit nurseries, garden centers, arboretums and botanical gardens, and never hesitate to ask questions. Two aids to locating these are the *Directory of American Horticulture* (American Horticultural Society, Mount Vernon, VA 22121; $5), and the excellent plant buyer's guide, *The Green Thumbook* (Valley Crafts, 168 Rainbow Lane, Cary, IL 60013; $2.95).

When buying plants, avoid bargains, which can be low-grade or nearly lifeless plants, and beware of flashy advertisements for "miracle" plants — these are usually weed trees and shrubs. In buying locally, look for healthy vigorous plants, well branched and nicely shaped, with good root systems and no sign of pest or disease injury. Mail-order purchases should be made whenever possible from a nursery in the same general climatic zone as your garden, for a plant grown in a southern nursery may not be as hardy and productive in northern gardens as the same species grown in a nursery up north.

When anything cannot be planted as soon as it is received, unwrap it and moisten the roots, then heel it in — plant it leaning at a 45° angle in a trench filled with moistened peatmoss and soil in a protected spot.

Don't be tempted to buy large plants for quicker results. You can make slow-growing trees grow fast, says horticulturist Richard B. Farnham:

> Do not even think to save time by buying a big size. A younger tree is usually in a much better condition to recover from transplanting and often catches up with the more costly specimen in a few years. The secret of fast growth after planting a tree is a wide hole, not a deep one, to be filled with soil mixed with one-fourth by volume of compost or moist peat.
>
> The floor of the hole must support the roots at a level where the trunk will be covered to the same depth as in the nursery. The loose soil of a deeper hole would allow settling later. Planting too deep kills more trees than anything else except too much water after planting. Following planting, place guy wires to hold the tree against swaying. Then saturate the loose soil with water running gently, cover the soil surface with a coarse mulch like salt hay or leaves, and forget it until summer drought when it should receive a weekly soaking the first year. Add fertilizer and reinforce the mulch each spring for three years. Your slow-growing tree will by then be growing fast. We have produced 5′ of growth on a red oak in a single year by such treatment.

Mr. Farnham also suggests that the least expensive fence post is a living one:

> Tree seedlings are common in most yards. Those with smaller leaves can be very ornamental fence posts. The elm, honeylocust and flowering crab, for instance, continue in health, without root spread, if allowed to develop a trunk to the desired height for your fence top, and then are clipped once a month to a foliage globe about 1′ in diameter at the top of the trunk. The secret of root control is that the roots of most plants are dependent on receiving the sugars made by the plant leaves. When the top is trimmed, one finds the roots limited in almost the same degree.

In flowers, give priority to long-blooming and/or long-lived, easy-care annuals and perennials that won't take time needed by major productive plants. Daylilies, hardy asters and iris go on forever.

Daffodils will bloom for 25 years when planted properly, and they can be naturalized in the lawn or groundcovers. In annuals, marigolds, zinnias, ageratum and several others will give bloom from late spring to frost, but even better are those that perpetuate themselves by reseeding. One of the best of these is nicotiana or flowering tobacco, which produces fragrant, long-lasting white, pink or rosy orange-blossom flowers all season and self-sows to repeat its impressive performance year after year.

Down to Earth

Developing a garden-homestead isn't an overnight proposition. But it can be done a lot more quickly than you might think. Vegetables and many dwarf fruits give almost immediate returns to encourage you while you're waiting for slower-growing plants to mature.

Be flexible — your master plan will probably undergo quite a few changes as you learn more about the plants you want to grow. But more important, organize your efforts and don't attempt too much at once, and you won't get discouraged, strain your budget, or miss any of the pleasure of watching each seedling develop into a plant of distinctive character.

All gardening, of course, begins with the soil. It's basic to all beauty and productivity, for there are no strong, healthy plants without strong, healthy roots. This means treating the soil for what it is: a living thing, not a sterile medium. It needs constant renewal, not only of its inert materials but also of its biological life. To supply the raw materials for this renewal in the most efficient way, we turn to natural gardening. This form of gardening operates in harmony with nature, and as we shall see in the next chapter, it grows superior plants with maximum satisfaction to the gardener and no harm to the environment.

Plotting Your Plantscape

The Dictionary of Useful Plants, by Nelson Coon (Rodale Press, Emmaus, PA 18049; $10.95)

The Earth Manual, by Malcolm Margolin (San Francisco Book Company/Houghton Mifflin; $10 hardcover, $5.95 paperback)

Edible Fruited Trees and Shrubs Combining Beauty and Utility, by the Morton Arboretum (Lisle, IL 60532; 10¢ plus stamped #10 envelope)

The Edible Ornamental Garden, by John E. Bryan and Coralie Castle (101 Productions, 834 Mission Street, San Francisco, CA 94103; $7.95 hardcover, $3.95 paperback)

Gardening For Good Eating, by Helen Morgenthau Fox (Collier-Macmillan; $1.95)

A Handbook of Edible Ornamentals, Research Report No. 2, R & D Group Publications (Rodale Press, Emmaus, PA 18049; $2)

Landscaping Your Home, by William R. Nelson, Jr. (University of Illinois Press, $8.95 . . . also available in paperback for $4 from the Office of Agricultural Publications, University of Illinois, 123 Mumford Hall, Urbana, IL 61801)

Nature's Guide to Successful Gardening and Landscaping, by William Flemer III (Crowell; $8.95)

Sturtevant's Edible Plants of the World, edited by U. P. Hedrick (Dover; $5)

Working With Nature, by John Brainerd (Oxford University Press; $15)

Wyman's Gardening Encyclopedia, by Donald Wyman (Macmillan; $17.50)

✎ 3 ✎

Making Soil Grow

NATURAL GARDENING is the oldest, and yet at the same time a brand new, way of gardening. Many a gardener and farmer practiced it instinctively down through the centuries, but we've had to rediscover it very recently.

About a hundred years ago, gardening and farming started to go off the track. The agricultural revolution that occurred along with the industrial revolution was based on solid new knowledge of the principles of plant growth — but as is so often the case with early research, much of the knowledge was fragmentary and gave only a partial picture. When the German scientist Justus von Leibig, for example, found that nitrogen, phosphorus and potash were the major constituents of plant matter, it was concluded that simply applying these three chemicals to the soil would keep it producing good crops indefinitely. In the field of pest control the same fragmentation prevailed, each new pesticide being hailed as a way to more and better crops without regard to any possible drawbacks.

Nature was no longer seen as a whole, as a balanced system in which each part complements or corrects others. The cycle of life which assures constant renewal of the soil by the return of all wastes to it was ignored, and the balance between destructive insects and the beneficial ones that keep them in check was disrupted. The results were depleted soils that required more and more fertilizer to keep them producing, and a never-ending battle to develop new and more powerful pesticides.

About 30 years ago, the idea that this approach might be wrong occurred to a man named J. I. Rodale. He published the first issue of a magazine he called *Organic Gardening* in May 1942, and vigorously promoted the heretical concept of working with nature

Soybeans fertilized with composted sludge
are analyzed by Agricultural Research
Service scientists studying the soil-improving
values of sludge. (Agricultural Research Service)

The gardener who follows nature's method
of replenishing the soil with every available
organic waste reaps many plant-growth and
health rewards. (*Organic Gardening and
Farming*)

instead of fighting her. For a quarter of a century afterward, controversy raged, with Mr. Rodale being labeled a faddist or worse by some, but attracting an ever-growing number of gardeners, farmers and eventually scientists to the common-sense logic of his position.

In the last few years, organic or natural gardening — the terms mean the same thing — has become accepted. Today it is practiced not only by millions of gardeners but also by small farmers, and as municipal wastes, biological insect controls and a whole new technology of natural methods develop, by a steadily increasing group of large-scale farmers. The late J. I. Rodale's ideas have been vindicated, natural gardening has proved itself, and we've found it can be more productive as well as ecologically safer and saner.

—————————————— Soil Food ——————————————

The first principle of natural gardening is soil building — an actual construction job that nature does very efficiently when the proper raw materials are supplied. Organic matter in many forms will build the ideal granular structure.

This vegetable and animal matter, known as humus in its more advanced stages of decomposition, is broken down by an incredible multitude of microorganisms, plus a few macroorganisms such as earthworms. In this breakdown process, humic substances are produced that bind the particles of clay, silt and sand into aggregates or "crumbs." Approximately 50% of a good soil is composed of these crumbs; the other 50% is pore space, the open space between the crumbs where air and water are held. This soil is spongy, does not compact or crust over, and holds large amounts of moisture on the surface of the soil crumbs, yet lets excess water drain away easily.

There are two ways to supply this vital organic matter. You can gather it and add it to the soil, or you can grow it right where it's needed. The second method, called green manuring, will rebuild the poorest soil with minimum expense and is the best method where large amounts of organic material are not available nearby or difficult to haul in.

A green manure crop — often called a cover crop when it is planted in the fall to build the soil and protect it from erosion over the winter — is usually composed of grasses and legumes. Grasses provide a great deal of bulk, while legumes enrich the soil with nitrogen "fixed" from the air by bacteria that work in special nodules on the plants' roots.

Many good green manure seed mixtures are sold in farm supply stores. Some excellent summer green manure crops are clovers, vetch, cowpeas, alfalfa, crotolaria, soybeans, Sudan grass, lespedeza and buckwheat. Two of the best for fall sowing, to turn under in spring, are rye and oats. Almost any locally adapted grass and/ or legume will improve the soil, but it's wise to choose a deep-rooted legume whenever possible — alfalfa, vetch, crimson clover, cowpeas — for its ability to break up packed subsoils and for the minerals it brings up from considerable depths.

If the soil is very poor, the first green manure crop may make meager growth, but even this will mellow the soil sufficiently so that each succeeding planting will be more vigorous. When fast-growing green manures are used, a new crop can be sown as soon as the previous one is turned under. Thus several can be grown in a year, and the poorest sand or clay will become loam in two to three years.

Green manures are best dug in while they are still succulent, before they near maturity, so they will decompose rapidly. But with some crops, such as oats, an early spring planting can be allowed to set some seed before it is turned under. This seed will produce a second crop for digging in late in the season.

A green manure crop should be planted whenever soil is bare, such as after the final harvest in the vegetable plot.

Another composting-in-the-soil method for improving poor soil is sheet composting. In this method, organic materials are spread on the soil and spaded or tilled in, at any season the ground is workable.

Just about any easily obtained material, from grass clippings, hay or leaves to pine needles, bark, sod and seaweed, is suitable. Sources are legion — farms, mills, stables, lumberyards, woodworking plants, street and highway departments, breweries, dairies, restaurants, and many types of food and fiber processing plants (the classified telephone directory can be a great aid) — and very often the materials are free for the hauling.

For rapid decomposition, coarse materials should be shredded or at least partially chopped up before turning them under. Mixing in animal manures or a high-nitrogen organic fertilizer will speed up the breakdown even further by stimulating the increase of decom-

Sanitation and highway departments are good sources of leaves, prunings and other materials for heap and sheet composting. (*State University of New York*)

position organisms. All the materials should be worked in as thoroughly and evenly as possible to 6″ depth and wet down well. Unless very coarse materials like cornstalks or tree prunings are used without shredding or chopping, everything should be sufficiently decomposed in two to three weeks to allow the planting of productive crops (the same waiting period is advised when green manures are turned under).

Some variations on this are trenching, undermulching and compostholing. Whereas in sheet composting the materials are incorporated into the upper soil and humic products slowly filter down to improve the soil below, trenching involves burying them deeply for faster enrichment of the lower levels.

The other two techniques are most useful around established plants. In undermulching, the organic materials are dug in very lightly to avoid injuring the plants' roots, then covered with a mulch. The mulch keeps them moist to hasten their decomposition. Compostholes are deep holes filled with organic wastes and soil. They can be made easily with a posthole auger, which will dig a hole 2′ deep and 6″ in diameter. The roots of nearby plants will grow quickly into these rich "cores" and multiply rapidly there, and improved growth of the plants will soon be noticeable. Compostholing is also valuable where there is a hardpan, a tightly packed layer a few to many inches below the soil surface. If the holes are filled with a mixture of soil and partially to completely rotted organic materials, vegetables and other small plants can be set in them and will thrive.

―――――――――――――― A Movable Feast ――――――――――――――

For a steady supply of rich ready-to-use organic matter, the compost heap is a concentrated fertility factory no real gardener would ever consider doing without. It produces a product that is invaluable for every link of the plant growth chain, from seed germination and planting to maintaining the health and productivity of all plants.

For a long time, only one method of heap composting was considered correct. Rigid rules had to be followed, and the process took a long time. It involved alternating 4″ to 6″ layers of animal and vegetable matter with 1″ layers of soil, then waiting several months to several years for this to be reduced to compost.

Though slow, this method has certain advantages. Diseased plant material can be used in this kind of heap, for it generates high temperatures that destroy most disease organisms. The same is true for kitchen wastes, particularly of root vegetables, which may carry nematodes that will be killed when the internal heap temperature goes above 120°. Even greasy meat scraps will decompose well (but should be buried deep in the heap to prevent odor and flies). And a gardener tells us that tin cans and other metal objects he buries in his long-term compost heaps crumble away in three years. He credits the superlative growth of his vegetables and fruits to the iron, zinc, copper and other trace elements these objects supply. Bones also break down completely, providing valuable calcium and phosphorus.

Much faster methods, however, are needed to produce the volume of compost food gardeners require. So while those who have the room will always maintain long-term heaps to recycle slow-to-decompose materials, "speed composting" is the answer to day-to-day production.

Here are four things you can do to accelerate the composting process:

1. Nitrogen is vital to feed the bacteria that break down the carbon materials in the heap. Most efficient decomposition will take place with a carbon/nitrogen ratio no higher than 3 to 1: 3 parts by volume of carbonaceous materials (sawdust, leaves, prunings, hay, cornstalks) to 1 part of nitrogenous materials (fresh grass clippings or other green plant residues, manure, high-nitrogen fertilizer such as dried blood, sludge or cottonseed meal, or dark finished compost from a previous heap).

2. Shred the materials to expose more surfaces to attack by the decomposition organisms. If you don't have a shredder-grinder, a rotary mower will do a fine job if tilted and run into a low pile of material.

3. Keep the heap moist, and aerate it by making some holes from top to bottom with a crowbar, or build it on a raised platform of wire or branches, or turn it over every month or so.

4. In winter, cover the heap with black plastic sheeting to hold in the heat and moisture so the decomposition process can continue. Some experts recommend using clear plastic, which admits more solar heat.

Here's a recipe for making compost in just 14 days: shred or grind up everything, using a high proportion of green materials or liberally sprinkling in high-nitrogen fertilizer, and make a heap about 4' x 8' x 4' high. Moisten the heap when necessary, and turn it over and mix it well on the fourth, seventh and tenth days. At the end of two weeks, it should be dark, crumbly and sweet-smelling, ready for use.

Commercial compost activators, which are billed as containing special strains of microorganisms essential to the breakdown process, are not necessary, since these bacteria will appear spontaneously and multiply at a fantastic rate when nitrogenous materials are present in the heap. Nor is lime needed, unless large amounts of acid leaves, pine needles or other acid materials are

Four panels of screen are easily latched together to make a neat compost container that is aerated from all sides. (*Organic Gardening and Farming*)

The Accelerator compost bin (Rotocrop, Inc., 58 Buttonwood Street, New Hope, PA 18938) has side and base ventilation, and sliding panels make it easy to remove the finished compost. (*Rotocrop, Inc.*)

used and the compost is intended for non-acid-soil plants. The practice of adding earthworms to the heap when it has cooled down is also unnecessary, for these valuable earth-makers will increase rapidly in the soil — which is where you want them working — when the compost is added to it.

There's no need for a compost heap to look unsightly. Attractive compost bins can be made of snow fence, picket fence, rough lumber, bricks, stone, cement blocks, wire or plastic mesh on frames, and metal drums. Since air circulation is vital to the composting process, the sides of a bin should not be solid. If they are, as in the case of a metal drum, cut out the bottom and replace it with wire mesh, then raise the container off the ground at least 6″ so air can enter through the bottom and be pulled up through the compost by convection. In some commercial composting operations, fans are used to force air through the mass of materials.

With only a 60-second turning each day, the Compostumbler (Kemp Shredder Company, Erie, PA 16512) produces dark, rich compost in 14 days. (*Kemp Shredder Company*)

Where space is very limited, compost can be made indoors in plastic bags. The 32-gallon garbage can liners are excellent. A couple of shovelfuls of plant wastes are put in the bag and sprinkled with a little soil and high-nitrogen fertilizer. Repeat this until the bag is full, then tie the top. Sufficient air passes through the plastic to allow decomposition to proceed at a good rate, and the compost should be ready in three to four months. In winter, keep the bags in a heated garage or cellar.

A compost heap, when screened, will yield both half-rotted fibrous material for working into the soil or mulching, and "fine" finished compost ideal for seed sowing, potting mixes and mixing with the soil in planting holes. The rule is to use the finished material, which will be dark, almost powdery-fine humus, for starting plants, and the cloddy, partially decomposed remainder for established plants and general soil building.

To screen compost easily, make a wood frame about 3' x 4' and cover it with ½" hardware cloth. Lay this horizontally on blocks. Shovel the compost onto the screen and rake across it with a hoe. Any material too rough to go through can be used for mulching or sheet composting or put into a new heap for further decomposition.

——————— Comprehensive Coverage ———————

Often a gardener-homesteader will come across a windfall of large amounts of one kind of organic material. A farmer may offer several loads of spoiled hay, a sawmill might decide to give away a mountain of wood shavings or sawdust, or various types of processing plants may make available huge quantities of peanut hulls, cotton gin trash, sugar cane fiber or other wastes. And in the fall, leaves are usually obtainable for the asking, from neighbors by the bagful, from the sanitation, street or park department by the truckload.

Chances are you won't have or can't immediately get enough nitrogenous material to balance such a large volume of carbonaceous material (unless you have the luck to be simultaneously offered a ton of pigeon manure by the breeder down the road). So you can't heap-compost it, and if your windfall occurs in a season when all your land is producing crops, you'll have no bare soil for sheet-composting it.

The solution is to use it as mulch. It's the easiest — and often the best — way to utilize many organic wastes. It's a soil builder, a soil and plant protector, and a great labor saver.

Except in the barren deserts and Arctic tundra, nature never leaves the soil uncovered. A mulch of grass, leaves, twigs and other plant residues is maintained constantly. This "compost on the surface" fulfills all the functions of compost made in the soil or added to it, and much more.

Often available free from utility companies,
wood chips build the soil's humus content
and encourage earthworms. (*Organic
Gardening and Farming*)

An organic mulch enriches the soil slowly, since decomposition is less rapid on the surface than when the materials are mixed with soil. When mulch is maintained constantly, however, the humus compounds produced as it rots filter down steadily, and the aggregating action builds good soil structure to considerable depths.

Mulch is also a marvelous moisture conserver. Like a loose-weave blanket, it soaks up the heaviest rain and lets it percolate into the soil beneath. A mulched soil suffers no destructive erosion from runoff (or from wind, either). Even more important, the mulch blanket reduces evaporation from the soil by as much as 90%.

Many gardeners first turn to mulching because it suppresses weeds and so eliminates the chore of weeding. But preventing weed growth benefits the plants, too, for weeds compete with them for moisture and nutrients. Even a moderate growth of weeds can reduce the growth and yield of productive plants by a third or more.

Mulch also maintains a more even soil temperature which is helpful to the plants. It can keep the soil beneath it as much as 25° cooler than bare soil on a hot day, and it holds in warmth on cool nights. The roots of most plants virtually cease their work of taking up food and water at soil temperatures below 45° and above 90°. In winter, a mulch reduces the penetration of cold into the soil so roots can continue to absorb moisture and nutrients, which the plants will store in their tissues ready for use when dormancy ends.

An organic mulch confers another little-known benefit: it produces carbon dioxide as it decays, increasing the air's supply of this gas which is essential to plants for use in photosynthesis, the basic food conversion process that goes on in plant tissues.

Finally, mulches cushion the soil against compaction by hard rains and foot or wheel traffic, and they prevent "splash inoculation" of plants' lower leaves with disease spores in heavy rains. And like all forms of organic matter, they act as a buffer against harmful substances — excess fertilizers, pesticides, even the salt used to de-ice roads. When splashed on the soil, this salt is very destructive of the biological life of the earth and of the tiny feeder roots through which plants take in their nourishment. A mulch locks up and hastens the degradation of these soil and plant poisons.

How to choose mulches and use them properly requires knowing only a few general rules. In spring, an organic mulch should be pulled back from planting areas a week or so before planting to let the sun hit the soil and warm it up. When the seedlings are well up, the mulch can be pulled back around them and more material added gradually as they grow; but do this slowly if the season is very wet, since the mulch could hold too much moisture around them and cause rot problems.

Most mulch materials are highly carbonaceous, and the microorganisms breaking them down will steal nitrogen from the soil unless this element is supplied by the gardener. So lightly work in a fertilizer that supplies 1 pound of nitrogen for each 100 pounds of mulch material before applying the mulch. Less will be necessary if the mulch contains some green material such as grass clippings. Later, if mulched plants appear to be growing slowly and have pale green leaves, more nitrogen may be needed and can be applied as a topdressing over the root zone under the mulch.

The texture of the material will determine the depth of the initial application of mulch. A very loose material like hay or straw can be piled 12″ deep and will settle to less than half this depth, but a dense substance such as sawdust is best applied 2″ to 3″ deep as it will settle very little. Those that tend to blow when dry or mat down when wet, like leaves or grass clippings, can be mixed or covered with wood chips, bark or similar heavier materials. Some — hay, straw, excelsior — pose a fire hazard and may need wetting down in a long dry period.

The permanent organic mulch system for vegetables, developed by Connecticut gardener Ruth Stout, is favored by many gardeners today. Miss Stout never tills the soil, simply mulching it with spoiled hay, and the only fertilizer she uses in her no-work garden is cottonseed meal. Over the years, the soil under the hay has become soft and mellow and produces good crops of all kinds. The Stout method has numerous advantages, but it should be noted that a poor soil will first need rebuilding with worked-in organic matter, unless one is willing to wait for years for the slow improvement the mulch will make. Also, for highest yields and intensive cropping of vegetables, more fertilizer is required.

Some partially organic materials are occasionally used for mulching. A ten-sheet thickness of newspaper will check evaporation and weeds, and will also add a small amount of organic matter to the soil (its basis is cellulose). Researchers report that no lead from the ink in newsprint has been found in vegetable plants mulched with newspaper, so there is no hazard in using them for this purpose.

Gravel is an efficient and attractive mulch for all kinds of plants, and large stones and rocks are especially good around perennial and woody plants. If they are closely spaced, few weeds grow between them, and the soil under them is always moist and teeming with biological life. They add no organic matter to the soil but do supply minerals as they weather. Some gardeners even use a

Newspaper is a great "stretcher" of other more attractive mulch materials, since only a thin topdressing of them need be applied over the paper to hide it. (*Organic Gardening and Farming*)

stone mulch on vegetables, valuing their ability to absorb sun heat and release it slowly at night to aid crop growth in the spring and fall. Light-colored stones also reflect light onto the lower parts of the plants to improve growth.

Organic gardeners also use certain inorganic mulches. Plastic sheeting, aluminum foil and fiberglass wool are three that give all the benefits of an organic mulch except the addition of organic matter and minerals to the soil. In a sense, they do aid the working of the soil, for they provide more uniform temperature and moisture conditions that stimulate soil microorganisms.

Black, clear and green plastic sheeting are widely used in growing vegetables (see the chapters on vegetables for specific techniques). New plastics for mulching are appearing: one, made by Polyagro Plastics (Box 236, Bridgeport, PA 19405), is coated with a lamination of white or silver paint or aluminum. The extra light this bounces not only boosts photosynthesis but also repels aphids and other harmful insects. A fiberglass mulch is Weed-Chek (Brighton By-Products Co., Box 23, New Brighton, PA 15066), a long-lasting ¼"-thick matting that allows easy penetration of air, water and nutrients.

Inorganic mulches are short-term or special-purpose materials. The soil still needs regular replenishment of its organic matter, and constant use of an inorganic mulch without additions of humus material will result in deterioration of its spongy structure —

Gravel, marble chips and stones are good mulches, conserving moisture and reflecting heat and light onto the plants. (*Vermont Marble Company*)

and this will be reflected in increasingly poor growth of everything planted in it.

———————————— Rich Refuse ————————————

If you're concerned about obtaining sufficient supplies of organic material, you'll be interested in several new sources that are being developed — and you may even want to promote their development in your community.

These sources are the wastes of population centers. Tremendous amounts of valuable organic matter are burned, dumped or flushed away every day by towns and cities all across the country. The waste of municipal wastes is one of the great environmental crimes of this century. It's only in very recent years that we have begun to be aware of (1) the pollution caused by these wasteful disposal methods, and (2) the vast soil-building potential of sewage sludge and household garbage.

Some three hundred communities today are spraying or irrigating cropland, parks, forests, golf courses and strip-mined land with municipal wastewater, but it is only recently that sludge — the material that settles out of the wastewater when it is treated at sewage plants — has been studied as a resource. Some 23,000 tons of sludge are produced nationally each day. Dried sludge is a fine soil conditioner and also, like compost, a low-grade but good slow-release fertilizer (its average N–P–K — nitrogen-phosphorus-potash — analysis is 2–4–.5). "Sewage sludge," an Environmental Protection Agency publication states, "conceivably can be used as a plentiful, cheap alternative or supplement to chemical fertilizer."

Knowledgeable gardeners have long picked up this material, often free for the hauling, at treatment plants, and some communities bag and sell it widely (Milwaukee's Milorganite, Schenectady's ORGRO, etc.). The latest trend is toward composting sludge rather than just drying or pasteurizing it.

Dr. Francis Gouin of the University of Maryland, who has been testing composted sludge from a District of Columbia plant, calls it "the most valuable material out of Washington, D.C." The rapid, odorless composting process, developed by the Agricultural Research Service (Beltsville, MD 20705), involves controlling the aeration of the sludge by mixing it with material like wood chips and blowing air through perforated pipes in the piles. The heat of composting destroys all disease-causing bacteria. The finished product is being used in Maryland state parks and the new Constitution Gardens along the Mall in downtown Washington. Dr. Gouin reports dramatic growth improvement from its use, and notes that it is also excellent in potting mixes (he recommends 2 parts composted sludge to 1 part leaf compost and 2 parts sand).

Bangor, Maine, is one of the first
municipalities to compost its sewage sludge,
mixing it with waste bark from local pulp
and paper mills. (*Agricultural Research
Service*)

Gardeners with access to local sludge should determine whether
it is digested, activated (pasteurized) or composted. Digested
sludge, which is simply dried, should not be used on land where
food crops that are to be eaten raw will be grown within a year.
The processed sludges are considered free of pathogens. Sludge
can be used liberally, in the compost heap, sheet composting, topdressing around plants, and in planting holes. Incidentally, if you
have a septic tank, *Maine Guidelines for Septic Tank Sludge Disposal on the Land* (Maine Agricultural Experiment Station, Orono,
ME 04473) provides standards for using its wastes.

For improved richness, sludge is being composted with other
wastes. In North Stratford, New Hampshire, Gregory MacDonald
produces Bambe, a sludge–bark–chicken manure compost-fertil-
izer. Experiments are being conducted in several states on the
feasibility of composting sludge mixed with industrial wastes such

Some rotary tillers can chop up cornstalks and mix them into the soil for on-the-spot composting. (*Garden Way Manufacturing Company*)

as the effluent sludge from paper manufacturing, or with cannery and other food-processing wastes.

Former Secretary of Agriculture Earl Butz recently stated that "it now looks as if composting comes closer to being technically efficient, economically sound, environmentally safe, agriculturally beneficial and politically feasible than any of the alternative methods for disposing of sewage sludge."

Garbage is the newest composting frontier. Many cities are discovering there's "gold in garbage" — Houston, Texas, St. Petersburg, Florida, and Mobile, Alabama, to mention just three of the leaders. Mobile is now marketing its garbage as Mobile Aid (tests of this material are detailed in *Utilization of Processed Garbage in the Production of Florist Crops*, from the Agricultural Experiment Station, Auburn University, Auburn AL 36830). Numerous other projects are described in the technical journal *Compost Science* (bimonthly, $6 a year), and in a book, *Garbage As You Like It* ($4.95), both published by Rodale Press (Emmaus, PA 18049).

One of the most interesting developments is a liquid compost-mulch made in 24 hours from household garbage by the Connecticut Agricultural Experiment Station (New Haven, CT 06504). Biochemists at the Station used an enzyme that causes soft-rot in plants by degrading the pectin that holds plant cells together; they applied this to chopped household food wastes and scraps. The enzyme made the garbage "collapse into a slush," which when sprayed on the soil around vegetables gave higher yields than equivalent amounts of chemical fertilizer. The liquefied garbage also served as a mulch, drying to a thin film on the soil surface, and this "dramatically suppressed weed growth and helped to conserve soil moisture."

———————————————— Tooling Up ————————————————

Hauling, processing and applying the organic materials a good-sized garden needs doesn't require a big investment in machinery. In fact, just two machines are considered essential by successful food gardeners, and a wide range of models of each of these makes it easy to get one suited to the size of your plot. Before buying any machine, carefully study the literature of all the manufacturers listed below.

A properly chosen rotary tiller will mix any green manure or crop residue into any soil, including heavy clay. For smaller gardens, the new lightweight folding Gilson Compact Tiller, only 51 pounds and 2 hp, may be more than adequate. Larger gardens and heavy soils could call for a machine of at least 5 hp and 300 pounds. Tillers with the tines mounted in the rear instead of the front are favored by many for their greater ease of handling and stability.

Here are some tiller manufacturers and dealers:

John Deere, Moline, IL 61265

Garden Way Mfg. Co., 102nd Street and Ninth Avenue, Troy, NY 12180

Gilson Brothers Co., Box 152, Plymouth, WI 53073

Merry Manufacturing Co., Box 168, Marysville, WA 98270

Montgomery Ward, Albany, NY 12201 (ask for Lawn-Garden-Farm catalog)

Precision Valley Mfg. Co., Box 1099, Springfield, VT 05156

The Roto-Hoe Co., Newbury, OH 44065

Should a tractor be needed for large-scale tilling, a highly recommended one is the Holder A-15, which has been called "the smallest, most powerful 4-wheel drive diesel tractor on the world market." This narrow-track 14 hp tractor has a track width adjustable to as little as 24″, allowing its use in very small spaces (Tradewinds, Inc., Box 1191, Tacoma, WA 98401).

The second indispensable piece of equipment is the shredder, which is usually a shredder-grinder-chipper. These "garden waste reduction units" use all sorts of knives, rotary blades, hammer-mills and flails to make compost and mulch material of wastes from grass and leaves to sizable branches. Besides sufficient capacity and power, be sure to get a machine that will handle both wet and dry material. The following are manufacturers:

Allis-Chalmers, Box 512, Milwaukee, WI 53201

Amerind-MacKissic, Box 111, Parker Ford, PA 19457

Atlas Tool & Mfg. Co., 5151 Natural Bridge Avenue, St. Louis, MO 63115

Gilson Brothers Co., Box 152, Plymouth, WI 53073

Jacobsen Mfg. Co., 1721 Packard Avenue, Racine, WI 53403

Kemp Shredder Co., Erie, PA 16512

Lambert Corp., 519 Hunter Avenue, Dayton, OH 45404

Lindig Mfg. Co., 1877 West County Road C, St. Paul, MN 55113

Magna American Corp., Box 90, Highway 18, Raymond, MS 39150

Osborne Mfg. Co., Box 29, Osborne, KS 67473

Red Cross Mfg. Co., 124 South Oak, Bluffton, IN 46714

Roof Mfg. Co., 1011 West Howard Street, Pontiac, IL 61764

Roper Sales Corp., 1905 West Court Street, Kankakee, IL 60901

The Roto-Hoe Co., Newbury, OH 44065

Royer Foundry & Machine Co., 183 Pringle Street, Kingston, PA 18704

Toro Co., 8111 Lyndale Avenue South, Bloomington, MN 55420

Winona Attrition Mill, 1009 West 5th Street, Winona, MN 55987

W-W Grinder Corp., 2957 North Market Street, Wichita, KS 67219

This should be the extent of the power equipment needed for food gardening on a small to quite large scale — except perhaps for a pickup truck for collecting and hauling organic materials from outside the garden. A cart for hauling them in the garden is also very useful, and from our own experience we recommend the famous perfectly balanced Garden Way Carts (Garden Way Research, Charlotte, VT 05445).

In hand tools, it pays to buy the best, but the best needn't be the most expensive. For many kinds of spadework, a U.S. Army entrenching tool (available at Army-Navy surplus stores) is ideal and costs only a few dollars. The best hoes we know are the very strong but lightweight Scovil Handled Eye Hoes, made since 1787 (from

Walter F. Nicke, Box 71, Hudson, NY 12534; catalog 25¢). Two versatile pruning and brush-cutting tools are the Woodsman's Pal (Oley Tooling Co., North Main Street, Oley, PA 19547), which can be used as a knife, draw knife or brush hook, and the Woodsman Pocket Saw (Gokey Co., 21 West 5th Street, St. Paul, MN 55102), a coilable length of three interwoven silicon steel blades held by hand grips. One of the best sources of garden tools and equipment is A. M. Leonard & Son (Box 816, Piqua, OH 45356).

The Casaplanta hand composter (Casaplanta, 16129 Runnymede Street, Van Nuys, CA 91406) is a manual shredder-grinder handy for daily preparation of kitchen and garden wastes for composting. (*Casaplanta*)

Some shredder-grinders will reduce tree limbs up to 3″ in diameter to fine-textured chips. (*Amerind-MacKissic*)

--------------------- Food Supplements ---------------------

Once your soil is in good shape, a constant mulch plus compost spread each year on the soil under the mulch, will generally provide ample nutrients to maintain adequately the majority of established woody plants. Compost and humus not only feed microorganisms that release minerals already present in the soil, but also add their own nutrient content to feed plants. Compost made of garden wastes contains about a 2–2–1 ratio of the three major plant food elements, nitrogen, phosphorus, and potash (N–P–K), plus trace elements that plants require in minute amounts.

Annual crops, however, need larger amounts of nutrients to make their rapid and productive growth. Many natural substances are available commercially to meet these needs: for nitrogen, dried blood (12–3–0), cottonseed meal (7–2.5–1.5) and hoof-and-horn meal (12.5–1.5–0) . . . for phosphorus, bonemeal (3–16–0), animal tankage (7–12–0), and fish meal (8–13–4) . . . and for potash, seaweed extract (3–1–5) and tobacco stems (2–.5–8). Some "free" materials are even higher in some of the major nutrients — wood ashes and banana peels, for example, are extremely rich in potash.

Eggshells are an excellent source of calcium, a "major minor" nutrient especially important to fruit crops and also a good soil "sweetener" that counteracts acidity.

Here are the approximate N–P–K percentages of some other plant and animal wastes that might be available in your area: alfalfa meal, 2.5–.5–2; antibiotic wastes, 3–3–1; apple pomace, 2–1–2; cannery wastes, 3–1–2; castor pomace, 5–1.5–1; cocoa shell dust, 2–1–3; coffee grounds, 2–.5–.5; incinerator ash, 0–5–2; spent hops, 2–.5–.5; tea leaves, 4.5–.5–0; wool wastes, 5.5–1.5–1.

Manures are regarded highly for both their organic matter and fertilizer value. The analysis of manure from large animals like cattle and horses is about 2.5–5–1.5, that from smaller animals and poultry is approximately 3.5–3–1.5. Fresh manures can be used for soil building on vacant land at any time, but they should be well rotted when applied around established plants or where planting will be done shortly thereafter.

All these materials can be used singly to provide specific nutrients, or combined to make up almost any formulation desired. A high-analysis balanced formula, approximately 12–12–12 in N–P–K, for instance, might be made with hoof-and-horn, tankage and fish meal. Compost heaps can be enriched by adding materials rich in one or more nutrients needed by the crops you grow. A gardener we know makes a special high-analysis "artificial manure," using 100 pounds each of cottonseed hulls, rough-cut alfalfa meal and fish meal (all obtainable at farm feed stores), mixed with a cubic yard of partially decayed leaves or similar organic matter and allowed to compost two weeks. Leaves, by the way, are rich in minerals, and a rich leafmold is quickly and easily made by shredding or grinding leaves and composting them in a heap with high-nitrogen fertilizer mixed in well.

Some materials are extremely valuable even though they may not be particularly high in the major nutrients. Sea products, from fish meals and emulsions to ground or liquefied seaweed, are rich in vital trace elements like boron, magnesium, manganese and zinc. Clemson University in South Carolina has found that seaweeds also produce, or stimulate soil organisms to produce, plant hormones that promote growth. The University's Department of Horticulture reports increased yields of crops from peas to melons to corn from the use of seaweed.

For easy, fast feeding, a standby is manure tea, made by soaking rotted manure in a cheesecloth bag in water. Fertile teas can be made of compost and many other organic materials. Another valuable fertilizer is earthworm castings, made by many gardeners in simple compost boxes to which earthworms are added when the initial heat of composting is dissipated — a gardener in Iceland uses partially decomposed seaweed as the medium and feeds his worms sour milk, and harvests vast amounts of rich castings.

Ground rocks or rock powders offer an easy way to insure ample phosphorus and potash in the soil. Phosphate rock and colloidal phosphate, and potash-rich granite dust and greensand, are long-lasting, and 10 pounds per 100 square feet worked in every three to four years will give the soil a good basic supply of these nutrients.

For trace elements, a new source is humates, the remains of plant matter deposited under water millions of years ago. Huge deposits of this "geological compost" have been found in Florida and New Mexico. Tests show that in addition to supplying numerous trace minerals, these materials are biologically active and improve soil structure, release locked-up nutrients and perform many other functions of organic matter to stimulate growth and yields. Clod Buster (Farm Guard Products, 701 Madison N.E., Albuquerque, NM 87110) is one of the first humate fertilizer-soil conditioners to be marketed.

To conserve fertilizer, always apply it where it is needed — where roots grow or will grow. A small amount of fertilizer placed 2″ deep directly under the row before seed is sown will promote rapid growth of the first roots the seedlings make. Any fertilizer added thereafter should be applied along the row to feed the roots as they spread out.

Learn to observe your plants for "hunger signs" that call for immediate application of fertilizer. When leaves turn light green or yellow, nitrogen is needed. A lack of phosphorus is indicated by stunted growth or purplish foliage. Older leaves that show yellow mottling and browned edges mean a potash deficiency.

It's a good idea to follow the farmer's practice of applying phosphorus and potash in the fall but holding off nitrogen, which is more easily leached out of the soil, until spring. Also, don't forget to rotate your crops. When leaf, root and fruiting crops are alternated in a given space, nutrient reserves are used up less rapidly, since each type of crop requires different proportions of each element.

A word about a fertilizer that is not often regarded as a fertilizer. Lime is an excellent source of calcium — and also magnesium, when dolomitic limestone is used. But many gardeners consider lime useful only to reduce soil acidity. It should be applied if a soil test shows conditions too acid for the crops you plan to grow (most vegetables do best at around pH 6.5, which indicates just slightly acid soil). The calcium will be an extra benefit. But if the test reveals that no correction of acidity is necessary, calcium can be supplied if needed by applying agricultural gypsum. Where the soil is too alkaline rather than acid, correct it with agricultural sulfur rather than with the frequently recommended aluminum sulfate, which can be very toxic to plants. Free or low-cost soil-testing services are offered by most state universities.

Water is the biggest single component of plant tissues, and fast-growing vegetables, as well as fruiting plants, need a great deal of moisture all through the season to produce to their fullest capability. Even mulched plants often will benefit from extra water: the mulch reduces evaporation from the soil, but plants grow bigger and faster under a mulch and so take up more water. Thus they can actually deplete the soil's moisture more rapidly than un-mulched plants.

Most gardeners think of sprinklers as the primary way of supplying water, but this is a wasteful method. Sprinkling usually applies the water over a larger area than necessary, and much of the water is lost to evaporation. Some sprinkling systems, however, are better than others: Chapin Spray Stakes and Spin Stakes (Chapin Watermatics, Box 298, Watertown, NY 13601), 10″ to 36″ high and covering areas from 3′ to 12′ wide, can be set up to water rows or beds quite efficiently.

An improvement on sprinklers is the soil soaker hose, which emits water through holes all along its length. This hose can be laid on the ground where it will supply water to the root zone of plants, with little wasted on paths or between-row areas.

Even better are the new drip or trickle irrigation systems. A more efficient version of the soil soaker, these systems use solid-wall hoses to carry the water to hose lines containing emitters that let water drip or trickle very slowly into the soil. The newest wrinkle is the "dew" or "ooze" hose which has thousands of microscopic holes through which the water seeps. Various fittings make

Jiffy-7 Peat Pellets expand in water to seven times their size and combine the functions of a pot and soil. (*Geo. W. Park Seed Company*)

it possible to set up the feeder and watering lines in almost any pattern so that water is applied only around the plants. A timer and solenoid valve can make the watering completely automatic.

These systems save substantial amounts of water, yet optimal moisture conditions for the plants are maintained constantly. There is none of the moisture stress, the alternating too-wet, too-dry situation, that occurs with rainfall or haphazard watering. Consequently the plants grow better, and vegetables and fruits produce 30% to 100% higher yields. Another advantage is that the hoses can be buried under mulch or even in the soil to almost totally eliminate evaporation and to keep them out of the way of gardening operations.

Many of the larger greenhouse suppliers, such as Brighton By-Products Co. (Box 23, New Brighton, PA 15066) and Chapin Watermatics, carry drip irrigation equipment. Some other sources are Roberts Irrigation Products (700 Rancheros Drive, San Marcos, CA 92069) and Submatic, Inc. (Box 246, Lubbock, TX 79408).

Sowmanship

Giving seed a good start is as important as anything you do later to the growing plant to make it vigorous and productive. Whether started indoors or in the garden, strong and healthy seedlings are the foundation of strong, healthy, high-yielding plants.

Cold-tender and slow-growing vegetables are usually started indoors. This can be done in peat pots, which you fill with a growing medium and plant, container and all, when the seedlings are ready to set out. Or you can use the new "grow cubes," blocks or pellets of peat or wood fiber that serve as both container and medium and are simply dropped into a hole in the soil at planting time. One of the best of these is Sea-Gro Cubes (Sudbury Laboratory, Sudbury, MA 01776), which are fortified with liquid seaweed to stimulate growth.

But for less costly production, flats are the answer. These can be the standard wood, fiber or plastic flats used by commercial bedding plant growers, or almost any fairly shallow container that has or can be provided with drainage holes — squat flower pots, halves of milk cartons, styrofoam cups, margarine tubs, clear plastic breadboxes and shoe boxes, etc.

The medium must be light and porous, almost fluffy in texture. Many materials meet these requirements, and mixes containing various combinations and proportions of peat, soil, compost, sand, perlite, vermiculite, calcined clay and other substances are used with good results. We prefer a mix of equal parts of good loamy soil, compost and sand, topped off with a ¼″ layer of milled sphagnum moss. Sphagnum is sterile, so prevents the growth of the

Use eggshells as "pots" for starting seeds, then crumble the shells and add them to the soil to supply calcium. (*George and Katy Abraham*)

damping-off fungus which can wipe out a flat of tiny seedlings overnight. Seed is sown on this, small seeds being merely pressed into the moss, larger ones covered with additional sphagnum.

A new seed-sowing product deserves special mention because it is an example of the development of a useful horticultural material from an all-too-common waste. Glass, ground talcum powder fine (available as Eco-Growth, by Castalco Associates, Box 262, Oakmont, PA 15139), has proved valuable for sowing and transplanting when used at the rate of 1 part to 4 parts of soil. In tests, vegetables sown in the glass-soil mix germinated as much as ten days earlier than seeds in plain soil, and the seedlings were more vigorous in growth. These results are attributed to the improvement in soil structure and the numerous trace elements provided by the glass.

When the seed is sown — as evenly as possible — water the flat thoroughly by standing it in a pan of water or from above with a sprinkling can that gives a gentle spray which does not disturb the seeds. Then put a glass or plastic cover over the flat and keep it in a light but not sunny place until the seeds germinate. Some seeds, like lettuce and cabbage, germinate best at 50° to 60°, but tomatoes, eggplant, peppers and most others need 70° to 80°, which can

"Grow cubes," which serve as both pot and soil, give seeds and cuttings a fast, sure start. (*Pullen Molded Products*)

be assured by placing the flats over an inexpensive heating cable.

When the seedlings start to appear, remove the covers and any bottom heat. Gradually move the flats into much stronger light, preferably full sunlight. Even better to insure constant even lighting is a fluorescent light setup. Two 40-watt tubes, of the cool or warm white or plant growth types alone or in any combination, will grow sturdy seedlings when lit 16 hours a day. Set the seedlings so their tops are 4″ to 6″ below the tubes; move them closer if the plants get "leggy," farther away if their leaves start to curl down.

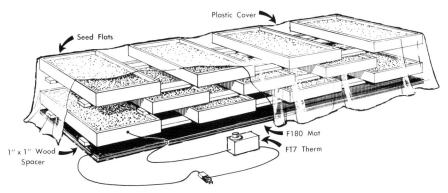

An efficient germination chamber can be made with a Famco electric propagation mat (Famco, Inc., 300 Lake Road, Medina, Ohio 44256), stacked flats and plastic sheeting. *(Famco, Inc.)*

Water carefully to keep the medium moist but not soggy, always using warm water. Michigan State University reports that growth is considerably retarded by lowered soil temperatures caused by applying cold water, whereas water at 90° will stimulate growth. Feed with weak manure tea or fish emulsion each time you water if your medium does not contain soil or compost.

Most gardeners transplant seedlings when the first true leaves appear, but we like to let them grow quite a bit larger, until they are really crowded in the container, for easier handling. If they are too crowded when they first appear, thin them by snipping some off at the soil line. Transplant into individual pots or space them well apart in flats. Continue to feed and water, and then about a week before it's time to plant them outdoors, harden them off to outside conditions by putting them in a protected spot in the garden for an increasing number of hours daily. If the weather isn't suitable when seedlings are ready to be set out, they can be "cold-stored" at 35° to 40° for as long as two weeks on a sunny porch or under lights in a cold cellar, where they will make little further growth but will stay in good condition.

An unusual transplanting aid, highly praised by many gardeners and commercial growers, is SUPERthrive (Vitamin Institute, Box 529, North Hollywood, CA 91603). A formulation of more than 50 hormones and vitamins, it stimulates rapid production of tiny feeder roots and so helps the plant take up more nutrients. Only 10 drops per gallon of water are needed in transplanting or to restore vigor to sickly or lagging plants, and gardeners often use a solution of 1 drop per gallon weekly on all plants to keep them growing well.

Food gardeners may want to try some of the new and exotic means of promoting plant growth now being investigated. Treating seeds with a magnet just before planting, for example, speeds germination and gives faster growth and higher yields, reports the Canadian Department of Agriculture. Magnetism appears to affect the seed's enzyme system, increasing the conversion of carbohydrates into energy-supplying sugars. Utah State University has found that tomatoes ripen much faster under a magnet, due to speeded respiration.

There is evidence that atmospheric electricity can improve growth. Gardeners who use metal posts, tin cans, wire trellises and other metal objects around their plants report more rapid germination, faster maturity, greater yields and even improved flavor. The ancient and still popular practice of planting by the moon appears to be based on taking advantage of electrical forces: Yale University has discovered that significant increases in electrical voltage occur each month in plants, correlated with the phases of the moon.

Sound also has a beneficial effect on growth processes. The University of North Carolina found that sound waves increase the germination rate of many seeds as much as 100%. Higher crop yields have been reported as a result of playing music to plants, one of the most spectacular examples being that of an English gardener who grew a world record 4-pound, 4-ounce tomato by fitting it with earphones and playing stereo music to it. Scientists believe the vibrations affect the metabolism of plant cells to make them synthesize large amounts of food.

Whether or not thought waves can influence plants is controversial, but one can't help but be impressed by the story of the Findhorn garden in Scotland where "mind power" is employed to grow enormous broccoli and cabbage on barren sand without fertilizer. However, we feel that in most cases any benefits that seem to result from good thoughts are mainly a matter of the gardener's total concern for plants. Careful observation of plants' responses and doing everything possible to meet their needs is the true key to a "green thumb."

A new method of accelerating growth to an amazing degree has been developed by the Agricultural Research Service. By greatly increasing all growth factors — light, temperature, water, fertilizer — the growth rate of vegetable and flower seedlings has been increased 10 to 50 times. The plants were given up to 4000 footcandles of light from fluorescent and incandescent lamps for sixteen hours a day, 85° day and 75° night temperatures, 65% minimum humidity, high-analysis fertilizer several times a day, and air enriched with up to 2000 parts per million of carbon dioxide. Lettuce grew to maturity in 25 days, petunias flowered from seed in five weeks. Furthermore, when the plants were removed from

A simple home-built fluorescent light unit
will raise hundreds of seedlings in the cellar,
garage or a spare room. (*Hertha Benjamin*)

these stimulating conditions, they continued to grow rapidly and were superior in every way to "normally" grown plants.

Not many gardeners will want to invest in the equipment for such accelerated growth. But a modification of the basic principles will give a worthwhile increase in the growth of seedlings and cuttings. Aim first at increasing the intensity and duration of light, perhaps with aluminum foil reflectors in the growing area plus artificial lighting to extend the day. Nutrients and water must be increased to match the growth stimulation of the stronger and longer light. Humidity should be higher than normal, and with most plants temperatures 5° to 10° higher than normal are advisable. Additional carbon dioxide can be provided with an open-flame burner.

This method works equally well with woody plants, and a Michigan grower of trees and shrubs tells us it gives him growth in three months that in the field would take two years. Incidentally, every gardener and homesteader should know how to propagate woody ornamentals and fruit plants. This is not only a fine way to save money but also makes it possible to add superior plants to your garden from the wild and from generous neighbors. An excellent course on propagating trees and shrubs is found in a two-part Guest Special Issue of *The Avant Gardener* by Alan D. Cook, Horticulturist at the Dawes Arboretum ($1 from *The Avant Gardener*, Box 489, New York, NY 10028).

Pest Control from the Ground Up

Few developments in horticulture and agriculture have been as sudden and revolutionary as the current "de-emphasis" on chemical means of controlling plant pests. Increasing insect resistance to these poisons, realization that some of them accumulate in the food chain from microorganisms to people, frequent population explosions of bugs when their natural predators are annihilated by pesticides — these and other revelations of proven or possible long- or short-term harmful effects on people and the environment are prompting the creation of a whole new arsenal of alternative control weapons.

We're beginning to see that the garden or farm is an ecosystem, a blend of interacting substances and forces that include the soil, light, air, water, plants and insects. When these are in a good state of balance, insect damage is held below severe levels by natural forces, with a little help from the gardener.

Good culture builds vigor into plants so they are less susceptible to insect attack. This starts with a soil that supplies all needed nutrients, hormones and other growth substances, with none deficient or present in excess. Too much nitrogen, for example, causes overly succulent growth attractive to insects such as aphids. Thrips are more numerous on plants suffering from lack of water. Destructive soil insects such as nematodes and root-worms are reduced by rotating crops, mulching, and tilling in green manures.

Second, the gardener can encourage or "import" biological control agents. Birds eat great quantities of bugs, and nesting boxes, hedgerows that provide food and shelter, and winter feeders are good investments. Snakes, toads and lizards are also very helpful and should not be destroyed.

Three insects that prey on harmful insects are the ladybug, praying mantis and lacewing. Equally valuable is the trichogramma wasp, which kills aphids, caterpillars and others by laying its eggs in them. These can be purchased (BioControl Co., Box 2397, Auburn, CA 95603; Gothard, Inc., Box 370, Canutillo, TX 79835; Vitova Insectary, Box 95, Oakview, CA 93022) and released in the garden. Avoiding the use of pesticides will conserve insects — ichneumon, syrphid, tachnid and robber flies, tiny braconid wasps, spiders, ground beetles, etc. — that eat or parasitize harmful bugs.

The minute trichogramma wasp, here piercing a cabbage looper egg, attacks several dozen major crop, orchard and garden pests. (*Organic Gardening and Farming*)

Two biological insecticides are the milky spore disease of Japanese beetle grubs (sold as Doom by Fairfax Biological Laboratory, Clinton Corners, NY 12514) and *Bacillus thuringiensis* (marketed as Dipel, Biotrol, Thuricide), a bacteria that infects the larvae of many caterpillars and worms. More such products are being developed as scientists study the diseases of pests, and also learn how to turn the bugs' own body chemistry against them: the first insect growth regulator, Enstar 5E, a hormone compound that kills several greenhouse pests by disrupting their growth cycles, is now on the market (Zoecon Corporation, 975 California Avenue, Palo Alto, CA 94304).

Certain plants help others by repelling pests, luring them away, or even killing them. This is called companion planting, and it's coming to be recognized as an important means of reducing insect damage. Numerous flowers and herbs are valuable in this respect and should be grown liberally in vegetable plantings. "Home brews," teas and sprays made with various plant parts and products, can also be effective in repelling or killing pests, and the gardener may also use certain natural insecticides derived from plants — rotenone, pyrethrum, ryania. (These methods are detailed in the chapters on vegetable and fruit culture.)

A new "mechanical" natural insecticide is diatomaceous earth, a talc-like powder made from the microscopic skeletal remains of algae. Rather than poisoning bugs, the minute fragments scratch and puncture their waxy protective outer coating, which makes them die by desiccation. The particles are harmless to the external and internal tissues of warm-blooded creatures, and diatomaceous earth is fed to cattle, poultry and pets for control of internal parasites, and is also used to coat stored grain to protect it from insects. In Perma-Guard Garden and Plant Insecticide (made by Bower Industries, Box 161, Orange, CA 92668), diatomaceous earth is mixed with pyrethrum to produce a quicker kill when first

These male European cornborer moths were lured to the sticky surface of a trap by a synthetic sex attractant. (*Agricultural Research Service*)

This sophisticated vacuum cleaner used by
an Agricultural Research Service technician
picks up many kinds of insects.
(*Agricultural Research Service*)

applied (a mail-order source is J. Mullin Nursery, 1173 Doylestown
Pike, Quakertown, PA 18951).

Some kitchen staples are useful repellents or insecticides. Salt
sprinkled or sprayed in solution on cabbage worms will eradicate
them. Hot red or cayenne pepper dusted or sprayed on vegetables
repels flea beetles, borers and others. Soap kills soft-bodied insects
like aphids, and gardeners say one of the best is Basic H, a clean-
ing compound made from soybeans. Aluminum foil used as a
mulch reflects short-wave light that repels aphids, thrips and Mexican bean beetles. Sprinkling flour on plants in early morning
when the dew is heavy will trap various worms and moths in a
sticky dough that bakes in the sun and kills them.

Simple mechanical and cultural controls can be very effective:

hand-picking larger pests (a gardener we know uses a vacuum cleaner), and hitting smaller ones with a strong hose stream . . . removing weeds that harbor pests . . . putting cardboard collars around seedlings to deter cutworms . . . digging or rototilling in early spring to expose the eggs of grasshoppers, slugs and others to drying . . . timing crops to avoid major pests, for example planting squash and melons very early to avoid borers which lay their eggs in midsummer, or planting cabbage late to escape maggots . . . trapping snails, slugs, cutworms and grubs with lettuce or cabbage leaves or wooden planks laid along the rows, earwigs with towel strips hung in shrubs, Japanese beetles with special traps such as the Ellisco (Ellisco, Inc., American and Luzerne Streets, Philadelphia, PA 19140), which is baited with a pheromone sex attractant that lures only Japanese beetles.

Netting is effective in keeping many insects off plants. A fine-mesh 100% nylon netting for this purpose is Insectinet, available from French Textiles Co. (835 Bloomfield Avenue, Clifton, NJ 07012) in 20′ widths and 30′, 60′, 90′ and 120′ lengths.

Traps such as this one for Japanese beetles, baited with the new pheromone sex attractants, are highly effective. (*Ellisco, Inc.*)

Healthy soil and plants plus these measures will reduce insect damage considerably. The aim is not to eradicate all destructive insects, for this would mean eliminating the predators that feed on them, leaving no natural controls for future infestations. A certain amount of insect injury is acceptable — some plants can lose as much as 30% of their foliage without reducing their yields. In fact, insect damage can actually make plants grow better. The Agricultural Canada Research Station in Saskatchewan found that "light pruning" by insects early in the season stimulates the production of growth hormones. Light infestations of aphids on beans and wheat and mites on cucumbers increased the yields of these crops.

Totally blemish-free crops are simply not necessary. Nutrition and flavor are not diminished by insect damage, and people are learning to welcome fruits and vegetables that are not absolutely perfect in appearance, but have the far more important virtues of superior taste and health value and freedom from chemical residues.

───────────── Down-to-Earth Guides ─────────────

The Basic Book of Organic Gardening, by Robert Rodale (Ballantine Books; $1.25)

The Biochemistry and Methodology of Composting, Bulletin 727, Connecticut Agricultural Experiment Station (New Haven, CT 06504; free)

The Encyclopedia of Organic Gardening, Rodale Press (Emmaus, PA 18049; $14.95)

Gardening With Nature, by Leonard Wickenden (Fawcett; 95¢)

Gardening Without Poisons, by Beatrice Trum Hunter (Houghton Mifflin; $6.95)

Handbook on Mulches, Handbook 23, Brooklyn Botanic Garden (Brooklyn, NY 11225; $1.75)

How to Have a Green Thumb Without an Aching Back, by Ruth Stout (Simon and Schuster Cornerstone Library; $1.45)

Natural Gardening Handbook, Handbook 77, Brooklyn Botanic Garden (Brooklyn, NY 11225; $1.75)

Organic Plant Protection, Rodale Press (Emmaus, PA 18049; $12.95)

An extensive listing of sources of natural fertilizers and compost and mulch materials is obtainable for a stamped self-addressed #10 envelope, from OGF Fertilizer List, Rodale Press (Emmaus, PA 18049).

≍ 4 ≍

Fundamentals for Vegetables

VARIETY FOR YOUR TABLE, savings for your budget, more wholesome food for your family — only vegetable gardening gives these rewards. And success will not elude the vegetable gardener who follows certain basic principles that, simply put, help the plants to do their best.

Full sun — at the very least, five to six hours a day — is the first essential. Many greens, such as lettuce and parsley, will stand some shade, but even these will grow better with full sun. Where crops are grown in rows, point the rows north and south to give the plants maximum sun. An exception: where vegetables must be grown on a definite slope, run the rows across the slope to prevent soil erosion, regardless of sun orientation.

Second, vegetables need a friable, well-drained soil. And except for the smallest, shallow-rooted crops, they will respond to good tilth and fertility to considerable depth. The Mississippi Agricultural and Forestry Experiment Station recently compared soybeans planted with conventional shallow tillage against soybeans grown where the soil was improved with sawdust, fertilizer and chicken litter to 30″ depth. Conventional tillage yielded 28 bushels per acre, the deep soil preparation yielded 39.

The third factor that determines success or failure is planning. First, look for all the possible areas for vegetables — not only back-yard or lawn areas large enough for a varied vegetable plot, but also all the spots in beds and borders, along fences and walks, or in foundation plantings where small numbers or even individual plants can be tucked in. Bulb beds are a fine place: a daffodil grower reports he plants everything but root crops in his beds. Daf-

Nothing compares to the flavor of home-grown vegetables — and the gardener can grow better varieties and get higher yields at lower cost than the farmer. (*U.S. Department of Agriculture*)

fodils need sun only until late June to mature their foliage, so May-sown seeds and June-planted seedlings are not large enough to shade them before the daffodil leaves die off.

Then consider the crops you want to grow. You won't want any vegetables the family dislikes (although the flavor of home-grown specimens may change their opinion!). If you don't plan on canning or freezing, be sure to include plenty of the "good keepers" for winter use — beets, cabbage, carrots, potatoes, onions, winter squash, Jerusalem artichokes, parsnips, turnips and the like.

Food value should be a prime factor in your choice. With careful planning, often you will be able to serve a leaf, a root and a fruiting crop from the garden each day to provide a good balance of vitamins and minerals. Certain vegetables are as rich in protein as high-priced meats. Black-eyed peas, for example, contain more protein ounce-for-ounce than sirloin steak. Other high-protein plants are navy beans, dried peas, peanuts and soybeans.

It should be noted that most vegetables, grains and nuts have "incomplete" protein: each of them is lacking in one or more of the eight essential amino acids that must be consumed together for health. However, this can be overcome by eating two or more of these products at the same meal, so that one supplies the amino acids missing in the other — *Diet for a Small Planet,* by Frances Moore Lappé (Ballantine Books; $1.25), has excellent details on this — or by supplementing them with milk, cheese or eggs.

Plant only as much of any crop as can be cared for and used before it is past its prime. Knowing just how much to grow comes mainly with experience, but a good rule for the novice, whether growing vegetables for the family or for local sales, is to plant less rather than more than you think you will need, and to devote the space saved to testing a new variety or an unusual crop.

--------------------- Succeed by Succession ---------------------

Two time-honored techniques for raising a lot in a little space are interplanting and succession planting. Practiced to their fullest, they can double or even triple the amount of produce from each square foot of growing area.

Interplanting is simply mixing fast-growing crops with slow growers, so that the first is harvested before the second has grown large enough to need the space. Examples are radishes, lettuce, early beans or spinach interplanted among melons, tomatoes or eggplant, or early corn with tomatoes, peanuts, bush sweet potatoes or okra. Tall and short crops that mature at the same time can also be interplanted, like squash or pumpkins around hills of corn.

Succession planting take several forms. Several plantings of a

An easily built plastic-covered frame can
keep a steady supply of seedlings coming
along to replace early crops. (*U.S.
Department of Agriculture*)

vegetable can be made at two- or three-week intervals to spread
out the harvest. A variation that also gives a long harvest period is
planting early, midseason and late varieties of a crop simultaneously. Most frequently, however, succession cropping involves re-
placing a crop as soon as it is harvested with another crop. Beans,
beets, leaf lettuce, chard, New Zealand spinach, carrots, turnips,
kohlrabi, radishes and the cabbage family are some of the vegetables that can be planted as early-crop replacements during the
summer.

Buy seed for summer crops early, for the seed racks may be depleted by planting time. For many crops, it's a good idea to start
the seed indoors or in a protected spot in the garden in early summer so as to have husky seedlings ready to plant out when needed.
Seed packets and catalogs tell the number of days to maturity, so
planting a crop that will not be ready to pick before frost is easily
avoided.

A point to remember is that succession planting is a form of crop rotation. When different crop types — leaf, root or "fruit" (corn, beans) — follow each other, growth is improved since each requires different nutrients and hosts different pests and diseases. So alternate the types of crop, and be especially careful not to plant one cabbage family member following another because of the soil-borne diseases common to them.

Later-than-ever summer plantings have been made possible by new fast-maturing varieties of many crops, plus the ease of protecting them with plastic or other coverings through those early frosts which so often are followed by lengthy mild periods. Some choice quick-maturing varieties for those last sows of summer: 'Seneca Zucchini' summer squash, 'Topcrop' bush bean, 'Full Heart Batavian' endive, 'Wando' heat-resistant pea, 'Italian Green Sprouting' broccoli, 'Shogoin' turnip (fine greens as well as roots), 'Green Wave' mustard, and winter radishes such as 'Chinese White,' 'Chinese Rose' and 'Long Black Spanish.' Lettuce, kale, spinach, Chinese cabbage, green onions and many others may also be sown quite late.

Even sweet corn is worth trying, planting a very fast growing variety like 'Polar Vee' (50 days). Slow-maturing root crops such as beets, carrots and rutabagas may be harvested while young, and quite a few crops will keep into winter under a deep mulch.

A good trick for sowing in the heat of midsummer is plug planting. Make a small hole or trench and fill it with a light soil mix or

Deep soil improvement, raised beds and close planting are keys to the very high yields produced by the Biodynamic/French Intensive Method. (*Organic Gardening and Farming*)

a soilless mix that has been well dampened. Sow the seed in this and cover with vermiculite, which both conserves moisture and reflects heat. Florida farmers now regularly use plug planting in their hot summer soils, and report that this method of providing a favorable microenvironment is helpful whenever drought, poor soil or other adverse conditions hamper seed germination and growth.

───────────── Concentrated Vegetables ─────────────

The big news in vegetable growing today is high-density or close planting. The idea is to plant everything closer together, so that with leafy vegetables in particular a "closed canopy" is formed over the soil by the time they mature. Several experiment stations have found that higher plant populations not only increase the per-acre yield but also often raise per-plant yields. A bonus benefit of close spacing is that the plants act as their own mulch, suppressing weeds by shading, reducing evaporation of soil moisture, and maintaining more even soil temperatures. For root crops, England's National Vegetable Research Station is now recommending spacings that give 20 carrots per square foot, 5 to 8 beets, 4 to 6 parsnips.

The new Biodynamic/French Intensive Method teams close planting with several other techniques to produce yields from 2 to 16 times the national average for beans, cucumbers, lettuce, soybeans, squash and other crops. The method calls for 24″-deep soil preparation, to permit roots to grow deep rather than spreading wide. The beds, 3′ to 5′ wide for leaf and root crops, 18″ wide for vertical vegetables like tomatoes, peas and beans, are raised to give improved aeration and drainage and faster warming of the soil.

With the aid of biodynamic techniques — a specialized form of natural gardening that combines organic fertilizing, companion planting for growth stimulation, and the use of certain plants for insect control — a vegetable plot only one-fifth acre in size can produce $6000 worth of crops a year, depending on the climate and the crops grown. So says the method's originator, Ecology Action of the Midpeninsula (2225 El Camino Real, Palo Alto, CA 94306), which offers a manual, *How To Grow More Vegetables Than You Ever Thought Possible On Less Land Than You Can Imagine* ($4 postpaid).

An essential element of the Biodynamic/French Intensive Method is deep soil improvement, which involves much hard labor initially but little in succeeding years. The bed is double-dug: first remove the soil and subsoil in a trench 24″ deep, then dig another trench right next to this. The soil from the second trench is improved with manure, compost and fertilizer and used to fill the first trench. This continues until the last trench to be dug is filled with the soil taken from the first.

────────────────── Boosting Bumper Crops ──────────────────

Although the organic materials and fertilizer you work into the soil or apply as mulch supply a considerable amount of nutrients, supplemental feeding is generally necessary for top production — and essential for close-planted vegetables.

Dr. Oscar A. Lorenz of the University of California says that close spacing without adding fertilizer during the season results in smaller and/or fewer fruits, tubers or leaf crops per plant. As a rule of thumb, when vegetables are planted twice as close together as normal, fertilizer rates should be doubled. Dr. Lorenz cautions that adequate phosphorus and potassium at seeding time are especially vital — a "starter" solution low in nitrogen but high in these two nutrients should be applied when sowing or transplanting. Nitrogen applications, however, are best spread through the season.

Leafy vegetables need large amounts of nitrogen through their growing period, while root crops require somewhat lower levels to avoid developing large tops and small roots. Fruiting crops such as beans and tomatoes must be given low nitrogen, especially during their later stages of growth, or they will make excessive vegetative growth at the expense of their fruits.

The best plan is to use a fertilizer with equal proportions of the major nutrients, such as 10–10–10, on all crops when the plants have been up about six weeks. Then repeat this in another six weeks for leaf crops, but make this second feeding a low-nitrogen formula, such as 5–10–10, for root and fruiting vegetables.

────────────────── Plotting Your Mulches ──────────────────

Close-planted leaf crops are not mulched but rather hand-cultivated or weeded until they are large enough to shade out weeds. Mulching, however, is recommended for all other crops and methods of growing.

If you use a year-round organic mulch, pull it back from planting areas at least ten days before sowing or transplanting, to let the soil warm up. And in a wet year, don't pile on too much of any material that tends to pack down and hold moisture, for a waterlogged deep mulch will restrict oxygen in the soil and also encourage root fungus diseases.

In normal years, even vegetables under a good moisture-conserving mulch will benefit from more water than the rains provide in many areas. Be prepared to water deeply when it has not rained heavily for some time and the soil an inch or two under the mulch

A mulch of stones absorbs sun heat and
warms the soil in spring and fall to aid plant
growth. (*Organic Gardening and Farming*)

feels dry. Sprinklers or soaker hoses are adequate, but for constantly near-ideal moisture conditions in the soil of a vegetable
plot, a drip irrigation system is a very worthwhile investment.

Inorganic mulches can be used for special purposes — to warm
or cool the soil as desired, and even to increase yields by increasing
light on the plants. To warm the soil quickly in early spring, lay a
narrow strip of green plastic film on the area where seed is to be
sown or seedlings planted. Clear plastic will warm the soil even
better, but weeds will grow under it. Then lay black plastic (which
admits almost no heat) or an organic mulch beyond the green plastic to keep the soil temperature stable later in the season when
roots have spread out.

This method, by the way, is very useful for lengthening the harvest of asparagus and rhubarb at both ends of the season for these
perennial vegetables. Lay green plastic over a portion of the beds

to stimulate early growth (cut holes to let the shoots through as they appear). Use black plastic over another section of the beds to keep the soil cool and delay the growth of the shoots beneath it.

A new idea is reflective mulching film (a good one is made by Polyagro Plastics, Box 236, Bridgeport, PA 19405). This provides "light enrichment" on the lower parts of plants which can boost yields and hasten maturity. Ripening of tomatoes, for instance, has been speeded as much as two weeks with a reflective mulch. Using the same film or aluminum foil mounted vertically on racks — if you don't mind the appearance of such a device in your garden — gives dramatic growth improvement by increasing light over the whole plant: at the University of Illinois, rack-mounted foil more than doubled corn yields, and at the Ohio Agricultural Research and Development Center it gave a 40% higher soybean yield.

Vegetables on Rye

A special technique that combines mulching and green manuring is used by horticulturist Richard B. Farnham. His method of making the entire vegetable garden into a year-long compost pile is simple and constantly builds better soil for better crop growth.

After fall's first killing frost, all crop residues are removed so they cannot serve as winter homes for insects and diseases. Then in early November, a strip is dug or tilled across the garden as

Glass jars make mini-greenhouses for individual seedlings to protect them against cold and speed their growth. (*Organic Gardening and Farming*)

wide as one can easily reach across with a rake. Limestone is applied, and the surface is raked smooth and crumbled. 'Balboa' rye (a grain, available at farm supply stores) is sown and stirred into the top inch of the prepared soil while the gardener stands on the undug soil. Mr. Farnham recommends at least 1 pound of seed to each 50 square feet of soil. As time allows, another strip is prepared, and so on until the plot is completely sown.

In the spring, as soon as the soil is crumbly and not sticky wet, a narrow strip is dug or tilled for each row. Turn under the rye and mix in a quart measure of 5–10–5 fertilizer to each 50' of row. This supplies nourishment for the soil organisms that decompose the rye.

For tall crops like beans and tomatoes, and for squash, zucchini, sweet peppers, chard, onions and New Zealand spinach, Mr. Farnham digs only a 15″ strip for each row, sowing a single line of the crop down its center. For smaller crops such as lettuce, radishes, turnips, beets and herbs like parsley, dill and chives, he digs a strip 24″ wide and in this places a double row, 18″ apart. In the center, between the two rows, he sows a single row of a very dwarf French marigold like the All-America 'Petite' (to protect the crops from nematodes), trimming their tops if necessary to prevent their crowding the vegetables. On each side of the triple row he allows at least 3' between it and the adjoining row.

As the crops grow, he walks the rye flat, in one direction, wherever it threatens the vegetables, but lets the rye continue to live and grow until lack of rain causes worry from dry soil. Then he walks the rye flat again in one direction and covers it with a strip of black mulching plastic (thick newspapers can also be used if held in place). All available weeds, leaves, and other organic refuse are immediately spread to form an insulating layer on the plastic, which should be slit with a knife here and there to admit rain and air. All pest-free plant garbage goes on the plastic throughout the summer and is quickly dried and deodorized by the sun. If sufficient organic material is lacking, Mr. Farnham recommends bagasse (Zorbit, Staz-dri), which is dried spent sugar cane, inexpensive and obtainable at farm stores.

Mr. Farnham fertilizes in June, but only if the plants show a lack of vigor. He suggests trying a teaspoonful of 5–10–5 on a square foot of soil and applying it at that rate (a quart measure to 100 square feet of soil) if growth improvement is noted. Except in a summer of heavy rains, there will seldom be further need for adding fertilizer.

After frost ends the garden, the remaining mulch is spread over the soil, the plastic is removed and hung to dry for storage, and the green manure crop is sown again. Thus the soil is constantly protected and improved, the green manure revitalizing the soil by steadily adding organic matter and by releasing nutrients slowly and safely in a well-balanced form.

——————— A Head Start and Late Finish ———————

For extra-early and extra-late harvests, cloches are the answer. These old-time devices — now appearing in many new forms — protect tender plants against late spring and early fall frosts.

Cloches can be as simple as paper hotcaps or bottomless glass jugs, or as imposing as "row greenhouses." Frames of varying lengths and widths and covered with plastic or glass are available ready-made, or the gardener can make cloches easily by laying polyethylene film over open-mesh wire fencing or opened wire hangers bent into semicircles. A new self-anchoring cloche is the Tico Tunnel (Williamstown Irrigation Co., Williamstown, NY 13493), which uses water-filled side tubes to hold it down so there is no need to bury the edges of the plastic in the soil. Crops can be planted quite close together under cloches, and the gardener can interplant early, fast-maturing crops with slow growers which will just be getting started when the fast ones are harvested.

New Hampshire vegetable grower Richard Clark uses row greenhouses to stretch his 120-day growing season into 200 days. These cover three rows of tomatoes in spring and fall.

Mr. Clark bends 21' lengths of ½" galvanized water pipe into semicircles. This makes a framing piece 16' wide with 5' headroom in the center. He stands these up 6' apart and forces the pipe ends 6" to 8" into the soil. Plastic cord tied from pipe to pipe at the top center interconnects them firmly. This frame is covered with two layers of 24'-wide construction-grade polyethylene sheeting. The inner layer is left loose so it hangs down slightly between the pipe frame members to give an air space for insulation, and the outer layer is pulled tight. The edges of the plastic are secured by burying them in the soil. Ventilation is provided when necessary by pulling back the plastic covering the ends of the greenhouses.

Mr. Clark plants sturdy tomato transplants in these cloches the last week in April, with a black plastic mulch on the soil. The greenhouses are removed about June 1. For the fall crop, he plants and mulches transplants the first week in July and puts the row greenhouses over them the first week in September. He reports the greenhouses protect the plants down to 25° outside temperature in spring; in the fall, when the soil has accumulated warmth, they protect to 17°. Last year he harvested tomatoes as late as November 22.

Water-filled plastic bags or tubing set around seedlings can provide helpful warmth. A used inner tube matured tomatoes much earlier for organic gardener Ellen E. Jantzen. She set an inner tube on the soil and filled it with water by making a small slit for the hose nozzle, then corking it with a wooden stopper. On April 1, she planted a seedling of a midsummer variety in the center of the "doughnut." An arch made of a bent coat hanger was placed over the plant to support a tent of plastic sheeting. The edges of the plastic were held down by simply tucking them under the outside of the tube, and pulled up slightly on one side when ventilation was needed. On sunny days the tube became very warm, and Ms. Jantzen reports it held considerable warmth in the soil and air in the mini-greenhouse all through the night. The plant grew vigorously, and the first tomato was picked on June 20, two weeks before neighboring gardens had ripe fruits (an early variety would have given even earlier harvest).

In autumn, frost protection can be provided with covers of loose mulch material, bags, baskets, etc., as well as with cloches. Watering will also protect against light frosts — water releases heat to the air as it cools. About $\frac{1}{3}''$ of water should be applied every three to four hours during the danger period. Even better is sprinkling, wetting each plant at least once a minute and continuing until rising temperatures melt the ice that forms. Spraying plants with liquid seaweed just before an expected frost also helps: at Clemson University, tomato plants given a foliar spray of dilute seaweed extract survived 29°, which killed unsprayed plants.

Vertical Vegetables

Sending vines up into the air has many advantages. Vertically grown squash, cucumbers, peas, tomatoes, pole beans, limas, small melons and others take one-tenth the space they need when allowed to sprawl. And they grow better because of better air circulation and exposure to light. On trellises, fences, walls, posts, frames and tepees, vine crops are cleaner, drier and often more ornamental. The glossy foliage of Malabar spinach and the scalloped leaves of cucumbers and squash make decorative screens — and the big yellow flowers of squash are as striking as those of many strictly ornamental vines.

A working trellis may be as simple as a wood frame with vertical and horizontal strings, or of all wood construction for plants like melons that bear heavy fruits. The tepee and A-frame are variations of the trellis. For a tepee, push four poles or bamboo canes into the soil a foot or so apart and tie them together near the top. An A-frame may be made of inexpensive lumber like lath, or of two old window frames nailed to posts so they form a high-pitched roof-like frame. Tomatoes can be planted just inside the bottom edges of the A and trained up the crosspieces, or cover the frame with chicken wire or similar mesh material for crops like cucumbers.

The new 'Tumblin' Tom' tomato was bred especially for hanging baskets. (*Stokes Seeds*)

Another good tactic is using stalks as living stakes. Corn, sunflowers and Jerusalem artichokes all have strong stalks, and climbers interplanted with these tall growers can be trained up them readily to produce two crops in the space ordinarily used for one.

A Vegetable in Every Pot

The patio, porch, deck, steps, along a path or the driveway, and in many spots in the garden where in-the-ground planting is not feasible or convenient — these are places for crops in containers. Salad crops and the new midget vegetables are natural choices, but even some vegetables of considerable size can be grown in containers. From windowboxes to planter boxes, from pots to buckets to baskets to flue tiles to plastic garbage cans and even children's wading pools, containers provide extra cropping space and often useful portability and decorative effects. Planter boxes and other containers attached to walls or fences are especially attractive, as well as often more productive because of the reflected heat and light.

Sufficient root room is the most important requirement: 8″ to 12″ soil depth for small vegetables like beets, lettuce, onions, chard, carrots and spinach, 12″ to 24″ depth for tomatoes, eggplant, peppers, cucumbers, squash and melons. All containers must have drainage holes covered with stones or crocks to prevent clogging, and the plants in larger containers will benefit if some holes are drilled in the lower sides as well as in the bottom. Home-built wood planter boxes should be given a coat of copper naphthenate or two coats of boiled linseed oil to preserve them, and they may be painted or stained on the outside.

A board-enclosed raised bed on a patio or apartment balcony can be considered a form of container gardening. Some gardeners construct a version of the strawberry pyramid, building one or more small raised beds on a large floor-level one. Plastic garden edging, 6″ to 8″ wide, can be used to make round or oval beds.

A soilless mix or a light soil mix containing large proportions of peat and perlite or vermiculite is best for containers. Watering will be needed almost daily in good summer weather, and the plants should be topdressed with organic fertilizer monthly.

Vegetable hanging baskets are unusual and practical, and the addition of flowers can make them spectacular. Some good crop subjects are dwarf tomatoes, cucumbers, zucchini and summer

Plastic sheeting stapled together and filled with planting mix makes an unusual and useful pillow pak container. (*U.S. Department of Agriculture*)

squash, lettuce, parsley, sweet potatoes, dwarf sugar peas, melons, strawberries and many herbs. A California nursery reports that two of its best sellers are a small hanging basket of cherry tomatoes, lettuce and alyssum and an elaborate "garden in the sky" containing a full-size tomato plant ringed by parsley, rosemary, two varieties of lettuce, cherry tomatoes and marigolds, with alyssum cascading over the edges (this one retails for $125!).

The most novel and versatile containers are pillow paks and moss walls. Pillow paks, developed by Cornell University, are

Biological, cultural and other natural controls will almost always eliminate all but a small, easily tolerated amount of insect damage. (*Community Environmental Council*)

tubes made by folding over and stapling the edges of a polyethylene sheet, then filling with the Cornell peat-lite soilless mix or a commercial version such as Jiffy-Mix or Redi-Earth (available at garden centers). The tube is stapled shut at the ends, laid down where wanted — it can even be curved — and planted through slits cut in the top. Pillow paks can also be hung vertically and planted all along their length to make "pillow pak pillars."

A moss wall container can be almost any length and height, any shape from cylindrical to half round to "wall" shape, and attached, hanging or free-standing (even on wheels). Free-standing moss walls should be 10″ to 12″ thick; those to be attached to a wall or fence are usually made 6″ to 8″ thick. A simple wood skeleton frame with a solid bottom is constructed of rot-resistant wood or wood treated with copper naphthenate preservative. Plastic-coated or chicken wire is stapled all around the frame, then it is lined with sphagnum moss (4-mil polyethylene may be used instead).

The container is filled with a soilless or light soil mix, which is moistened well before planting. Holes are made in the liner and the plants are set rather deeply, at a slight upward angle, and close together, as they will not spread out as much as they would in horizontal planting. Water from the top whenever the medium around any of the plants feels dry, and feed as you would with any soilless mix. A surprising number of vegetables will thrive in a moss wall garden — lettuce, parsley, spinach, herbs, strawberries, even tomatoes.

Some mini-varieties that are gardeners' favorites for all kinds of containers are 'Little Finger' and 'Short 'n Sweet' carrots, 'Dwarf Morden' and 'Little Leaguer' cabbages, 'Golden Midget' sweet corn, 'Cherokee' and 'Patio Pik' cucumbers, 'Tom Thumb' butterhead lettuce, 'Morden Midget' eggplant, 'Mighty Midget' pea, 'Baby Crookneck' and 'Chefini Zucchini' summer squash, 'Golden Nugget' winter squash, 'Minnesota Midget' muskmelon, 'New Hampshire Midget' watermelon, and 'Pixie,' 'Patio,' 'Tiny Tim' and 'Small Fry' tomatoes (the new 'Tumblin' Tom' tomato is great for baskets).

Making Bugs Buzz Off

The late J. I. Rodale, father of organic gardening, often said that insects and disease are nature's censors — their job is to weed out unfit plants. Good culture that provides all the necessities for growth in proper balance makes strong plants that resist pests and disease.

Other means of minimizing these problems on vegetables are planting disease-resistant varieties, such as tomatoes certified to

Squash yields were almost doubled when an
aluminum foil mulch repelled aphids, which
transmit virus diseases that reduce growth.
(*USDA*)

be resistant to verticillium and fusarium wilts, or mosaic-resistant
cucumbers . . . rotating crops so that the same crop is not grown in
the same space year after year . . . practicing scrupulous sanitation, promptly removing infected or infested plant parts through
the season, and all crop residues at the end of the season . . . and
using cultural, mechanical and biological controls as described in
Chapter 3.

A special technique for crop protection is companion planting.
Some plants help others when grown near them by repelling pests
or by acting as "trap crops" which are more attractive to the bugs.

Garlic is one of the best repellent plants, effective against
aphids, Japanese beetles and many other pests. Catnip, chives,
chamomile, feverfew, dill, tansy and shallots also repel a variety of
pests. Basil protects tomatoes, nasturtiums lure aphids from other
plants, radishes attract onion maggots. Mint, mustard and sage
guard members of the cabbage family. Asters, cosmos and savory
repel bean beetles. The roots of marigolds exude substances that
kill nematodes. Many other beneficial plants and plant combinations are detailed in *Gardening Without Poisons,* by Beatrice
Trum Hunter (Houghton Mifflin; $6.95).

Two of the most important principles of companion cropping are

Israeli gardeners produce high yields of
vegetables on bales of fermenting straw.
(*Organic Gardening and Farming*)

the use of strong-smelling plants — the volatile oils or other substances which produce the odor drive away pests . . . and the more varied and mixed your garden plantings, the less pest damage you'll have. As Professor R. B. Root of Cornell University has observed, "The confusion of chemical stimuli offered by a mixture of plants can cause the breakdown of an insect's orientation, feeding habits, and population numbers."

When serious problems threaten, the safest insecticides are those derived from plants. Rotenone and pyrethrum are two of the best. Both are fast-acting and have very short residual effects. They are very safe for warm-blooded animals, but highly toxic to fish, and so should not be used around streams or ponds.

Horticulturist Richard B. Farnham uses rotenone to prevent bug problems: "For double-safe dusting, for years I have used nothing on vegetables except rotenone dust (¾% or 1%). I apply it before I see any pests, starting promptly in spring's first warm days, repeating every three or four days for several early weeks, when the foliage is dry and at twilight.

"To make pest control easy and quick, quite necessary when done frequently, I use a hand-pumped duster with a long small spout having a device to direct the dust either up or down. It stands always behind the kitchen door, ready to use at a moment's notice. Prompt use far offsets the greater killing power of sprays, because young pests are more easily killed than mature ones. Also, dust, well applied with gentle short strokes of the handle, drifts to points often missed by the average sprayer. More important is the fact that dusts are far less likely to injure plant foliage and to be absorbed by the skin of the gardener."

Often the pest controls you make yourself may be the best of all. Slugs are attracted to and drown in saucers of beer, and both slugs and snails literally dry up when they encounter wood ashes sprinkled on the ground. Wood ashes also deter cutworms, and when sprinkled on foliage they prevent damage by squash bugs, bean beetles and many others. Nematodes can be killed by watering with the water in which asparagus has been cooked.

Many organic gardeners swear by sprays made with ground-up garlic, green onions, hot peppers, mint and other strong-flavored plants. Aphids, mites, bean beetles and flies are killed or repelled by a spray of mashed turnips and corn oil, the University of Wisconsin reports. "Teas" made by boiling tomato stems and leaves or the foliage of wormwood (artemisia) are effective against aphids and other soft-bodied bugs. And the old-time quassia spray is said to be one of the best: two ounces of quassia chips are soaked in a gallon of water for two days, then simmered three hours, and strained. Blend two ounces of soft soap into the solution.

Creative Cropping

Inventive gardeners come up with many ways to save work or time, or to make vegetable growing possible in unusual situations. Here are some of them:

If you're "stealing" a section of lawn for a vegetable plot, the sod needn't be dug up and removed or even turned under. Simply cover the grass with black plastic, roofing paper, several thicknesses of newspaper, or a 3" layer of partially rotted organic materials. Any of these will smother the grass and make it decompose to add its richness to the soil. To plant, make holes or shallow trenches through the cover and decomposing grass, and add some fertilizer and compost when sowing or transplanting. This method gives crops immediately with little work, and deep soil improvement can be done at the end of the season.

Where soil is very poor or poorly drained and you don't have the time or materials at hand to improve it, try planting on a bale of straw. Israeli growers spread a layer of poultry litter mixed with wood shavings and sawdust on the top of the bale and water frequently until heat in the interior of the bale indicates that decomposition of the straw is well under way. Vegetables are then planted on the top, and they send their roots deep into the bale. Growth is lush and rapid due to the heat at the roots and the growth-stimulating carbon dioxide rising from the rotting straw. For many vegetables, yields are twice as high as for ground-planted crops. Instead of the poultry litter, any high-nitrogen fertilizer watered in well should spur decomposition of the straw, and a thin layer of soil spread on the bale will make planting easy.

Volunteer vegetables — those that spring up from self-sowing crops or from seed in scraps tossed on the compost heap or buried in mulch — often supply valuable free plants. Sometimes volunteer plants actually seem to be improved because only the sturdiest seeds have managed to come through the winter. Asparagus sows itself, birds may sow sunflower seeds, lettuce will produce volunteers if a plant is allowed to go to seed. Some herbs also self-sow readily. Usually volunteers are easily transplanted. And don't forget another source of free plants — the side shoots you remove from tomatoes, which will root easily and grow rapidly.

Many crops can be started indoors — even corn, in peat pots — and transplanted to the garden when the soil and air have warmed

Even corn can be started indoors in a sunny window or under lights for an extra-early harvest. (*Organic Gardening and Farming*)

up. But if time or space for indoor sowing is lacking, try extra-early direct sowing outdoors. Planting one to four weeks ahead of recommended planting dates can pay off if the weather cooperates, and can be especially successful if the planting is on high ground (not a frost pocket), protected from chilling winds, or near a southern wall that reflects extra warmth. Sow large-seeded crops twice as deep as normal, and they will be likely to escape light frosts that barely penetrate the ground. And in summer, risk later-than-recommended planting, for vegetables started in summer heat usually mature more rapidly than the notations of days to maturity on the seed packets indicate.

A few more tips: in windy areas, windbreaks improve yields by protecting crops from drying or chilling winds — on the Texas plains, cabbage yields were 143% higher when a taller crop or shrubbery shielded the rows . . . don't sow seed of salad crops, carrots, beets and the like too thickly; if not overcrowded, the thinnings you take out later will be large enough for transplanting or delightful eating . . . a spading fork is a wonderfully versatile tool for incorporating all sorts of material into the soil, mixing organic materials, turning compost, loosening the soil, etc. . . . take time to observe your garden, learning something every day, and keep a notebook record of layout, planting dates, problems, varieties that performed best or were tastiest — such facts and figures will be invaluable when you plan next year's garden.

Pick of the Crop

Learning to pick vegetables when they are at the peak of flavor and texture means maximum enjoyment at the table, as well as better sales at the roadside stand when customers discover that your vegetables have been harvested at just the right stage of maturity.

This takes practice, for many crops are at their peak for only a short time. Corn, for example, is best when the kernels are at the milky stage. Pull back a section of the husk when the silk has become fairly dry, and press your thumbnail into a kernel. It should be quite milky — a doughy texture indicates it is past its prime.

Tomatoes and melons are two crops that should be fully ripe before being picked. But many others are best harvested when young. Carrots and summer squash are succulent when half grown, beets and kohlrabi when no larger than golf balls, cucumbers while still moderate size, snap beans before the beans show through the pods, cabbage as soon as the head is firm. Peppers and eggplant are two that are excellent over a long period from youth to maturity.

Daily picking and tasting are a good rule until you recognize the appearance and size at which each vegetable is at its eating prime. If not used immediately, most crops keep best when refrigerated at as near 32° as possible. The Agricultural Research Service also has found that plastic wrapping greatly prolongs the freshness of many vegetables, and that some vegetables keep better if stored unwashed — kale packed without washing in plastic bags stayed fresh twice as long as washed kale.

Because of the superior flavor of home-grown vegetables, gardeners naturally tend to eat more of them raw, a very healthful practice. In cooking, to preserve maximum nutrients as well as flavor, use a minimum of water and cook as rapidly as possible, just to the "tender-crisp" stage. Six to eight minutes is sufficient for many vegetables. Add the vegetables to boiling water, cover immediately and lower the heat to a simmer. Or put them in a very small quantity of water in the top of a double boiler over the flame, cover and steam them for a minute, then put the top section over boiling water in the bottom section to complete cooking.

Stir-frying is another fine quick-cooking technique. Bite-size pieces of many vegetables are cooked over high heat in just enough oil to allow free stirring. Lower heat is used for soft vegetables like tomatoes and squash, while the hardest vegetables — broccoli, cabbage, cauliflower, carrots, corn and peas — are best stir-fried at high heat for a few minutes, then steamed by adding a very small amount of water and covering the pan.

Incidentally, an excellent and inexpensive hand grinder for making baby food from your home-grown vegetables and fruit is the Happy Baby Food Grinder, from Walnut Acres (Penns Creek, PA 17862).

A special caution for urban gardeners: if you garden in an area of heavy auto traffic, it may be wise to wash your vegetables in a vinegar solution. Fruits and vegetables from gardens in several cities have been found to be contaminated with large amounts of lead, mainly from auto exhausts, states Gil Friend of the Institute for Local Self-Reliance (1717 18th Street, N.W., Washington, DC 20009). While the lead on home-grown produce is generally only a small part of the total lead intake of an urban dweller — dust and inhalation are two primary sources — it can add appreciably to the total amount consumed. In some areas — such as in a community garden tested in St. Louis — the levels of lead on crops may be so high "that eating it would be of questionable safety and a clear danger to children."

Mr. Friend recommends "maximizing the distance between gardens and sources of emissions, such as heavily traveled roads; screening gardens with trees, buildings or fences; situating gardens so prevailing winds carry pollutants away before they can settle; and washing produce." Washing with a vinegar solution will remove lead. Hilltop and rooftop garden vegetables, incidentally, usually have the lowest lead accumulations.

Recycling Seed

Save carefully selected seed from your own vegetables, and you'll have better crops, says C. H. Nissley, Vegetable Specialist at the New Jersey Agricultural Experiment Station. Constant improvement will result from continually propagating the healthiest, highest-yielding, most vigorous plants of open-pollinated or self-pollinated (nonhybrid) crops. Also, of course, mutations that show valuable characteristics should be preserved.

Many gardeners are especially interested in saving tomato seed. Mr. Nissley advises choosing a healthy plant yielding a high number of uniform, well-shaped fruits of good color, with thick, meaty outside and inner walls. The seed should be squeezed out into a nonmetal container with some water, and allowed to ferment for 24 hours to separate the seed from its mucilaginous cover. More water is then added and stirred vigorously. The good seed will settle to the bottom, and the lighter pulp can be poured off. The seed is then washed clean and spread to dry on absorbent toweling that is placed in shade with good air circulation.

When the seeds are completely dry, store them in a cool place — as low as 50° — in packets in clean, closed containers with some calcium chloride as a dehumidifier in the bottom.

Preserving Your Produce

Some vegetables are very easy to store — just leave them in the ground. Given a thick layer of straw, hay or leaves after the first hard frost, many will supply harvests long into winter. Carrots and parsnips will keep almost until spring, and dug from under February snows are better than any from storage. Even way up north, Brussels sprouts can be harvested from snow-covered gardens, the firm green sprouts almost frozen solid. Parsley and multiplier onions will winter over in many areas under a light, loose mulch.

Turnips and rutabagas keep for months under a mulch cover (but most gardeners say they are better dug early in the winter and stored). Beets keep well at least until early winter, as do winter radishes. Kale and corn salad leaves can be harvested even when frozen. Salsify is good until the ground freezes, then again in spring. Broccoli, cauliflower, late cabbage, collards and Chinese cabbage are others that stay in good condition through many light frosts.

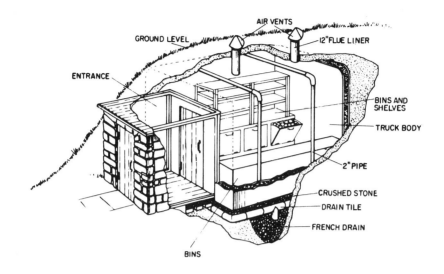

If you have a large garden, a root cellar is a worthwhile investment to provide optimal temperature and moisture conditions for stored crops. (*Organic Gardening and Farming*)

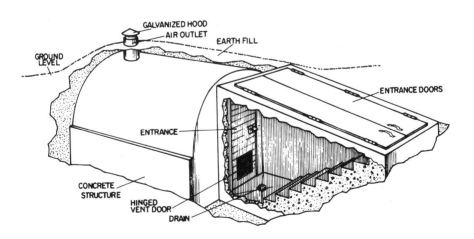

Food gardeners have worked out many ways of storing late-harvested crops. Temperature and moisture conditions in the storage area are the vital considerations. Beets, carrots, Brussels sprouts, cabbage, Chinese cabbage, Kohlrabi, salsify, parsnips, rutabagas, potatoes and turnips keep best at from slightly above freezing to 40°, with very high humidity. Onions, peppers, cucumbers, squash, sweet potatoes, melons, pumpkins, and tomatoes need temperatures of 50° to 60° and drier conditions.

Root crops like carrots which shrivel easily can be kept in a dry atmosphere if they are sprinkled occasionally or stored in closed containers such as large crocks, tight boxes or barrels, or metal or

Solar or electric driers preserve the nutritional value and flavor of vegetables at lower cost and with less work than canning. (*Organic Gardening and Farming*)

plastic cans. Celery is best buried in sand. Sweet potatoes, pump-kins and squash should be "cured" at about 70° for a couple of weeks before putting them in storage. All vegetables must be harvested before they are overripe, and handled very carefully to avoid bruising. Apples, which give off a gas that causes ripening, should not be stored with vegetables.

Partitioning off part of the basement, away from the furnace and including a window for ventilation, may provide a good storage room. A pit several feet deep in a well-drained spot in the garden is also good for root crops, which are piled in the pit on a layer of straw or dry leaves, then covered with straw and soil or with bales of hay. A barrel, sewer tile or galvanized metal can buried in the ground serves well, too. A root cellar is a larger and sturdier structure, roofed over aboveground and covered with soil or other insulation.

Excellent details on these structures and methods are found in USDA Home and Garden Bulletin 119, *Storing Vegetables and Fruits in Basements, Cellars, Outbuildings and Pits* (30¢ from Superintendent of Documents, Washington, DC 20402), and in *Stocking Up*, by the editors of *Organic Gardening and Farming* (Rodale Press, $8.95).

Deciding whether to can, freeze or dry vegetables takes careful weighing of the merits of each method. Canning somehow is more creatively satisfying, but it does take time and demands careful use and maintenance of equipment, and the cost of equipment and supplies does mount. Overcooking that destroys vitamins is inevitable when you take the precautions necessary to destroy toxic organisms.

The USDA warns:

> Don't take shortcuts or experiment in home canning: use only jars, cans and lids made especially for home canning . . . do not reuse sealing lids . . . do not use overripe food . . . do not over-pack foods . . . follow exactly the time and temperature specifications for foods and container sizes listed in instructions . . . test the seal according to instructions . . . do not use canned food showing signs of spoilage . . . boil home-canned vegetables covered for at least ten minutes before serving.

Approved methods of canning are detailed in two excellent references, the *Ball Blue Book* (Ball Corporation, Muncie, IN 47302; 50¢), and the *Kerr Home Canning and Freezing Book* (Consumer Products Division, Kerr Glass Mfg. Corp., Sand Springs, OK 74063; $1).

Canning does have one undeniable advantage over freezing: you don't run the risk of loss through power failures. Canning is also less expensive — or is it? Not if you consider that freezing retains more of the food value (vegetables to be frozen only have to be steamed or "blanched" for a few minutes). Also, freezer costs are not as high as one might think: an Ohio Extension Service publication states that costs are 11¢ to 19¢ per pound of frozen food, depending on local electricity rates, how efficient your freezer is, and the extent to which it is fully utilized.

Some vegetables, of course, are better suited to canning than to freezing, and some varieties of a vegetable freeze better than others. The seed catalogs are beginning to provide notations of this.

Drying vegetables, almost a lost art, is returning to favor. Drying preserves food values quite well, and the flavor is unique, — "better than fresh" to many people. Some vegetables that dry well are lima and snap beans, corn, carrots, onions, peas, chard, spinach, peppers, cabbage and tomatoes.

Some, like corn, are blanched before drying, while beans and peas are allowed to dry on the plant, then shelled and dried further. Most vegetables are sliced or chopped (tomatoes are cooked and pulped), then spread on boards in the sun or dried in homemade or commercial driers that use either sun or artificial heat (a popular unit is the Solar IV Food Dehydrator by Western Botanical Co., 710 Wilshire Boulevard, Santa Monica, CA 90401). Dried vegetables are best stored in airtight freezer bags. A good reference book is *Home-Drying Vegetables, Fruits and Herbs*, by Phyllis Hobson (Garden Way Publishing Co., Charlotte, VT 05445; $2.95).

Many gardeners delight in making pickles, relishes, sauerkraut and chili sauce. One of our own special favorites is the dill crock. Here's a "recipe" supplied by the late Euell Gibbons:

Any container from a 1-gallon jar to a crock of 10-gallon or larger capacity can be used. And almost any crisp, firm vegatable can be "dilled", and some fruits, too. There's no standard recipe — each crock should be an individual creation — and the only basic ingredients are dill at the bottom and in occasional layers, ¼ cup of cider vinegar per gallon of crock capacity, and ¾ of a measure of sea salt (a source is Natural Sales Co., Box 25, Pittsburgh, PA 15230; also sold at health food stores) to each 10 measures of water.

Some fine subjects for dilling: small green tomatoes, wax or green beans (the only vegetable to be cooked before putting it in the brine, and only for three minutes), onions, cauliflower, leek, Jerusalem artichokes, sliced cucumbers, peppers, halved peaches, cherries, even wild plants such as purslane stems and pokeweed sprouts. A few grape or cherry leaves add flavor and aid curing. Since large green tomatoes and whole cucumbers cure very slowly, these are best dilled separately rather than in a mixed crock.

Mr. Gibbons said dilled vegetables, besides being ideal for hors d'oeuvres, snacking and buffets, are superb served by the bowlful at lunch or dinner. Dilled nasturtium buds, incidentally, make marvelous "capers."

————— Guides to Gastronomic Gardening —————

A to Z Hints for the Vegetable Gardener, Men's Garden Clubs of America (5560 Merle Hay Road, Des Moines, IA 50323; $2.95)

All About Vegetables, edited by Walter Doty (Chevron Chemical Co., Box 3744, San Francisco, CA 94119; $3.98 — specify West, South or Midwest-Northeast edition)

Burrage on Vegetables, by Albert C. Burrage (Houghton Mifflin; $8.95)

The Food-Lover's Garden, by Angelo M. Pellegrini (Knopf; $6.95)

Gardens Are For Eating, by Stanley Schuler (Collier/Macmillan; $3.95)

The Green Thumb Book of Fruit and Vegetable Gardening, by George Abraham (Prentice-Hall; $7.95)

The Home Vegetable Garden, Handbook 69, Brooklyn Botanic Garden (Brooklyn, NY 11225; $1.75)

Making Vegetables Grow, by Thalassa Cruso (Knopf; $8.95)

The New York Times Book of Vegetable Gardening, by Joan Lee Faust (Quadrangle/New York Times Book Company; $9.95)

Putting Food By, by Ruth Hertzberg, Beatrice Vaughan and Janet Greene (Stephen Greene Press, Brattleboro, VT 05301; hardcover $8.95, paperback $4.95)

Step-by-Step to Organic Vegetable Gardening, by Sam Ogden (Rodale Press; $3.95)

⚜ 5 ⚜

Vegetables, Herbs and Grains Galore

---— Vegetables ---—

Artichoke — The Edible Thistle

The globe artichoke originated in the Mediterranean region, which makes it almost a semi-tropical vegetable. But gardeners north of Chicago and in New England and Quebec are raising this unusual crop successfully. They harvest smaller artichokes, but these "baby chokes" are especially tender and delicious.

The plants are handsome enough for border use, growing to 4' and bushy, with big velvety silver-green leaves. A perennial best grown from roots (seed-grown plants can vary considerably), it will bear in 90 to 110 days from spring planting. The best crops are produced in the second and third years, and the plants should be replaced with suckers from the roots every three years. High humidity helps the thistle-like flower heads, which are the crop, develop good size and succulence, so misting frequently with a fog nozzle once the flowers begin to show is a good idea.

Plant 4' apart after the soil has warmed up, setting the roots 5" to 6" deep in a well-drained soil liberally enriched with compost and manure, plus several handfuls per plant of bonemeal and a high-nitrogen fertilizer. Frequent feedings and an organic mulch are recommended through the growing season, but mulch is not advisable in winter as any sogginess could cause rotting of the dormant

Corn is always worth the space it takes, for its finest flavor can only be enjoyed within minutes after picking. (*W. Atlee Burpee Company*)

roots. The plants are cut to within a few inches of the ground after frost and covered with an inverted box or basket with leaves or hay mounded over this, plus 6″ or more of soil in the far North. Artichokes can also be grown in large tubs and taken into a cool but frost-free building for the winter.

Deep Subject — Asparagus

The controversy over shallow versus deep planting of asparagus is one that every vegetable gardener eventually hears about. Much hard labor is saved by planting only a few inches deep — but are the results as good?

No, say gardeners who have tested both methods. Roots set deep

Although the globe artichoke is a southern vegetable, northern gardeners can grow it by covering the plants in winter. (*W. Atlee Burpee Company*)

A properly made asparagus bed will produce
a high-quality crop every spring for a
lifetime. (*USDA Extension Service*)

give much greater yields of higher quality spears. No amount of
fertilizing or mulching will bring a shallow bed up to the productivity of one planted by the old-time trench method. And since an
asparagus bed can last 30, 50, 100 years, it pays to give it the best
possible start.

So plant it deep, preferably in a rich, well-drained sandy loam.
Make the trench 14″ deep and 14″ wide. Line the bottom with 3″ of
finished compost, well-rotted manure or a rich mix of soil, peatmoss and complete fertilizer, covered with 3″ of soil. Set one-year-
old roots — the 'Washington' varieties are recommended — on
this, 15″ apart, allowing about 25 roots per person. Cover the roots
with 2″ of soil. Then as the growing tips begin to break through,
add more soil, continuing this until the trench is filled. A mulch of
hay or straw will hold down weeds and conserve moisture.

Asparagus should not be harvested the first year and only mea-
gerly the second. Thereafter a well-grown bed will yield heavily
over a period of eight weeks. Asparagus is a heavy feeder, so
spread 20 pounds per 1000 square feet of 8–16–16 fertilizer early in
the spring and again after the harvest is completed. If manure is
available, apply it fresh in early winter or rotted in early spring.
The fern-like tops can be left on the plants through winter and cut
off in early spring for use as mulch.

Dr. S. A. Garrison of Rutgers University tells how to save a year in growing asparagus from seed. Seed is much less expensive than crowns, and Dr. Garrison's method results in bearing in two years instead of the three usually required from seed.

The seed is first sterilized by a two-minute soaking in a 20% Clorox solution to prevent fusarium infection. Then it is sown — in late February in the New Jersey area — ¾" deep in flats, in rows 2" apart and 1" apart in the row, or in small pots at two seeds per pot. The seedlings must be given all possible sun, preferably in a south window and with fluorescent lights to extend the day. A 20–20–20 fertilizer is used every four weeks.

Twelve weeks after sowing, the seedlings are transplanted into the garden, set 12" apart in trenches 8" deep. Fill the trenches in gradually as the plants grow. The first year, Dr. Garrison recommends sidedressing with a 5–10–10 fertilizer in midsummer and watering in dry weather. Use dolomitic lime if necessary to maintain pH 6.5 to 6.8.

Bamboo Shoots

The edible bamboos have been grown for centuries in the Orient for their delicious shoots or sprouts. Called *take-noko*, these are cut off as they break through the soil, and the outer sheaths are peeled off. The shoots may be sliced and eaten raw, parboiled and then sautéed, or used in Oriental dishes.

The genus *Phyllostachys* provides the finest shoots, but several other edible types are listed by specialists such as Pacific Bamboo Gardens (4754 Vista Lane, San Diego, CA 92116; catalog 35¢) and Palette Gardens (26 West Zion Hill Road, Quakertown, PA 18951; catalog 50¢). There are dwarf bamboos for groundcover use, and

Beets will always be tender if grown in a soil rich in organic matter and given plenty of water. (*W. Atlee Burpee Company*)

Broccoli is very easy to grow and will
produce several heads per plant. (*All-America Selections*)

tall (30′ or more) species that make handsome screens, hedges and
accents, so this is an excellent ornamental edible. Many are hardy
to at least –20°.

Bamboos need a deep fertile soil, full sun, ample moisture and
feeding in early and late spring. Runner types often need their
spreading rhizomes confined by edging. Many bamboos are fine
container plants, and the canes make good stakes and fishing
poles.

Beans — Plain, Fancy and Epicurean

Beans are among the least particular of vegetables, culturally
speaking, and produce huge harvests. Two important points:

beans are legumes, taking nitrogen out of the air to enrich the soil, and treating the seed before planting with an inoculant such as Legume-Aid will assist in developing the root nodules where this is done . . . and sprouting beans may break up if they must force their way through a soil crust, so cover the seed with vermiculite or other light material to prevent crust formation. Soaking the seed overnight before planting, incidentally, will prevent "chilling injury" of early-planted beans.

Snap beans — they were called string beans until all the "string" was bred out of them — are a mainstay of gardens everywhere. 'Kentucky Wonder,' 'Blue Lake' and 'Italian Romano' pole beans are climbers that yield over a long season and take up little space trained on a wire or string trellis, pole, fence, tepee or cornstalk. Bush beans mature more quickly and should be planted every two weeks for a long harvest. Some top varieties are 'Topcrop,' 'Bush Blue Lake,' 'Bush Kentucky Wonder' and 'Tendergreen' in the green types, 'Eastern Butterwax,' 'Midas,' and 'Kinghorn Wax' in wax (yellow) sorts. 'Royalty' is a purple-podded bush snap bean (the purple disappears in cooking) that is said to be shunned by the Mexican bean beetle.

Limas require a warmer soil for germination, so are generally planted two to three weeks later than the first snap beans. In northern areas with short summers, the faster-maturing bush limas are preferred to pole limas. Good bush varieties are 'Fordhook 242,' 'Dixie Butterpea' and 'Prizetaker' in the big "butter bean" type, and 'Baby Fordhook,' 'Evergreen,' 'Thorogreen' and 'Henderson' in the "baby lima" type. Among the best pole limas are 'King of the Garden,' 'Sieva,' and 'Christmas' (pink-striped white beans).

Try at least one unusual bean every year. An especially ornamental one is the scarlet runner, a climber that produces long sprays of bright red flowers and long green pods — when young, pods and all are eaten like snap beans, or the beans are harvested like limas when mature. The fava, Windsor or broad bean is shelled like limas but has a pea flavor; this bush bean grows best in cool weather and is planted as early as peas — 'Long Pod' is a standard variety. A climbing bean (actually a type of cowpea) with asparagus flavor is the asparagus pea or yard-long bean, which needs a hot, moist summer and bears striking red-brown flowers and squarish pods which are best picked young and cooked like snap beans.

Some beans are grown mainly for drying. Navy, kidney and pinto are the best known, but there are many others. The garbanzo (chick pea) is a bush type with unusual feathery foliage, a long-season bean with a nutty flavor. Montezuma red beans, a prehistoric strain still grown by Guatemalan Indians, are superb for baking. From the Orient comes the Adzuki, a very sweet red bean containing over 20% protein and used for cakes and candies as well as soups and stews.

Some others are the French horticultural bean, which actually originated in New England . . . 'Wren's Egg,' a horticultural bean delicious as snap beans when young and baked beans when dried . . . dwarf French haricot 'Comtesse de Chambord,' a white bean whose young pods are eaten raw . . . and 'Maine Yellow Eye,' perhaps the finest of all baking beans. Beans for drying are harvested when the pods are fairly dried out, hung in a dry place until the pods are brittle, then shelled and heated in the oven for an hour at 140° before storing in closed containers.

If you become a bean fan, get *The Bean Book*, by Crescent Dragonwagon (Workman Publishing Co., 231 East 51st Street, New York, NY 10022; $2.45), for its many fascinating recipes.

Unbeatable Beets

Beets are bothered by fewer pests and diseases than almost any other vegetable. They're also easy to grow, take little space, and are a "totally edible" as well as high-vitamin crop. Since beets stand both cold and heat (except midsummer heat in the far South), succession sowings can be made all season long from six weeks before the last spring frost until six weeks before the first fall frost.

Each beet seed produces several plants, so the seedlings must be thinned when about 4″ or so high. The thinnings can be cooked, tops and all, or used in salads. Or transplant them to stand 4″ apart in a new row about 4″ from the original row; if watered well, they will soon continue growing. For succulence and flavor, beets must never be checked in growth, so mulch and be prepared to supply moisture if rains are short. Nonfibrous extra-large beets — up to 4 pounds each — can be grown by planting a variety like 'Detroit Dark Red,' thinning to 8″ apart, and growing them in a friable, fertile soil with ample moisture. Two large long-season beets are 'Winter Keeper' and 'Lutz Green Leaf.'

Several dozen excellent varieties of beets are available. 'Little Egypt' is one of the best of the fast-maturing types. A very sweet beet is 'Sweetheart,' a cross between a table beet and a sugar beet made by the University of New Hampshire. There's a white beet and a yellow beet, and even a cylindrical one ('Formanova') that is very easy to slice. And while almost any variety's leaves can be used for greens, some have especially good foliage for this purpose, such as 'Beets for Greens' and 'Tendersweet.'

Broccoli — Vitamin Powerhouse

Although it has been grown in Asia for 20 centuries, broccoli is a "new" crop to American gardeners, who have recently discovered its exceptional vitamin and mineral values. A cool-season crop, it is planted in spring for summer harvest, in summer for fall harvest. In the North, the early crop is best started indoors. Broccoli is a "cut-and-come-again" vegetable: the center head is picked first, then smaller side heads as they grow. Abundant moisture is important through the growing season.

'Green Comet,' 'Bravo' and 'Early Spartan' are fast-maturing. 'Italian Green Sprouting,' 'Waltham 29' and 'DeCicco' are highly recommended standard varieties. There is also a very early variety, 'Raab,' that does not develop a central head, a white broccoli of delicate flavor, and several purple-headed types that turn green when cooked.

Several hundred kinds and varieties of beans are available, and it's fun to try at least one new type every year. (*Joseph Harris Seed Co.*)

Brussels Sproutlets

Americans have never prized Brussels sprouts as the French do, mainly because those in the stores have been picked at top size and have a strong cabbage flavor. But the home gardener can harvest them when they are much smaller, tender and mild. And they are a marvelous in-the-garden keeper, providing a succulent midwinter crop for harvesting from beneath the snow.

Jeannette Lowe, a horticulturist at W. Atlee Burpee, says that seed of hybrid 'Jade Cross' was sown at Burpee's Fordhook Farms, 30 miles north of Philadelphia, in mid-July in rows 2½' apart, and the seedlings were thinned to 2' apart. By October, sprouts could be picked at the bottom of the plants, with many more forming higher up on the stems. In early January, when the plants wore snow-ice caps, Miss Lowe found lots of firm green sprouts, many frozen almost solid, nestling under the leaves. New sprouts forming near the tops soon enlarged to gourmet size, and were picked as late as mid-February. All had unusually delicious flavor.

Miss Lowe says the "snow sprouts" should be cooked within a few hours after picking, or else stored temporarily in the freezer. Being partially frozen in the garden, they tend to get soft and spoil if kept long above freezing.

A long-season crop, Brussels sprouts are often started indoors in the far North. Harvesting begins at the bottom of the plant, and the leaves beneath the sprouts are removed at each picking. If you want a full harvest before severe cold weather, pinch out the growing tip in early autumn — this will force all growth into the sprouts to mature them rapidly.

Cabbages Are Kings

Some catalogs list almost as many cabbages as they do tomatoes. You can grow early to late green cabbage, red cabbage for pretty salads and pickling, and crinkled-leaf Savoy and multicolored flowering cabbage as edible ornamentals.

Early green varieties such as 'Emerald Acre' or 'Early Marvel' can be followed by midseason types like 'King Cole,' 'Bonanza' and 'Stonehead,' and finally by the late 'Ballhead' and 'Green' varieties. 'Meteor' and 'Red Acre' are the best of the red cabbages, and 'Storage Red' is the finest keeper. Savoy cabbage, which has more vitamins and a sweeter taste than other cabbages, is represented by 'Chieftain' and 'Savoy King.'

It's a good idea to grow only as much early cabbage as you can use quickly, since it likes cool weather. Start some indoors for extra-early harvest, then make a couple of succession sowings outdoors. If hot weather makes the heads start to crack, pull up the plants slightly and slow growth by loosening the roots, or root-prune them by pushing a spade down one side of the plant.

The stubby 'Chantenay' carrot will grow to perfection in even heavy clay soils. (*W. Atlee Burpee Company*)

Midseason and late varieties are sown directly in the garden. Mulch and watering if necessary are very important to steady growth. In harvesting, cut out the head but leave the big outer leaves, and several more small heads will grow from the base.

Cardoon — The Celery Thistle

Grown since ancient times in southern Europe, cardoon is an artichoke relative grown for its stalks instead of the flower buds. It has beautiful silvery fern foliage, grows 3′ to 4′ tall and bears large blue-purple flower heads. A long-season crop, it should be started as early as possible in the North, and is grown as a perennial in the

South. Cardoon requires high fertility and much moisture, but the soil must be well drained.

In early autumn the leaves are bunched together and wrapped with burlap or paper to blanch the stalks. The 18″ to 24″ blanched heart is boiled, deep-fried or sautéed, or used in salads, soups and stews. The flavor is unique, and the slight bitterness to which some people object is easily removed by parboiling before using. French and Italian cookbooks contain many recipes for this unusual and delightful vegetable.

Top Carrots

Carrots come in all shapes and sizes, and they're as culinarily versatile as any crop you can name — besides their numerous raw and cooked uses, they'll make carrot wine, carrot cake, even carrot marmalade. The tiny, extra-sweet "baby" carrots are very popular, but there are also coreless red carrots, beet-shaped carrots, and "stubbies" only 1½″ long.

Carrots in general like a loose sandy soil, but this is not an inviolable rule. Minneapolis gardener Bob Smith notes that there are top-quality types for all soils.

The stubby 'Chantenay,' 'Nantes' and 'Danvers' varieties have no trouble penetrating all but the heaviest soils, but 'Imperator,' 'Gold Pak' and similar long tapered types must have a deep loamy soil to avoid 'stumping" and loss of flavor and texture. Mr. Smith recently tested the new 'King Imperator' and found that in deep loose soil it grew as long as 14″. A thick mulch is especially important where the soil is less than ideal to the proper depth for the variety, to cover roots that may force up above the surface, becoming green and bitter, when the carrot has difficulty growing downward.

Given only one carrot to grow, Mr. Smith would choose 'Scarlet Nantes' for its fine quality in most soils. He sees no particular value in hybrid over standard varieties, and grows both types regularly. For finest flavor, he recommends June sowing for major growth in cool autumn weather, and harvesting as late as possible.

Cauliflowering

Like broccoli, cabbage and other cole crops, cauliflower is usually at its best when grown as a cool-season vegetable. Some of the 'Snowball' varieties and the new 'Stokes Early Abundance' mature in as little as seven to nine weeks. Seedlings started indoors can be planted out four weeks before the last frost date; for a fall crop, seeds are sown in June and the seedlings set out in July. The purple-headed types (which turn green when cooked) take twice as long to mature, so can be sown in spring for a fall crop. The long-season green-headed variety 'Chartreuse' has very fine flavor, and another unusual, the French 'Metropole,' produces heads weighing up to 20 pounds.

Cauliflower needs a very fertile soil and must never be short of moisture. White-headed varieties are blanched as the heads begin to mature by pulling the leaves over the head or "curd" and tying them. Stokes Seeds reports that "some growers are experimenting with a 16″ x 18″ mass planting . . . forcing a more upright plant which shadows the head throughout the day, to eliminate tying the heads." Purple and green varieties do not require blanching.

The fall crop of cauliflower can stand several freezes. A good way to store cauliflower for several months is to lift the plant, roots and all, and set it in loose soil in a pit.

Celeriac — Turnip-Rooted Celery

Celeriac is related to celery and grown just like it, but the edible part is a bulbous root that looks like a turnip and tastes like a

The new 'Self-Blanche' cauliflower curls its leaves over the head, making it unnecessary to tie them up to blanch the head. (*Joseph Harris Seed Company*)

The "celery" hearts of celtuce can be eaten
raw or cooked, and its "lettuce" leaves have
four times the vitamin C content of lettuce.
(*W. Atlee Burpee Company*)

combination of celery and parsley. This root is sometimes eaten
raw, but more often it is boiled and used in soups, stews, and
salads.

'Large Smooth Prague' is the most widely grown variety. It
takes four months to mature, so should be started indoors in the
North. The roots are harvested when 2″ or more in diameter.
They store well in a pit or in moist sand in the basement.

Tender Celery Isn't Tough

Celery is an easy — though not carefree — crop if its special needs are met. To grow abundant, tender and tasty celery, the gardener must supply: a deep, rich, loam soil . . . considerable phosphorus and potash but not too much nitrogen . . . and moisture, moisture, moisture.

A marsh or muck plant, celery requires a moisture-retentive but nevertheless well-aerated soil, high in organic matter and fertility. If the soil is not naturally of this quality, add compost, leafmold or peat and manure liberally to 12″ depth, plus 5 pounds of 5–10–10 or 5–10–20 fertilizer per 25′ of row. Wood ashes are an excellent source of potash and should be used if available.

Set seedlings, started ten weeks earlier indoors, in rows 24″ apart with each plant 6″ to 8″ apart. Water well when transplanting. If the soil is not very rich, sidedressings of dry fertilizer several times during the growing season will benefit the plants. Since the soil for celery must never be dry, mulch to conserve moisture and water deeply during drought, or use one of the best new aids — a trickle irrigation system which will keep constant moisture in the soil.

Seed of many good varieties, including self-blanching and golden types, is widely available. An unusual celery is 'French Dinant,' which makes many narrow, thin stalks with uncommonly full flavor.

Celtuce — The Celery-Lettuce

A variety of lettuce, celtuce's young leaves (very rich in vitamin C) are used like lettuce or as boiled greens. But later its stalk when peeled is a delicious "celery with a slight cucumber flavor," as one gardener describes it. This is harvested when about 1″ in diameter, and used raw or cooked just like celery.

This unusual double-harvest vegetable, much prized in its native China, does best in cool weather and will stand some light shade. It is almost totally untroubled by pests or disease. Sow it when you sow lettuce, and thin to 8″ to 10″ apart.

Chard — Triple-Treat Green

A beet grown for its big leaves and stalks, chard thrives in summer heat that makes lettuce and spinach go to seed. It's a "cut-and-come-again" vegetable from which outer leaves are harvested all season and through early frosts (even longer under a heavy covering of hay or straw). The leaves are an excellent "spinach," the stalks serve as "celery" or can be treated as "asparagus."

Chard roots can go down 6′, so prepare the soil deeply. It makes a good container plant if given a 24″-deep tub. It's extremely pest-resistant, and the foliage is decorative, especially in the crimson-stalked 'Rhubarb' variety. 'Lucullus' and 'Fordhook Giant' have white stalks. Chard is often called Swiss chard or the Swiss beet, although it originated in the Canary Islands. It is very high in vitamin A, calcium, phosphorus and iron.

The Vegetable Pear — Chayote

Gardeners in the South and California have discovered a new vegetable, the chayote, mirliton, or vegetable pear. An evergreen perennial in frost-free areas, this Mexican squash-type vegetable produces as many as 100 green furrowed fruits, weighing up to a pound apiece, on each vine. It is now being grown as far north as southern Oklahoma, the vines cut off in autumn and the plants heavily mulched with hay, covered with a basket and mounded with leaves. Farther north, chayote is treated as an annual, but it needs a long warm season to fruit.

The whole one-seeded fruit is planted, the broad end slanting downward and the tip just slightly above the surface. At least two plants should be grown, spaced 10' apart, to insure pollination. Chayote requires a rich, well-drained soil, full sun, and generous watering and feeding. The vine grows rapidly, with big lobed leaves that soon cover a trellis, fence or wall. The fruit harvest begins in late September.

Delicate in flavor, the fruits — as prized by modern gourmets as they were by the Aztecs and Mayas — can be boiled or baked, stuffed, used in salads, made into soups or desserts, or pickled. Excellent recipes are found in *Cooking With Vegetables*, by Alex D. Hawkes (Simon and Schuster; $4.95). Young tender shoots are cooked like asparagus, and the large root tubers produced in the second year are used like potatoes.

A source is Reuter Seed Co. (New Orleans, LA 70119). Fine varieties can be propagated by cuttings of the shoots taken at the crown of the plant.

Chic Chicory

Gardeners most often grow the leaf or Witloof form of chicory, but there is also the parsnip-rooted "Italian dandelion" ('Magdeburg') type, which provides leaves for salads and cooking like spinach and also large roots which are dried, roasted and ground as a coffee substitute. This is further subdivided to an "asparagus" form ('Cicoria Catalogna'), which has tender stalks that can be eaten like asparagus.

Witloof chicory, often called Belgian endive, is forced in winter for salads. It is sown in spring and thinned to 6″ apart, and the tender young leaves are harvested. Then after several frosts in autumn, the roots are dug and trimmed to 8″ long, the tops to 2″, and it is stored in a cool place. Whenever the forced heads or "chicons" are wanted, the roots are planted upright in moist soil, then covered with 6″ of sand and kept at 60° to 70°.

The tips of the blanched oval heads will appear above the sand in three to four weeks and can be uncovered and twisted or cut off. For a homesteader with a root cellar, forcing Witloof chicory can be profitable, for the heads bring high prices in specialty markets.

Chinese Cabbage

Because it can't tolerate hot weather, Chinese cabbage is best grown as a fall crop. Sown in summer, it will produce crisp, tender heads from early fall until the first hard frost. They have a mildly pungent flavor, something like celery crossed with lettuce, and are suited to salads and slaw, or they may be steamed and served plain or sauced, stir-fried, or used in soups and stews.

'Michihli' makes a tall cylindrical head, while 'Pac-Choy' is loose-leafed like chard and very fast-maturing, and the Wong Bok types like 'Burpee Hybrid' produce rounded heads 12″ tall and 8″ across. Chinese cabbage is a gross feeder, so give it your most

The blanched heads of Witloof chicory, a gourmet salad crop, are easily produced by forcing indoors. (*W. Atlee Burpee Company*)

An increasingly popular cool-weather crop, Chinese cabbage adds intriguing flavor to salads and many dishes. (*Joseph Harris Seed Company*)

fertile soil and plenty of moisture. Plants of the Wong Bok varieties dug before frost store well for as long as three months in moist sand.

Collards — Headless Cabbage

Of the many southern vegetables currently being "discovered" by northern gardeners, collards are among the most flavorful, useful, and easy to grow. This "hardy headless cabbage," a variant of kale, has mild-tasting, broad wavy blue-green leaves. They are very high in vitamin A and calcium, and can be cooked like cabbage, used in soups, or boiled with bacon, ham, salt pork or pig's knuckles.

Collards are sown in late summer in the South for a fall crop, but in the North they are best planted in spring. Sow 1/4" deep and thin to 5" to 6" apart, then to 18" apart. The young plants removed can be transplanted or used as food. Thereafter lower leaves are harvested over a long season when light green in color and 8" to 10" high. Leaves touched by frost in the fall have an especially sweet flavor. The plants grow up to 3' tall.

The standard variety is 'Georgia,' a more compact new one is 'Vates.'

Incomparable Comfrey

A new perennial vegetable is Quaker or Russian broadleaf comfrey. Its big deep-green leaves, very high in protein as well as vitamins and minerals, are used as a salad or cooked vegetable when young. It's a soil-building crop, too, sending roots as deep as 10′ to bring up minerals, and its older leaves make valuable mulch and compost material. In New Zealand, where comfrey is fed to livestock, as many as a dozen cuttings are made a year, producing over 100 tons of forage per acre.

Comfrey roots should be spaced 3′ apart and may be planted in spring or fall. In harvesting, the plant is cut back to 2″ above the ground, and it will make new growth large enough to cut again in two to three weeks. A healthful tea can be brewed from fresh or dried comfrey leaves, and dried leaves are often used for seasoning.

Sweeter and Quicker Corn

Corn isn't exactly a space-saving vegetable, so it pays to grow only the best varieties. And even the high-sugar varieties like 'Early Xtra Sweet' and the late white 'Silver Queen' should be picked only after "the water is boiling in the pot." If you must defer cooking for a while, hydrocool the corn as farmers do: carry a bucket of ice water or ice slush with you when picking, immediately plunge the ears in this, then wipe them dry and refrigerate as soon as you get indoors.

White-and-yellow-kerneled bicolor sweet corns such as 'Butter and Sugar,' 'Sweet Sue' and 'Honey and Cream' are now among gardeners' and consumers' top preferences. But old favorites like 'Golden Bantam' and 'Country Gentleman' are still widely grown. Among the newest varieties, 'Tendermost' is one of the finest yellows and 'Tokay White' is a very sweet white hybrid.

Everyone wants to be the first gardener in the neighborhood with corn. Here's how to do it: plant the fastest-maturing varieties like 'Polar Vee' or 'Hybrid 4th of July' . . . start the seed indoors three weeks early in peat pots, or sow outdoors as much as four to five weeks ahead of the usual planting time, first warming the soil with a green plastic mulch, which is later replaced by aluminum foil to bounce extra light on the plants . . . use cloches to protect the seedlings until frost danger is past. Another trick farmers use is planting the seed on 3″-high narrow ridges, which will warm up several degrees higher than level soil. Also, the largest kernels in a batch of seed will usually produce the fastest-growing plants.

Corn should be planted in blocks of a few short rows, rather than in a single row, for good pollination. Don't crowd corn — 8″ apart is sufficient for small early varieties, but later ones need 15″ for proper ear production. Space rows 2′ apart. Mulching with compost in various stages of decomposition is beneficial to supplying nutrients as well as conserving moisture. The worst pests, earworms, are easily controlled by applying a few drops of mineral oil down into the silk as soon as it appears.

If you have room for it, grow some popcorn. It's a surprisingly nutritious snack, containing 12.7 grams of protein per cup. If you'd like to make your own hominy, plant some hominy corn (directions for processing are given in the catalog of Nichols Garden Nursery). Parching corn, another good snack, is dried, then heated in a pan with oil until golden brown and served cool. Best of all, make your own cornmeal — it won't be degerminated and will therefore be more flavorful and nutritious than commercial cornmeals. 'Black Aztec' and 'Indian Flint' are two of the best varieties for cornmeal.

Cool Greens — Corn Salad

An early-late salad green that has as many worthy traits as it has names is corn salad. This hardy annual, which often sprouts in cornfields in Europe after harvest, is also called mache, doucette, fetticus or lamb's lettuce, and is easily recognized by its small rosette of vivid green spoon-shaped leaves.

Corn salad is a cool-season crop, sown in spring at the same time peas are planted or in late summer for a fall crop. The seedlings should be thinned to stand 6″ apart. Succession sowings every two weeks will extend the harvest, although even a single sowing will give long cropping — the plants mature in six to eight weeks, but some outer leaves can be picked in as little as four weeks, and the foliage stays succulent long after maturity. Corn salad has a very mild flavor and can be used in salads with other greens and salad vegetables, or quick-cooked (only two or three minutes) like spinach.

Peppy Cresses

The cresses are mildly to strongly pungent greens, valued for the piquancy they impart to salads and sandwiches.

Upland cress resembles watercress but has larger leaves and grows 18″ tall. A hardy biennial, it will survive the winter under a loose mulch and supply greens in thaws and in the spring. Peppergrass, which has a "hotter" flavor, grows very rapidly to 6″, and cutting of the leaves can begin three weeks after sowing. The plants are decorative, the lacy foliage making an attractive edging. Both of these cresses do well in almost any garden soil.

Watercress is one of the very few foodstuffs that is almost a balanced diet by itself. And it is way ahead of other salad crops in nutritional value: it has twice the protein, 4 times the vitamin C, and 300 times the calcium content of lettuce.

This zesty green is usually grown commercially in quietly moving streams. It will, however, grow well in a garden pool — very well if there is a fountain that keeps the water just barely moving. Watercress can also be grown quite successfully in pots of sandy soil with a little ground limestone and leafmold added. The pots must be wet at all times, so they should be set in a tub or tray of water. Sink this in a cool, partly shady spot, and change the water often. Cool conditions are important, and in the South watercress is most successful in the winter.

Cucumbers Unlimited

Cucumbers have gotten so much attention from plant breeders in recent years that it's hard to keep up with all the new types and varieties. Dwarf, burpless, nonbitter, all-female — these new developments are making cucumbers more productive and more fun to grow and eat.

The new all-female hybrid cucumbers produce tremendous yields, especially when grown on trellises. (*Joseph Harris Seed Company*)

The all-female (gynoecious) hybrids have very few male flowers, so almost every flower becomes a fruit. 'Spartan Valour' and 'Gemini Hybrid' are two of these, while 'Pioneer' is a gynoecious pickling variety. A midget for limited space or containers is the gynoecious 'Patio Pik.' 'Burpless Hybrid' is very easy to digest, as is the unusual 'Lemon,' which produces golden lemon-shaped fruits with a "sweet lemon" flavor. Two that never develop bitterness are 'Sweet Slice' and 'Armenian Yard-Long' — the latter is often coiled and is most delicious when 12″ to 18″ long, but even when nearly a yard in length it becomes only slightly woody rather than bitter.

Grow cucumbers on trellises and you'll not only save a great deal of space but also get higher yields of better fruits. This is due to more light reaching the plants and better aeration that reduces disease problems. Dr. T. R. Konsler of North Carolina State University recommends a 6′-high trellis with posts set no more than 15′ apart. Top and bottom horizontal wires are connected with plastic twine tied between them at each plant. The plants are set 8″ to 10″ apart, and the main stem is trained up by intertwining it with the twine. Highest yields, Dr. Konsler says, result when the first six lateral runners at the base of the vine are pruned off. A variation of this is made with wire mesh fencing, which can be curved or even set up in a circle (but leave an opening so you can get inside for harvesting).

Dandelion Gains Status

Dandelions, gardeners are beginning to realize, should really be respected as a valuable vegetable rather than despised as a weed.

The young tender leaves or "dandelion greens" are a salad delicacy, and nutritionally they excel most garden greens: a cup provides over five times the minimum daily requirement of vitamin A (better than spinach), plus respectable amounts of vitamin C and iron and calcium — and contains only 80 calories. Connoisseurs also brew a tea from dandelion roots, and make dandelion wine from the flowers and a rich "coffee" from the roasted and ground roots.

A cabbage-leaved dandelion, with leaves spreading up to 2′, is now offered by several seedsmen. For improved flavor, the leaves are tied together to blanch the hearts, which are then eaten like endive.

Eggplantings

One way to extra enjoyment of vegetable gardening is to make a specialty of one vegetable, to explore all the differences in flavor and appearance among its varieties. You'd be surprised, for example, at the wide range in eggplants.

Eggplant does best on a light, rich soil and develops its best flavor when given plenty of water. (*Joseph Harris Seed Company*)

There are white eggplants — 'White Beauty' and 'White Italian' — mild in flavor and decorative. The green varieties such as 'Applegreen' are flavorful and high-yielding, and do not develop any bitterness if growth is slowed by lack of water or fertilizer in summer.

The diminutive eggplants bear many fruits: 'Morden Midget' is excellent far north, 'Hybrid Pickling Purple' makes better pickles than cucumbers, and 'Golden Yellow' bears lemon-size fruit and makes a handsome winter pot plant indoors. Finally, the elongated varieties, bearing fruits up to 12″ long and often only 1″ in diameter, are also high-yielding dwarf plants good for limited space . . . some of the best are 'Long Black,' 'Long Tom' (good for cool-summer areas), and 'Chinese Long Sword.'

Start eggplants indoors six to eight weeks before planting time in the garden. A warm-weather vegetable, eggplant must not be set outdoors until daytime temperatures settle down at around 70°. Pick the fruits when they have developed a high gloss. They are at their eating best beginning when they are one-third their full mature size.

Endive and Escarole

Endive and its broadleafed form known as escarole are popular crops, adding a special zest and many vitamins to salads. Both are grown just like lettuce, but sowings can extend from late spring to midsummer at three-week intervals for a long harvest. They can be blanched to reduce the slightly bitter taste: simply tie the tips of the leaves together a few days before harvesting . . . or in late fall, cover them with a loose mulch, which will both blanch the plants and protect them from considerable frost.

'Green Curled' and 'Salad King' are good varieties of endive, and 'Full Heart Batavian' is the finest escarole. You can begin to pick young leaves while the plants are still quite small, before they have formed a central rosette.

Florence Fennel or Finocchio

A superb but little-known vegetable, Florence fennel is related to the herb fennel, but it resembles a feathery-foliaged celery.

The leaves are used as a garnish and the stalks like celery, but the most important part of the plant is the big bulbous base. This has a sweet anise flavor and may be cooked alone or used in recipes. If the bulb is blanched by mounding soil around it two to three weeks before harvest, it is delicious raw in salads.

Florence fennel, often called finocchio, can be started indoors in peat pots, but in areas with hot summers it is best sown in the garden in summer for a fall crop. It takes about three months to mature. Space the plants 8″ apart so they can form large bulbs.

Essential Garlic

Garden-fresh garlic cloves are far superior to the packaged garlic in the market. This member of the onion family is also beneficial to your health — it lowers blood pressure — and to the health of other plants in the garden through its insect repellency.

Except very far in the North, garlic is usually planted in late summer or early fall, mulched over the winter, and harvested the following summer. Some of its spear-shaped leaves can be snipped occasionally and used green like chives. The flower heads are cut off when they appear so they will not take energy needed to develop large bulbs. Harvest the bulbs when the tops start to dry and fall over, pulling up the whole plant and hanging it to dry.

The mammoth 'Elephant Garlic,' a strain that produces bulbs weighing as much as a pound, is quite mild-flavored and is often eaten raw or made into pickles. In smaller varieties, there are the standard white Mexican and pink Italian, and the very "hot" German red garlic.

Berry Tomato — The Ground Cherry

The "Chinese lantern" genus, *Physalis*, offers several delightful unusual vegetables, known variously as ground cherry, husk tomato, cape gooseberry, and strawberry tomato. The plants are quite similar, growing 18″ to 36″ high and bearing small yellow fruits, each enclosed in an inflated calyx. These berries are most often used for pies and preserves, but they can also be eaten raw in salads, stewed or fried, made into a sauce for meat or desserts, or even candied (recipes are included with seed from Glecklers Seedmen). The flavor is an intriguing combination of sweet and tart.

Culture is the same as for tomatoes, and the seed may be started indoors for early bearing. The fruits are ready for harvest when they turn deep yellow and somewhat soft. Should they fall before ripening, they can be kept in a warm place, where they will continue to ripen. The plants are quite decorative, much branched, with hairy, toothed leaves.

Home Horseradish

Homemade horseradish sauce, to those who like it, is a delight. It's easily made in a blender, with a little white vinegar and water added. The plants are easy to grow, too, but beware: this is a spreading perennial plant that can take over cultivated areas, so relegate it to a back corner.

Cuttings of the parsnip-like branched roots are planted in spring, 2″ to 3″ deep with the small end slanting down. Harvest can begin in summer, and the roots may be dug till late fall and stored, or left in the garden all winter. When harvesting again in the spring, break off some of the smaller roots that are attached to the large ones and plant these for a new crop.

Herbaceous Huckleberry

A fruit that, like the strawberry, is grown in the vegetable garden is the garden huckleberry. Actually, this is not a true huckleberry (which is a member of the genus *Gaylussacia*), but a relative of the eggplant and potato (which are species of *Solanum*).

But if you like huckleberry pie, this easy-to-grow 3′ annual plant will give you an abundant crop of blue-black berries. These are too tart for eating raw, but when baked in a pie they taste like extra-tasty blueberries. Each plant produces enough berries for a pie (and they won't stain your teeth). Some gardeners can or freeze the berries, and they make fine preserves or jelly combined with grapes or apples.

Jerusalem Artichoke

A native American vegetable with a mixed-up name but unusual health value is one of the best new garden crops. A member of the sunflower family, the Jerusalem artichoke has nothing to do with

Jerusalem or artichokes — the Jerusalem derives from the Italian *girasole,* meaning "turning to the sun," and the taste of the tubers is only very slightly reminiscent of artichokes.

The plants look like sunflowers and grow to 6' or more. They are remarkably productive, each yielding at least 10 pounds of knobby, white-fleshed tuberous roots. An excellent substitute for potatoes, they are high in vitamins and minerals but have only 75 calories per pound compared to potato's 300. They are especially recommended for diabetics because they contain no starch, their carbohydrates being in the form of inulin and levulose. They are also very low in fat and sodium.

The tubers have a crisp texture and delicate nut-like flavor, sweeter than potatoes. Cook them, without peeling, in any way that you prepare potatoes, or use them raw in salads. They are dug through the fall — frost seems to improve them — or left under mulch for harvesting during thaws. Even with careful harvesting, enough tubers are always left in the ground to provide new plants the next spring. To start Jerusalem artichokes, plant cut-up tubers, each with an "eye," 6" deep and 12" apart in either fall or spring. For best tuber production, they should not have high fertility. The plants make a decorative background or screen and bear small golden sunflowers.

Kale — Winter Green

A handsome looseleafed cabbage with broad, very curly and ruffled leaves, kale matures in only eight or nine weeks and can be grown as a very early source of vitamin-rich greens. But more often it is planted in summer for fall harvest. Frost improves its flavor, and you can pick it all winter even in the North if you mulch it over.

The plants grow 12" or more tall and wide. Use the tender young leaves like lettuce, and all the leaves as cooked greens. The new 'Curled Vates' as well as the standard 'Dwarf Green Curled Scotch' and 'Siberian Curled' are excellent varieties.

Kohlrabi — Hard-Headed Cabbage

Kohlrabi is the "turnip-headed" member of the cabbage family. It makes a round bulb — actually the swollen stem — just above the soil surface. This should be harvested when no more than 3" in diameter, before it gets too old. In flavor it resembles a mild-tasting turnip. Cut it in strips for use in salads, or steam it whole, sliced or diced. It's also a prized ingredient in vegetable soups.

A very easily grown cool-weather crop for spring or fall, kohlrabi is planted 4" apart and matures in eight weeks. For tender bulbs, supply ample moisture and fertility. 'Early White Vienna' and 'Early Purple Vienna' are widely available varieties.

A fast-maturing crop, kale can be sown in
very early spring, then again later for fall
and winter use. (*W. Atlee Burpee Company*)

Unstoppable Leeks

The leek is truly a gourmet onion, with a subtle flavor that has
been relished since the days of the Pharaohs. It gives an extremely long harvest, the early thinnings being used as garnishes
and the mature plants from early fall through winter. Leeks under
a heavy winter mulch will thaw out perfectly when dug out with a
garden fork. Refrigerate them, and don't remove the roots until
you're ready to use the stalks. Leeks are superb stir-fried or
steamed and buttered like asparagus, invaluable in vegetable
soups, a fine addition minced into salads, and a wonderful ingredient in scores of other recipes.

Seed is started in flats or peat pots or sown directly in the garden.
Leeks take a little extra work: they must be sown or transplanted
into 4"-deep trenches, to which soil is added as they grow. This

blanches the stems. Some gardeners plant them on the surface and hill up soil around them as the stems elongate, and others simply add mulch close around the plants to accomplish the blanching. Thin when the seedlings are about the diameter of a pencil, so that the remaining plants stand 6″ apart.

'London Flag' is a long-popular variety, but even better are new ones such as early 'Titan,' long-season 'Giant Musselburgh' and 'Elephant,' and the thick-stemmed, very hardy 'Unique.'

Lettuce Unlimited

Good gardeners keep lettuce coming all season. The earliest crops are started indoors, making succession sowings at ten-day intervals. Bolt-resistant varieties, which are slow to go to seed in hot weather, are chosen for summer maturity, while a great many varieties produce excellent crops late into the fall from summer sowings.

Of the four types of lettuce, head or Iceberg takes longest to mature — 70 to 90 days. 'Great Lakes,' 'Ithaca' and the new 'Portage' resist bolting, and 'Stokes Evergreen' has considerable cold tolerance. Butterhead lettuce, which has a loose head, matures in about 70 days; 'Matchless,' miniature 'Tom Thumb' and the 'Bos-

The newest varieties of crisphead lettuce resist bolting in hot weather. (*W. Atlee Burpee Company*)

ton' varieties are widely grown; and 'Buttercrunch' and 'Summer Bibb' are especially favored for their heat-resistant qualities.

Looseleaf or bunching lettuce, which needs only 40 to 50 days, is represented by 'Black Seeded Simpson,' bolt-resistant curly-leaved 'Salad Bowl,' bronze-leaved 'Prizehead' and the even more decorative 'Oakleaf' and 'Ruby.' The fourth type, Cos or Romaine, has elongated upright heads, matures in about 70 days, and is notably heat-resistant. 'Paris Island Cos' is one of the best varieties.

Lettuce is shallow-rooted, so mulch it early to conserve moisture and water if there is little rain when the heads are forming. Be sure to thin lettuce adequately, allowing 6″ or more between leaf types, 12″ for head lettuce, so they can form properly.

Here's a trick to produce good head lettuce in the hottest summer, when even bolt-resistant types will go to seed: make a simple frame of wood, wire or wire mesh over the plants and cover this with two layers of cheesecloth. This "tobacco shading," plus a sprinkler that applies water very lightly and slowly, will produce sufficient cooling to allow the plants to form good heads.

And here is a way to have sturdy, very early transplants for spring. Sow lettuce in the fall, and gradually cover the seedlings with a heavy mulch of straw, leaves, etc., as cold weather approaches. A Michigan gardener reports that September-sown 'Evergreen' lettuce came through temperatures near –20° to make beautiful heads he harvested the following May.

Malabar — The Hot-Weather Spinach

Spinach won't take summer heat, but Malabar spinach thrives on it. This vine is not related botanically to spinach, but its foliage used fresh in salads or cooked is much like that of a mild-flavored spinach.

Trained on a string or wire trellis, it grows rapidly — as much as a foot per week — and the broad glossy leaves are a rich green and heavy-textured. Thus Malabar spinach is a good ornamental for screening or greening up a fence or wall. Pinching the stems when the plants reach about 2′ in height will make them branch. The youngest leaves can be harvested liberally. Malabar spinach also makes a decorative trellised container plant.

Mastering Melons

New fast-maturing varieties and speed-up growing methods have made it possible to grow all sorts of melons way up North. Today we have 75-day cantaloupes, midget and seedless watermelons that can be harvested in 65 to 80 days, and even 90-day honeydews and crenshaws.

'Gold Star,' 'Canada Gem,' 'Samson,' 'Pride of Wisconsin,' 'Min-

'Gold Star' is one of the finest new hybrid cantaloupes for home gardens. (*Joseph Harris Seed Company*)

nesota Midget,' 'Charantais,' 'Saticoy' and 'Burpee Hybrid' are among the best cantaloupes grown everywhere. 'Early Crenshaw' and 'Honey Mist' honeydew are quick-maturing varieties of two melons that formerly were restricted to warm climes. In watermelons, northern gardeners do best with the short-season 'New Hampshire Midget,' 'Sugar Baby' and yellow-fleshed 'Yellow Baby' and 'Honey Cream' in the "icebox" size, and 'Fordhook Hybrid' and 'Northern Delight' in the large-fruited class.

Try some unusuals, too, such as the banana melon, 18″ long with salmon-pink flesh, or the egg-shaped 'Gold Crown,' a Casaba-type hybrid that grows farther north than do Casabas.

Sow melon seed indoors three to four weeks early, and harden off the seedlings carefully. Use a green plastic mulch to speed warming of the soil in the planting area, and lay black plastic or aluminum foil in the area where the vines will spread — tests have shown this can speed maturity by as much as 10 days, as well as preventing soil-borne disease by keeping the fruit from touching the ground. Put hotcaps or cloches over the plants to protect them until the weather has become steadily warm. Then be sure the plants have plenty of moisture until the fruits begin to ripen (dry soil then will increase their sweetness).

Cantaloupes are ripe when the stem breaks off with a very slight twist of the fruit, watermelons when the "ground spot" on the underside turns pale yellow and the tendrils nearest the stem are dry.

For all but the big watermelons, growing on trellises is practical and a great space-saver. Use a strong wide-mesh wire fencing, and support the fruits when they begin to get big and heavy with cloth slings tied to the wire.

Speedy Greens — The Mustards

A southern staple, mustards are well worth growing in the North, for they are quick, easy and very rich in vitamins and minerals. They mature in four to six weeks and go to seed fast in hot weather, so mustards are a crop for early spring and fall. Make three or four sowings at 10-day intervals, and thin to 6″ apart. The thinnings and plants 4″ high can be used for salads, but for cooked greens mustards are harvested when 6″ tall. Today's mustards are quite mild in flavor, with just a slight peppery tang.

An All-America Selection, the yellow-fleshed 'Yellow Baby' watermelon is one of the new midget hybrids that mature rapidly, making them practical for northern gardens. (*All-America Selections*)

Best smooth-leaved varieties are 'Florida Broad Leaf' and the heat-resistant 'Tendergreen.' 'Southern Giant Curled' and 'Fordhook Fancy' have curled leaves. Some dealers offer mustards with reddish-purple leaves or broad white stalks.

New Zealand Spinach

Another mild-flavored hot-weather spinach substitute, New Zealand spinach is related to neither true spinach nor Malabar spinach, and it's easier to grow than either of them.

This is a low, wide-spreading plant — give it at least 24″ spacing after thinning. The small pointed young leaves and stems can be picked all summer and fall. Pick about 3″ to 4″ of the tips each time you harvest it. The seeds are slow to germinate, and it is best started in peat pots indoors.

Okra Is More Than Okay

A southern vegetable that is becoming a northern favorite is okra. It's a fast-growing (seven to eight weeks) hot-weather crop that requires only moderate fertility, and there are many more uses for the green fleshy pods than the traditional gumbo. They can be steamed, fried, deep-fried, broiled or roasted, made into pickles, and used in many recipes. Okra is rich in minerals and also contains a digestive aid called mucin. A species of hibiscus, it bears beautiful large yellow flowers that add to its ornamental value as a hedge or screen.

Sow the seed when the soil has warmed up, 15″ apart for dwarf varieties such as the 30″ 'Long Green Pod' or 'Emerald Green,' 24″ for the 5′ 'Clemson Spineless' and 'Perkins Mammoth Long Pod.' The pods must be picked while young, almost daily, for they quickly become stringy and tough on maturing. They should snap off easily. The plants will continue to bear over a long period. Some seedsmen offer white- or red-podded okras.

Basic Onions

To grow good onions of all kinds, there's one essential: a soil rich in organic matter. Onions are a high-organic sandy loam to muck crop, so dig in all the well-rotted manure or compost you can.

Onions are started from seed, transplants or sets. Any standard onion can be harvested young as green bunching onions (scallions), although there are special bulbless 'Bunching' varieties bred for this purpose. From seed, onions take a long time and so must be planted very early in spring. In the North, either seedlings or the stunted bulbous plants called sets are preferred for a head start (but of course not all varieties are available in these forms). Sets may be planted 1″ to 2″ apart and the thinnings used

In a moist, high-organic soil, 'Sweet
Spanish' onions grow to a pound or more.
(*W. Atlee Burpee Company*)

as scallions, leaving the rest about 4″ apart to develop fully. Any
seedstalks that appear should be snipped off immediately.

You can grow your own sets by sowing seed very thickly in July,
breaking off the tops in early fall, and digging them a few weeks
later. The little sets are dried and stored in a cool dry place until
spring planting time.

To harvest full-grown onions, knock over the tops with a rake as
soon as some of them start to fall over naturally. Pull up the bulbs
and let them dry in the sun for a day or two, then out of the sun
until cold weather, when the tops are clipped off and the bulbs put
in storage.

The white or yellow 'Ebenezer,' 'Globe' and 'Sweet Spanish' are very popular varieties, but there are many more. The 'Bermuda' varieties are mild but do not store well. 'Barletta' and 'Silver Queen' are excellent pickling and cocktail onions.

An unusual onion is the top-multiplier or Egyptian tree onion. It produces little bulblet onions on the tops of fat hollow stalks. This hardy perennial self-sows, the bulblets taking root when the stalks fall over. They provide fine scallions in the spring. The little top onions are delicious for all onion uses, and the stalks are used in salads when young or cooked as leeks when they get fatter.

Katy and George "Doc" Abraham, the famous *Green Thumb* authors and radio and TV columnists, provide this helpful tip:

> There can be three reasons for onions that are almost too "hot" to eat: overcrowding slows their growth and makes them hot — if you sow seed, allow 3 or 4 per inch and thin to 1″ to 1½″ apart; sets can be planted 3″ apart (thicker if small early green onions are wanted); onion plants of the "hamburger" type should be spaced 4″ to 6″ apart . . . lack of water — in dry spells onions need daily watering to avoid slowing of growth . . . low fertility . . . onions do best on a rich sandy loam, with plenty of humus, compost or muck (well-rotted manure is great for onions). In short, anything that slows the growth of onions makes them hot.

Progressive Parsleys

Parsley is one of the most versatile ornamental edibles, the smaller kinds being good for edgings and the larger ones attractive in borders. And parsley can be grown all year — in the garden from early spring through fall and in a kitchen window in winter.

There are flat-leaved parsleys with foliage much like that of celery ('Plain,' 'Dark Green'), and curly-leaved types ('Moss Curled,' 'Paramount,' 'Evergreen'). More unusual is the choice 'Mituba' Japanese parsley which grows 2′ tall, and the 3′ 'Giant Italian' that has thick stalks which are used like celery. And for a fast-growing "parsnip," grow 'Hamburg' parsley, which produces 6″ fleshy roots with parsley flavor and parsnip uses.

Parsley seed is slow to germinate, so soak it for 24 hours before planting, or pour boiling water over it after it is sown. Sow very early in spring and thin to 6″ apart for the smaller types. Cutting can begin as soon as sprigs are well formed. A biennial, parsley will winter over under a light mulch. In spring, cut off the flower stalks to prevent the plants from going to seed, and they will produce a good crop until your new spring-sown parsley is ready to harvest. Plants can be dug up and potted in the fall, or seed started in pots in late summer, for growing and harvesting indoors all winter.

Rooting for Parsnips

Parsnips are a more versatile — as well as more delicious — vegetable than most gardeners realize. Garden-grown and especially when dug after frost, they have a sweet, delicate flavor and crispness, wonderful alone or "singularly appropriate with a great many things," to quote botanist-gourmet Alex D. Hawkes. They can also be harvested earlier, however, before the center core has formed, to make an excellent substitute for carrots in a soup or stew. One cup of parsnips supplies almost one third of an adult's daily requirement of vitamin C. And the celery-like stalks and leaves, which are fine for winter and spring salads, are rich in minerals.

Best quality in parsnips results when the soil is light, rich and moist. It should be dug, compost-enriched and soaked to at least 12″ depth. Sow the seed early, no deeper than ¼″, and thin to 3″ to 4″ apart. Harvest begins in late summer and can continue through winter if a deep mulch of hay is applied.

New green tops will sprout in thaws, and stalks will form in spring for an extra crop — use the latter chopped like celery in salads and soups. But don't leave too many plants until spring, for the roots become woody when left this late. Where the winter is very frigid, parsnips are dug early and stored in cold cellars in sand. A fine variety is 'All American.'

Peanuttiness

Though they're a long-season crop, peanuts are grown successfully by gardeners as far north as Ontario, Canada. They are fun to grow, far tastier when home-grown and freshly roasted, and very high in protein and minerals. A legume, peanuts add nitrogen to the soil, and the 18″ plants bear showy yellow flowers — try combining peanuts with petunias for a pretty border for the vegetable plot.

The small-kerneled 'Spanish' takes 110 days to mature, and the newest varieties of the large-kerneled 'Virginia' require only slightly longer. Give peanuts a light sandy soil, a green plastic mulch for fast soil warming before planting, and cloches over the seedlings for early cold protection. Plant the shelled nuts no deeper than 2″ in the North.

When the plants start to flower and send down the shoots that produce the "goober peas" underground, hill up the soil and apply a loose mulch such as hay or grass clippings. Before frost, lift the vines with a fork and either hang them or remove the peanuts and put them in shallow trays for curing in a dry place indoors for a month or so. They can be roasted shelled or unshelled, 20 minutes at 350°.

Cool Peas to Cowpeas

Peas are the top early crop in most vegetable gardens, but the season can be extended much longer than most gardeners realize.

'Little Marvel,' 'Laxton,' 'Lincoln,' dwarf 'Burpee's Blue Bantam' and the new extra-sweet 'Green Arrow' are cool-weather peas, sown as soon as the ground can be worked, with several succession plantings made every ten days or varieties chosen for early to late maturity. Treat the seed with legume inoculant before planting, and be sure to move aside winter mulches at least ten days before sowing so the ground can warm up.

Even dwarf varieties need the support of a chicken wire trellis or twiggy brush from winter prunings — unless you plant them in wide rows or patches, so that the plants grow very closely together and hold each other up. The 5' 'Tall Telephone' or 'Alderman' can be staked; this very productive long-bearing variety takes longer to mature than the others, so plant it as early as possible.

Edible-podded peas are eaten pod and all when young. (*W. Atlee Burpee Company*)

Peppers come in many shapes and colors
and are among the most ornamental
vegetables in the garden and in containers.
(*W. Atlee Burpee Company*)

A heat-resistant pea is 'Wando.' It can be planted late in the spring for summer cropping, or sown in summer for harvest in the fall. For cool-weather varieties that fail to begin bearing before hot weather, try the tobacco shading and evaporative cooling technique suggested for lettuce.

The Chinese edible-podded sugar or snow peas are delicious pod and all. There are dwarf ('Little Sweetie') and tall ('Mammoth Melting Sugar,' 'Super Sweetpod') varieties. They are harvested when the peas are just beginning to form in the pods. Fast cooking, or adding the pods only during the final two or three minutes when making Oriental dishes, retains their unique crisp texture. If the peas develop in the pods before they can be picked, shell them and use as you would ordinary peas.

The colorful and nutritious southern field peas or cowpeas, which include blackeye, crowder, lady and other types, are easily grown in the North, even in Minnesota. 'Blue Goose,' 'Pink Eye Purple Hull,' 'Calico Crowder,' 'Mississippi Silver' and 'Early Ramshorn' are superior varieties (H. G. Hastings is a good source) of these peas, which do well in poor soil and hot summers. They are planted when the soil has warmed up and picked when the bean-like shells are still green or allowed to ripen for dried peas. The plants are bushy vines and do not require support.

Pepper Pep-Up

Gardeners who grow only one or two common sweet peppers miss much gardening and eating pleasure. The fruit forms and colors of many unusual peppers add beauty to the vegetable garden, and there are zesty differences in flavor.

Some we especially like are the long yellow 'Sweet Banana' . . . red 'Cubanelle,' the finest for frying . . . red 'Hot Portugal,' very large, hot, fast-maturing . . . yellow 'Romanian Wax,' sweet-hot, dwarf, heavy-bearing . . . 'Sweet Cherry,' small rounded fruits excellent for salads and pickling . . . 'Chili Jalapeno,' a superb pickling type . . . 'Pimento,' very sweet, heart-shaped . . . 'Hercules Sweet Red' and 'Yellow,' both huge, extremely sweet . . . and two University of New Hampshire introductions, 'Pinocchio,' bearing upturned clusters of long red fruits, and 'Sweet Chocolate,' which actually turns a rich brown when ripe.

Peppers are a warm-weather crop, started indoors six to eight weeks before planting out. For extra-early bearing, use a green plastic mulch to warm the soil around the plants when you set them out, put hotcaps or cloches over them, and set wide boards on end in the rows to deflect wind and reflect sun heat and light onto the plants. Peppers are very ornamental in containers.

Easy No-Dig Potatoes

Don't plant potatoes — just lay them on the ground and cover them with a thick loose mulch. The vines will grow quickly through 8″ or more of hay, straw or similar material. This is the modern, easy, works-everywhere method.

Buy certified seed potatoes, cutting them into 1½″ sections with at least one good "eye" in each. The soil should be moist and friable, almost "fluffy," and slightly acid (lime increases potato scab). Space the seed pieces 12″ to 14″ apart. Small "new potatoes" can be harvested while the vines are green (just reach under the mulch), those for storage are generally left until the tops have been withered for a couple of weeks.

Early varieties start maturing in about 90 days, late ones take 110 days or more. Ten pounds of seed should yield 100 to 150 pounds of potatoes — but Dr. Ray Crawford, in upstate New York, harvested a national record of 423 pounds from 2 pounds of seed. He attributed this to planting in almost pure leafmold (all the leaves from his street are dumped on his garden every autumn).

'Irish Cobbler' is an excellent early potato, 'Norgold Russet' is one of the finest for baking, and late 'Katahdin' is very high in vitamin C, but there are many other fine varieties. Some potatoes have unusual shapes and colors: lavender-skinned 'Black Chenango' is a very high quality potato but little known, while the yellow-fleshed 'German Fingerling,' regarded by connoisseurs as the finest of all for salad and German-fried potatoes, produces great quantities of 2″ to 4″ long potatoes only 1″ in diameter.

Winning Pumpkins

Pumpkins are a fascinating crop. If you're short of room, you can grow a bush type like 'Cinderella.' For the best pumpkin pies, grow the sweet 'Spookie' or 'Small Sugar.' For Halloween, 'Big Tom' ('Connecticut Field') and 'Jack-O'-Lantern' are big and popular. If you want to grow a really huge pumpkin, well over 100 pounds, choose 'Big Max,' and allow only one fruit to develop (it won't be eating quality, but you may win a prize at the county fair). And finally, to grow those healthful pumpkin seeds without the arduous chore of hulling them, plant the new "naked-seed" variety, 'Lady Godiva.'

Varieties that bear small fruits can be trained on a fence, trellis, tree or cornstalks. Pumpkins need a great deal of moisture, so mulch and water heavily in extended droughts. Incidentally, pumpkins make other delicious dishes besides pumpkin pie, from custards to casseroles, and an unusual pudding is made by scooping out the seeds and fiber, filling the cavity with milk, and baking the pumpkin until the milk is absorbed.

Radishes That Rate

Radishes are an easy and popular crop — but they're also a neglected one, in the sense that few gardeners have tried the great variety available.

In standard radishes, the best for cool weather are 'Burpee White,' 'Cherry Belle,' 'Comet,' 'French Breakfast,' 'Sparkler' and 'White Icicle.' For hot weather, grow 'All Seasons White,' 'Champion,' 'Red Boy' and 'White Strasburg.' Best for remaining in the ground without becoming pithy: 'All Seasons White' (keeps up to six weeks, and usable from 6″ to 12″ long), 'Burpee White,' 'Champion,' 'Comet,' 'Firecracker' and 'Scarlet White Tip.'

Some fabulous radishes are found in the Oriental, French and Spanish winter types. 'French Golden' is piquant and gold-colored, 'De Gournay' is sweet and violet, 'Nerima Long Neck' grows 24″ long, 'Shogoin' has turnip shape and weighs up to 5 pounds, and 'Sakurajima' sown in May will reach 50 pounds or more. Sweetest of all is 'White Celestial,' a Chinese stump-root variety. All winter radishes store well for months in moist sand in a cool place.

Radishes are rich in vitamins A and C, and all kinds are superb

'Big Max' pumpkins will grow to over 100
pounds if only one fruit is allowed to develop
per vine. (*W. Atlee Burpee Company*)

cooked. Slice and sauté them in butter and onion, then add a
little water, salt and parsley, and simmer 10 to 15 minutes.

A growing tip: if your radishes are often infested with maggots,
use a tarpaper mulch to repel them. Or as George "Doc" Abraham
suggests, dip the seed in kerosene before planting — "the radishes
will not have any taste of kerosene, and will be completely free of
maggots."

Regal Rhubarb

Only a half-dozen plants are needed to produce ample rhubarb for
a family. Since it's very ornamental, this many plants are easily
accommodated almost anywhere in the garden. A long-lived perennial crop — a bed should last at least twenty-five years — it
needs only dividing every six or seven years to prevent crowding.

Rhubarb is most often grown from crowns. These are planted in
early spring in rich, well-drained soil. Moderate harvesting begins

The home gardener can grow not only red
and white radishes of superb flavor, but also
some big and very sweet winter radishes.
(*W. Atlee Burpee Company*)

the year after planting crowns, the second year from seed. Pull the
stalks with a slight twist. The leaves should never be eaten, as
they contain toxic oxalic acid. Cut off seedstalks as soon as they
appear, to conserve the plant's energy for production. Large
amounts of rotted manure or compost applied very early in spring
and again after harvest will supply the high fertility rhubarb requires (it's almost impossible to overfeed it). 'Valentine,' 'Victoria'
and 'MacDonald' are leading varieties.

To force extra-early stalks, put a bottomless box or basket over
the clump and cover it with clear plastic or glass. This will trap
warmth and draw up the stalks rapidly. Rhubarb can also be
forced indoors in winter, by digging up a clump, letting it freeze,
and then planting it in a box of soil or sand that is kept in a dark
basement at 60°. Stalks will be ready for harvest in a few weeks.

Rutabaga — The Lapland Turnip

Rutabagas haven't as yet quite reached the gourmet class, but
they're on the way. The Swede or Lapland turnip is being up-

graded by the development of new home-garden varieties such as 'Altasweet,' which has an unusually mild, sweet flavor.

The rutabaga, says Robert Rodale of *Organic Gardening*, even surpasses the true turnip in vitamin C content, and has more vitamin A plus some B vitamins and many minerals. It is best planted 90 days before the first fall frost, thinned to 8″ to 10″ apart, and harvested after a few nights of light frost. One of the best storage crops, it will keep for months packed in boxes of straw in a cellar at temperatures just above freezing, or buried in sand in an outdoor pit. Or the plants may be left in the garden and dug when needed.

Rutabagas can be used in almost any recipe that calls for turnips. The delicate-flavored 'Altasweet' should be especially good for soups and ragouts, or serve it raw, cut in slivers, in salads.

Salsify, the vegetable oyster, has an unusual sweet flavor prized by gourmets. (*Organic Gardening and Farming*)

Salsify Is Satisfying

Salsify, scorzonera or the vegetable oyster produces a 6″ to 8″ white-fleshed carrot-like root that has a delicate oyster flavor. It is delicious both raw and cooked — gourmets recommend first parboiling it and then browning in butter.

Salsify is a long-season crop. Seed is sown early in spring in a sandy soil. The roots can be left in the ground under a mulch for winter or spring harvest, or dug and stored in moist sand indoors. 'Mammoth Sandwich Island' is the most widely available variety.

Shallots — Aristocrat Onions

The shallot is considered a very special onion — distinctive and mild in flavor, indispensable in French cookery, and very expensive in the markets. It is planted in the fall or very early spring and harvested and stored like other onions, but the shallot is a multiplier onion that produces a clump of small bulbs or cloves like garlic. The smaller cloves are saved for replanting. Thinnings make especially delicious scallions, and the leaves can be chopped and used like chives.

'Zucchini Elite' produces tremendous yields of the most popular type of summer squash if kept picked. (*Joseph Harris Seed Company*)

A marvelous seasoning spread, says Alex D. Hawkes, is made by blanching peeled cloves until they are tender, then grinding them in a mortar with butter. They also make very fine pickled onions, and their delicate flavor is a welcome change from ordinary onions in every sort of recipe.

Soybeans instead of Steak

Soybeans are a terrific crop, nutritious (when heated they supply complete protein, and sprouting greatly increases their vitamin content), soil-improving (they're a nitrogen-fixing legume), and as easy to grow as beans even in the North (varieties like 'Early Green Bush' mature in only 12 weeks).

Treat the seed with a soybean inoculant and sow in peat pots in early spring in the North, in the garden in late spring in the South. A reflective mulch of aluminum foil or white polyethylene film has been shown to boost yields dramatically. Harvest when the shells are green and plump.

For easy shelling, pour boiling water over them and let stand for two or three minutes before draining and cooling. Soybeans are cooked rapidly and served alone with seasonings or in salads, casseroles and many other dishes. Dried soybeans are added to meat recipes, or they can be roasted for a snack or for grinding into a meal for baking or even making coffee.

Dynamic Spinach

Popeye does get his strength from spinach, says the National Academy of Sciences: it tops all popular vegetables in iron, calcium and vitamin C.

Spinach is a cool-weather crop, and varieties like 'Cold Resistant Savoy' and 'Winter Bloomsdale' will actually winter over under mulch for an early spring harvest. These are also often planted in late summer for fall harvests. 'America,' 'Bloomsdale Long Standing' and other standard varieties are planted in early spring, and although some are reputedly slow-bolting they should be timed to mature before the onset of hot weather. Grow spinach in a light soil, and thin to 3″ apart if every other plant will be harvested before it is fully grown — a good way to stretch the harvest.

Squash for All Seasons

Seed catalogs list a fabulous array of both summer and winter squashes. Most summer squashes come in space-saving bush form, but nearly all winter squashes are vines. All are planted when the soil — preferably a light one high in sand and organic matter — has warmed up. Summer squash is picked while a fingernail will still pierce the skin with very little pressure. Only a

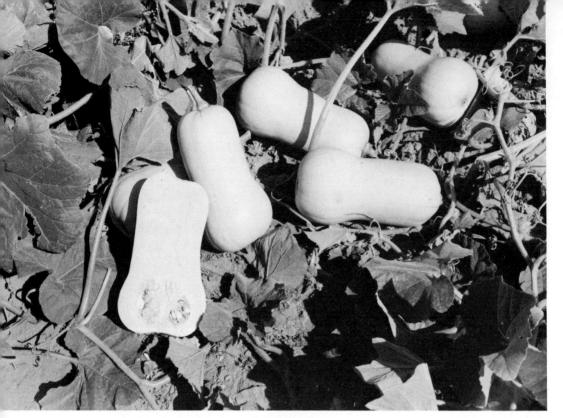

The best winter squash is 'Waltham Butternut,' which keeps its rich flavor for a long time in storage. (*Joseph Harris Seed Company*)

few plants will supply enough for a family, for the more you pick the more they bear. Some winter squashes, like 'Butternut' and 'Hubbard,' can be harvested young, but for storage all must be fully ripe but not exposed to frost. Always leave a piece of stem on when harvesting them to prevent rotting in storage.

With squashes, the rule for a small garden is to try a new kind each year, for there are subtle flavor differences among the summer crookneck, zucchini, patty pan, cocozelle and other summer squashes, and even greater differences among the acorn, hubbard and other winter varieties. Several of both types have received All-America awards and are especially valued for productivity and quality. One many gardeners would never be without is 'St. Pat Scallop,' a patty pan that is delectable when picked no larger than a silver dollar.

Some of the old varieties, however, such as 'Umatilla Marble-head,' a winter squash with fruits up to 40 pounds, are still well worth growing. A deservedly popular novelty is the spaghetti squash or vegetable spaghetti — its 8″ fruit is boiled whole for 30 minutes and the long fibers inside are delicious with spaghetti sauce.

For extra-early squash, try this special technique. Plant seed, presprouted by wrapping them in a wet towel overnight, in bottom-less square bands made by cutting 3"-wide strips out of a one-gallon milk carton. These strips are placed on a board and filled with soil mix. Keep them in a sunny window, and when it's time to plant outdoors, lift each banded seedling with a pancake turner, drop it into a 3" deep hole and pull the band up and away. Because the roots are never disturbed, the seedlings suffer no transplanting shock and continue growing rapidly.

Squash blossoms are a special culinary treat. Cook them for no more than five minutes in butter or oil in a covered pan over high heat, or dip them in batter and cook over medium heat until golden brown.

Strawberry Patch-Work

Botanically, strawberries are a fruit (so are tomatoes), but these herbaceous plants are most often grown in the vegetable plot — and in Japan, where strawberry growing and forcing are practically a fine art, the strawberry is classed as a vegetable.

This is not important to the gardener, who is more concerned with the confusing multiplicity of growing methods. Books recommend all sorts of systems — from hill to matted row and spaced row and myriad variations on these. The result is that few gardeners get the big yields of top-size fruit they want, and they also work too hard at growing America's favorite fruit.

In very recent years, commercial growers have developed methods that give yields of 40,000 to 50,000 quarts per acre. The gardener can adapt their system by planting in beds of three rows, the rows 12" apart and the plants spaced 30" in the row, and allowing two of the earliest runners from each plant to develop, one up and one down the row. These are encouraged to root by placing a small stone on them or covering them with soil. They will replace the original plants the second year, and thereafter only single runners from occasional plants will be needed to keep the row filled. All flowers should be removed from June bearers the first year, but remove them from everbearers only until early summer so they will bear a crop later the same year.

This method diverts energy that would have gone into making many runners into producing a strong heavy-bearing plant. For highest production, very high fertility and humus levels are essential. A strawberry planting should have a great deal of rotted manure, compost, leafmold or other organics, plus bonemeal and bloodmeal or cottonseed meal, worked in when it is first prepared, and additional fertilizer applied each spring. Also important is a 2" mulch of wood chips, sawdust, straw, grass clippings or similar material to keep the berries clean, conserve moisture and reduce

Plant the best varieties, give them very high
fertility and prune out excess runners, and
you'll get big yields of sweet strawberries.
(*Organic Gardening and Farming*)

weeds. A protective mulch of straw or hay is placed over the
plants in the North after a few hard frosts. For plants to start a
new bed, simply let runners root in peat pots or bottom sections of
milk cartons, cutting them off the mother plant when they are well
established.

Early spring planting is recommended for strawberries except in the South. Some varieties are fairly widely adapted — 'Catskill,' 'Earlidawn,' 'Sparkler' and 'Fletcher' in the June-bearing types, and everbearing 'Ozark Beauty' — but most do better in certain regions and locales than in others. So check with your extension service office for the best recommendations for your area.

A fascinating, truly everbearing perennial strawberry you can grow from seed is the wild alpine strawberry. It will bear the first year from early spring sowing and continue to produce small but wonderfully sweet berries each year from early summer to frost. The plants produce no runners, so make neat edgings for borders. 'Baron Solemacher' is the best-known variety, and a yellow-fruited type is occasionally offered. Equally good are the European woodland strawberries sold as *Fraises des Bois* by White Flower Farm (Litchfield, CT 06759; catalog $4).

Sunflowers Are for the Birds — And You

Considering the soaring cost of birdseed, sunflowers would be worth growing just to supply your birdfeeders. But they're also supremely nutritious, especially rich in protein, the B vitamins, vitamin E and several important minerals, and their fat content is in the form of polyunsaturates. Robert Rodale has called the sunflower "one of the most remarkable and useful plants in the world" and sunflower seeds "perhaps closest to being the perfect food."

'Mammoth Russian' often grows to 12' or more and produces heads 30" across (the giant stalks, of course, are great for compost and mulch when chopped or shredded). Sunflowers are drought-resistant and will grow even in poorer soils. The broad leaves quickly shade out weeds. Thin the plants to stand 18" to 24" apart. Harvest when the base of the flower head has turned yellow and the florets in the center are shriveling. Cut with a foot of the stalk attached and hang up in a dry, airy place for the seeds to cure. They are easily rubbed out of the head when dry, and store well in a dry place in nonairtight containers.

Since sunflower seeds are so nutritious, only a small amount need be eaten at a time, and in this case the seeds can be hulled by opening them with a thumbnail or cracking the shell with your teeth or a clothespin. For larger quantities, a small farm hammer-mill does a good job with the screen removed and the mill set at 350 revolutions per minute. Occasionally speed it up to 1200 to 1500 rpm to prevent clogging. The kernels can be roasted dry or with oil if desired, or ground for use in baking.

Solid Gold Sweet Potatoes

Northerners can grow as good sweet potatoes as Southerners — if they give them the right soil and head-start methods.

Sweet potatoes must have a warm sandy soil low in nitrogen (farmers use a 1:4:5 ratio fertilizer). A green plastic mulch to warm the soil before planting, plus cloches over the young vines, will make it possible to set out the plants earlier than the usually advised three weeks after last frost. Most important, start your plants indoors: sprout the tubers at room temperatures in moist sand or suspend them with toothpicks in jars of water with about one-third of the root end under water. In four to five weeks, rooted

Sunflowers grow as easily as weeds, and a few plants will produce a large harvest of nutritious seeds. (*Organic Gardening and Farming*)

sprouts can be gently pulled off. These are planted about 15″ apart in the row.

Harvest before or immediately after the first frost. Dig very carefully to avoid bruising. "Cure" the potatoes for a couple of hours in the sun, then in a warm but airy and shaded place for two weeks. They will keep until spring stored at 55°.

Good varieties are 'Centennial,' the fast-maturing 'Buncho Porto Rico,' and 'Allgold,' which contains three times the vitamin A and 50% more vitamin C than other sweet potatoes.

Tampala — Tropical Spinach

A tropical Asian relative of the amaranthus grown in the flower garden, tampala or Fordhook spinach is an excellent hot-weather spinach substitute. It's regarded by many as better than spinach, not only in flavor — it's closer to artichoke than to spinach — but also in its ability to stay tender longer and to supply stems that are cooked like asparagus.

Seed of tampala is sown when the ground is warm, making succession sowings for a long harvest. Picking of the tender young leaves can begin six to eight weeks after planting. They are good raw or cooked.

Tomatoes — America's No. 1 Garden Obsession

Tomatoes that will germinate and grow in the cold of Canada's prairie provinces ('Swift,' 'Early Fireball,' 'Coldset') . . . tomatoes for Hawaii's heat ('Pearl Harbor') . . . yellow ('Jubilee,' 'Sunray,' 'Golden Queen'), pink ('Ponderosa') and white ('Snowball,' 'White Beauty') tomatoes, very low in acid . . . giant tomatoes ('Big Boy,' 'Big Girl') . . . tomatoes with several times the vitamin C of other tomatoes ('Caro-Red') . . . tomatoes for canning, purée and paste ('Veeroma,' 'San Marzano') . . . tomatoes for containers ('Pixie,' 'Small Fry,' 'Stakeless') . . . cherry, plum and pear tomatoes . . . tomatoes that don't need staking or pruning (determinate types) . . . plus a host of great early, midseason and late varieties that bear medium-size red tomatoes — these are all available today due to the vast amount of selection and breeding work that has been directed toward improving America's favorite vegetable.

Tomatoes will produce well with casual care, lavishly with a little extra effort. Their two great needs are lots of water and lots of fertilizer. The planting holes should be prepared 2′ deep, with compost, dried or rotted manure, bonemeal and a nitrogen fertilizer such as bloodmeal mixed in thoroughly. Seedlings started indoors develop into stocky, sturdy plants if the medium has a good proportion of compost in it and they are fed with a fertilizer high in phosphorus and potassium, such as seaweed. And be sure to grow your tomatoes with a deep mulch to conserve moisture and stabilize soil temperatures.

Set the plants deeply, so that only a few leaves are above the soil surface, and the buried stem will make roots all along its length to strengthen the plant. To get the earliest tomatoes, prune off all the suckers that form in the leaf axils, or leave just one to make a two-stemmed plant — this produces an earlier but smaller crop of larger fruits.

A method that gives very high yields is suggested by Iowa gardener Robert V. Fisher, a member of the Men's Garden Clubs of America: he lets suckers grow until a bloom cluster forms on each, then pinches out the growth beyond the cluster, as well as all side branches that start to grow on the sucker. Instead of suckers rampant with leaves that shade the fruit and reduce its growth, he has bloom clusters that produce fine fruit, giving him as much as triple the normal yield.

Indeterminate tomatoes can be trained on tepees and A-frames as well as staked. A "tomato cage" gives high yields with less work. A 48″ length of concrete reinforcing wire, 30″ high, is bent into a circle and set over the plant. This serves as its support as the vines grow up through the mesh, and the plants are left unpruned since they will spread out naturally in the cage and shade the fruits just enough to prevent sunscald.

For easy feeding and bountiful production, plant your tomatoes around a compost ring. A 13′ length of 5′-wide small-mesh wire fencing is made into a circle of 5′ diameter. This is set upright on the ground and filled with vegetable wastes, grass clippings and other compost material, with an occasional sprinkling of soil and fertilizer. Plant four to six tomatoes around the outside of the circle. Water the compost regularly to supply a constant flow of nutrients to the plants' roots, which will spread out under this core of fertility.

A few more ideas from the best tomato growers:

Crushed eggshells added to the soil around your tomatoes will help prevent blossom end rot (a calcium-water stress problem) . . . in windy areas, plant tomatoes in the bottom of a 6″-deep trench, and they'll give earlier and bigger yields . . . take cuttings from your best plants in the fall, pot them up and root them, then take and root more cuttings from these, and you'll have quite a few plants to set out in spring — this practice can add 30% to 40% to the productivity of your tomato patch, says a gardener who follows it.

Don't be too quick to pick your tomatoes: horticulturist Richard B. Farnham says that " 'Heinz 1350' — a really fine tomato, well formed, noncracking, very flavorful if harvested at the right stage" — is usually picked when it turns scarlet, but if left until it be-

A few plants of almost any modern tomato variety will produce more than enough for the family if some special techniques are followed. (*Ball Seed Company*)

comes a bright, rich red, the flavor will be greatly improved . . . Tomatoes still green when frost comes can be stored by hanging the vines in a frost-free indoor area, or the tomatoes can be wrapped in paper and held for several weeks at 50° to 55°. Bring them into warmer temperatures (but not sun) when you want them to ripen quickly for use.

Toothsome Turnips

As easily grown as radishes, turnips thrive in a light soil and the cool of spring and autumn. The recent All-America Winner, 'Tokyo Cross Hybrid,' matures in only five weeks, but it can be left in the ground until it is 6″ in diameter without becoming pithy. For a late crop, grow the 'Shogoin' foliage turnip, which produces greens in 30 days, roots in 70.

Turnip greens are very high in vitamins A, B₂ and C and calcium, and are tasty in salads or as cooked greens. 'Just Right' is another good variety for greens, and thinnings of standard varieties like 'Early Purple-Top Milan' and 'Purple-Top White Globe' are also prized for this purpose. For some unusual turnips, try 'Presto,' the little white turnip that can be pickled overnight . . . 'Longue de Caliure' from France, with long black-skinned roots and very sweet flesh . . . and 'Gros Longue d'Alsace,' which produces extremely long fat roots.

Turnips can be planted quite close together, with those that are harvested while small leaving room for the rest to grow to full size. Given ample mulch and moisture, many varieties can be allowed to grow large without loss of flavor and texture.

Herbs for All Seasonings

A selection of the culinary herbs is indispensable not only to the good cook but also to the gardener, for many herbs are valuable for their insect repellency and growth-stimulating effects on other plants. So grow them throughout your garden (but for a wonderful decorative feature, make an herb wagon wheel or knot garden near your terrace or patio). Since seasoning herbs go a long way, only one to a few plants are needed of each kind you want.

Herbs have few special cultural demands. Some will thrive in smog-plagued, sooty city gardens or in shady, acid, poorly drained situations anywhere — mints, basil and rosemary in particular. Most herbs, however, prefer full sun and a neutral to moderately alkaline, light, dry soil low in fertility. Many are annuals — anise, basil, chervil, coriander, dill, fennel, safflower (false saffron), summer and winter savory and thyme. Caraway is one of the few biennials (but it self-sows readily), while borage, marjoram, oregano, the mints, rosemary, sage and tarragon are perennials.

Herbs dry quickly hung in loose bunches, laid on wire screens, or in the oven at a very low heat. When the leaves are crisp, strip them from the stems and store in tightly closed jars. For intriguingly flavored salt, alternate ½″ layers of one or more herbs with thin layers of salt in a jar and store in the refrigerator. Herb butters are made by creaming lightly salted butter, mixing in finely cut herbs, and creaming again. "Sugared" herbs are a delightful garnish: brush single leaves or small clusters with egg white, dip them in sugar, and let them dry for two days before storing in tight containers.

The special class of herbs known as potherbs supply salad and cooked greens. French sorrel, a perennial, has succulent leaves

One of the prettiest annual herbs, basil has
shiny leaves and dainty lavender-white
flowers. (*W. Atlee Burpee Company*)

cut when young for salad, steamed when older in combination
with other greens or made into delicious sorrel soup. Rocket, ro-
quette or arugula is a strong-flavored annual member of the mustard family that requires rich soil, does best in cool weather, and
self-sows. The gray-green leaves of borage, another hardy annual,
are cucumber-flavored when young but taste much like spinach
when mature, and its bright blue flowers are often candied.

Lovage is the most versatile of the potherbs. Young leaves of
this handsome 4' to 5' perennial are used in salads, curries, soups
and stews, the round hollow stalks when blanched serve as celery,
dried leaves enhance many dishes, and the dried seeds are good in
salads, bread and meat pies. Lovage grows best in part shade and
rich soil.

Two very useful publications are the *Handbook on Herbs*, Handbook 27, and *Herbs and Their Decorative Uses*, Handbook 68,
from the Brooklyn Botanic Garden (Brooklyn, NY 11225; $1.75
each). One of the most complete books, covering herbs for heal-
ing, cooking, dyeing and pest control, plus culture and landscaping
and a 300-page encyclopedia of herbs, is *The Rodale Herb Book*,
edited by William H. Hylton (Rodale Press; $12.95).

Anise has lovely yellow flower heads,
followed by gray-brown seeds that add
intriguing flavor to breads, cakes and soups.
(*Ferry-Morse Seed Company*)

Garden Grains

Robert Rodale has said in *Organic Gardening*, "The hottest trend
in American homesteading today is the growing of grain on small
areas." Besides its practical value as human and animal food,
there's something unusually satisfying about planting, harvesting
and threshing grain and baking your own bread.

Buckwheat is very easy to grow, maturing in 60 days, and 10
pounds of seed sown on a 50' x 100' patch will yield at least two
bushels of grain. A spreading plant that produces more when
thinly planted, it does not require rich soil or fertilizer. Sow it in 7"
rows from early to midsummer, and harvest after the first frost.
Cut it with a scythe or sickle, bunch and tie it in sheaves, and

stand several sheaves together in shocks. In 10 days it can be threshed, by beating it on a hard surface with a wooden flail — one gardener recommends a toy plastic baseball bat. Winnow out the chaff by slowly pouring from one bucket or basket into another in a good breeze or in front of an electric fan.

Buckwheat is high in the B vitamins. It makes a fine cereal, and fine-ground into flour is unsurpassed for pancakes and pasta. Small hand or electric mills are available from R & R Mill Company (45 West First North, Smithfield, UT 84335), Lee Engineering (2021 West Wisconsin, Milwaukee, WI 53201) and many mail-order houses, but many blenders will do an excellent grinding job. Buckwheat, by the way, is a fine soil improver, and if you keep bees it makes a rich dark honey. A seed source is Farmer Seed & Nursery Co.

Wheat takes much less space, a 1500-square-foot plot yielding a couple of bushels. There are winter and spring wheats, several types within these categories, and over 200 varieties. Your state experiment station can tell you the best for your area, and seed is available at farm supply stores. Winter wheat is sown around the date of the average first fall frost, spring wheat at the time of the average last spring frost, usually by broadcasting the seed and raking to cover it lightly. Winter wheat is harvested in early summer, spring wheat 90 to 110 days after planting, when the grains are hard (not milky) when chewed. It is cut, threshed and ground like buckwheat.

Three more grains worth growing are rye, oats and millet. Rye is

Wheat is productive, easy to grow and the most versatile grain for the home baker. (*Organic Gardening and Farming*)

planted and harvested just like winter or spring wheat and yields about the same. Oats for home-grown oatmeal are also fall- or spring-sown (but a month earlier in the fall than winter wheat).

The little-known pearl or grain millet is grown like buckwheat but does best in a somewhat richer, moister soil. Millet is richer in vitamins than other cereals and contains seven of the eight essential amino acids that make up protein. It is slightly alkaline, so is easier to digest than other grains. Millet has a bland, slightly nutty flavor, and is used by itself or combined with other grains in cereals, bread, and stuffing, and as an ingredient in stews, casseroles and other dishes. 'Hansen White Proso' millet is offered by Hansen New Plants (Whitewater, WI 53190), other varieties are obtainable from Game Food Nurseries (Omro, WI 54963; catalog $1).

Amaranth grains are a "new" crop offered by Thompson & Morgan. Known as the food of the Aztecs, amaranth is highly productive — 1 square meter yields ½ pound of grain, says Thompson & Morgan — and rich in protein. The grain is very easily threshed, and when ground it may be added to cereals, bread, baked with honey as a confection, or used in many dishes. The leaves are also a valuable food, tasty and equal to or better than spinach or beet greens in their content of protein, iron and several vitamins.

A good book on growing and using grains is *The Book of Whole Grains*, by Marlene Anne Bumgarner (St. Martin's Press; $4.95).

―――――――――――― A Crop of Catalogs ――――――――――――

Archias Seed Store, 106 East Main Street, Sedalia, MO 65301

Burgess Seed & Plant Co., Galesburg, MI 49053

Burnett Brothers, Inc., 92 Chambers Street, New York, NY 10007; catalog $1

D. V. Burrell Seed Growers, Box 150, Rocky Ford, CO 81067

W. Atlee Burpee Co., Warminster, PA 18974; Clinton, IA 52732; Riverside, CA 92504

Comstock, Ferre & Co., Wethersfield, CT 06109; catalog $1 — vegetables and herbs

De Giorgi Co., Council Bluffs, IA 51501; catalog 35¢

J. A. Demonchaux Co., 225 Jackson Street, Topeka, KS 66603 — French vegetables

Evans Plant Co., Ty Ty, GA 31795 — vegetable plants

Farmer Seed & Nursery Co., Faribault, MN 55021

Henry Field Seed & Nursery Co., Shenandoah, IA 51602

Germania Seed Co., 5952 North Milwaukee Avenue, Chicago, IL 60646; catalog $3

Glecklers Seedman, Metamora, OH 43540 — unusual vegetables

Gourmet Garden, Box 88, Danville, VT 05828 — unusuals and herbs

Grace's Gardens, 100 Autumn Lane, Hackettstown, NJ 07840; catalog 25¢ — unusuals

Greene Herb Gardens, Greene, RI 02827; catalog 10¢

Gurney Seed & Nursery Co., Yankton, SD 57078

Joseph Harris Co., Moreton Farm, Rochester, NY 14624

Charles Hart Seed Co., Wethersfield, CT 06109

H. G. Hastings Co., Box 4088, Atlanta, GA 30302

Johnny's Selected Seeds, North Dixmont, ME 04932; catalog 25¢ — northern, imported and heirloom varieties

J. W. Jung Seed Co., Randolph, WI 53956

Kitazawa Seed Co., 356 West Taylor Street, San Jose, CA 95110 — Oriental vegetables and unusuals

Landreth Seed Co., 2700 Wilmarco Avenue, Baltimore, MD 21223

Le Jardin du Gourmet, Ramsey, NJ 07446 — shallots, French vegetables, herbs

Earl May Seed & Nursery Co., Shenandoah, IA 51603

Natural Development Co., Bainbridge, PA 17502

Nichols Garden Nursery, 1190 North Pacific Highway, Albany, OR 97321; catalog 25¢ — unusuals and herbs

Olds Seeds, Madison, WI 53701

Geo. W. Park Seed Co., Greenwood, SC 29647

Piedmont Plant Co., Albany, GA 31702 — vegetable plants

Roswell Seed Co., Box 725, Roswell, NM 88201 — southwestern varieties

Seedway, Inc., Hall, NY 14463

R. H. Shumway, Rockford, IL 61101

Stokes Seeds, Box 548, Buffalo, NY 14240

Thomas Seeds, Winthrop, ME 04364 — northern varieties

Thompson & Morgan, Box 24, Somerdale, NJ 08083 — English varieties

Otis S. Twilley, Salisbury, MD 21801

Vermont Bean Seed Co., 2 Ways Lane, Manchester Center, VT 05255 — the largest selection of beans in the country

Vesey's Seeds, Ltd., York, Prince Edward Island, Canada — northern varieties

⚔ 6 ⚔

Fruit Culture

To THE TRUE GARDENER, producing one's own fruit is the crowning achievement, for this branch of horticulture is generally considered to require a higher degree of husbandry than any other.

Actually, home fruit growing has been greatly simplified in recent years, but the thrill of harvesting fresh, top-quality tree-ripened fruit from the garden has not been diminished. And it's a great incentive to be able to grow fruits, such as some of the berries that are rarely available in markets, and others that are available only in limited variety and insipid quality. The home grower is not restricted in his choice of varieties by commercial "handling" considerations such as suitability to mechanical harvesting and long shipping.

There's also an important contemporary reason for the new interest in home orcharding. Americans are becoming health-conscious, and fruits have unique health values. They are low in calories and fat, high in vitamins (especially A and C) and minerals (iron, calcium, potassium), and are superb digestive aids through the cellulose they contain (which supplies "bulk" for intestinal health) and their ability to neutralize acid residues from protein-rich foods. Fruits are protective foods, and an apple a day really does keep the doctor away — at Michigan State University, 1500 students who ate apples daily had far fewer respiratory, skin and digestive ailments, and even suffered less from tension.

Picking Fruits

Growing a wide variety of fruit has become practical in even the small suburban or city garden. Fruit trees are getting dwarfer and dwarfer, and new techniques of training make them useful as gar-

Pear trees are one of the best subjects for espalier training, in formal or informal styles. (*Horticultural Society of New York*)

den architectural features without reducing their productivity. In bush as well as tree fruits, new varieties are appearing that suit colder or warmer climates, extend the harvest season, or are especially adapted to container growing. The amount of room you have and your taste preferences, plus perhaps storing, canning and freezing qualities, will be foremost considerations in choosing the kinds and varieties of fruit to grow. Check next for cold hardiness if you garden in the North, or for a sufficient cold period to satisfy chilling requirements in the South. With many fruits, early, mid-season and late varieties can stretch the harvest, but with early varieties bloom before the last spring frost can be a problem (blankets over the plants on frosty nights may be enough protection). Pollination requirements are also important: most apples, pears, plums and sweet cherries need at least two compatible varieties for cross-pollination, while most peaches, apricots, sour cherries and others are self-pollinating.

The better nursery catalogs specify much of this information, and the Cooperative Extension Service in every state provides bulletins describing the best varieties for local use.

With apples, the rootstock on which the variety is grafted determines the size of the tree. Choose M9 for the smallest tree. M26 is slightly larger, and M7 will be 50% as large as a standard apple tree at maturity. M9 and M26 are shallow-rooted and need staking. The new naturally dwarf spur-type trees grafted on dwarfing rootstocks produce the small, high-yielding "double dwarfs." Peaches and nectarines are available in genetic dwarfs that can be kept as low as 4'. The new sweet cherries on 'North Star' rootstock grow only 6' to 9' tall.

Functional Fruiting

In commercial orcharding today, the word is intensive planting. Orchardists are adopting some methods long used by gardeners, and gardeners are finding useful ideas in new "high density" techniques developed by orchardists.

The centuries-old European art of espalier, or training on wood or wire in a flat plane, is the most efficient gardening-by-inches ploy ever devised. Espalier fruit trees, to quote expert Henry Leuthardt, are not only beautiful in design but also "yield unusually excellent, large-sized fruit, and of much better flavor than ordinary fruit due to the greater sun exposure penetrating through all the branches." The initial training is not at all difficult and begins when the tree is only a year old — usually the nursery does the early training. Once the fan, U, cordon, palmette or other form is developed, maintenance pruning is simple and goes very fast: in late winter or early spring, the terminals of all branches or arms

"Fruiting fences" of dwarf trees on trellises
are beautiful, take almost no space — and
never need painting. (*Pennsylvania State
University*)

are headed back as necessary, and through the summer side
shoots are frequently pinched back to induce fruiting spurs.

Espaliers are most often trained against a wall, but they are
equally striking and even more functional when grown free-standing to line a path or serve as a screen or garden divider. An apple,
pear, peach, plum or nectarine "fence" is made by driving pipes or
cedar posts 2′ deep and passing galvanized wires, spaced 18″
apart, through holes in these, tightening with turnbuckles at the
end post. The trees are spaced 4′ to 8′ apart, depending on variety,
and branches are trained and tied horizontally or at a 30° to 40°
angle to the wires. Commercial orchardists are now using this
method, which they call trellising, to greatly increase their yields
per acre.

Another new system is called the hedgerow. Dwarf trees are
planted as close as 4′ to 6′ apart and pruned to form a dense hedge.
Both dormant and summer pruning are practiced as with espaliers. Like all formal hedges, the hedgerow should be kept narrow
at the top and wide at the bottom to expose more of the foliage and
fruit to light.

The ultimate in concentrated cropping is the single-shoot
method developed in England to produce up to 75 tons of apples
per acre. This variation of the cordon espalier grows apples, on a
very dwarfing rootstock, as single unbranched shoots for a year.
Then flowering and fruiting are forced by applying the growth re-

Trellising on two, three or four horizontal
wires is one of the new methods for high
production in limited space. (*Michigan
State University*)

tardant B-9, and the orchard is harvested and mowed down. When
the stumps sprout, the cycle is repeated.

———————————————— Pomologistics ————————————————

Three essentials for all fruit plants are full sun and good air and
water drainage. Avoid any shade, soils known to have a hardpan
or impervious subsoil, and low sites to which cold air drains to
form frost pockets that can cause spring freeze injury to buds and
blooms. Sloping land is good if available — for early-blooming
trees, preferably a northern or eastern slope where they will re-
ceive less winter sun and so blossom later when there is less

Many dwarf fruits can be planted close
together and pruned to form dense, high-
yielding hedgerows. (*Pennsylvania State
University*)

chance of late spring freezes. Some growers advocate planting cold-sensitive fruits like peaches against a west wall for wind protection and the heat the wall radiates at night, and also because it blocks the morning sun and so allows slow thawing of blossoms if frost occurs.

Most fruits are best planted in early spring. Soaking the roots of bare-root plants in a tub of water or vitamin-hormone solution such as SUPERthrive (Vitamin Institute, 5409 Satsuma Avenue, North Hollywood, CA 91603) for several hours before planting aids establishment. Any broken or overly long roots should be cut away.

If the soil in the fruit area is poor, the plantings will benefit from additions the year before of organic materials and/or growing a green manure. Agricultural gypsum, mixed in at 3 pounds per cubic foot of soil, will lighten heavy clay. Except for blueberries, which require a more acid soil, fruit plants do best at pH 6.5, which is just barely acid.

Dig a hole for each plant at least 6″ deeper and wider all around than the spread-out roots or root ball. Mix peatmoss, compost and/or leafmold liberally with the soil, and tamp it down well as you fill under and around the roots. With dwarf and interstem trees, plant so that the bud union is 3″ to 4″ above the soil level. Water well and leave a saucer depression to catch rainwater, or mulch immediately. Only slow-release fertilizer can be mixed in with the soil when planting, but a high-nitrogen fertilizer watered in at half-strength following planting and monthly thereafter through early summer the first season will give improved growth. Kraft paper or tree wrap around the lower trunk will protect the tender bark from sunscald and rodents.

One-year-old whips should be cut back to 3′ to 4′. With older branched apples, pears and cherries, prune off all but three to five strong branches at least 6″ apart, at wide angles to the trunk and pointing in different directions; cut these back to 10″ but leave the leader 16″ long. With peaches, plums, nectarines and apricots, the central leader is pruned out, as well as all side branches except three to five which are cut back to 2″ to 4″ long. In later years, weak, crowding and competing limbs should be removed and, on all except apples and pears, excessive shoots thinned out. Prune in late winter or early spring, and always prune to an outward-growing bud. Remember that horizontal branches are more fruitful than upward-growing ones.

Mulch-Feeding

Fruit trees and bushes may or may not need regular feeding. The general rule for fertilizing fruits under clean cultivation or in a lawn or groundcover is one pound of 10–10–10 or 12–12–12 per inch of trunk diameter (as measured 12″ above the ground) in early spring.

With an adequate mulch, however, the need for fertilizer may be eliminated. In addition to conserving moisture, suppressing weeds, maintaining soil structure and keeping roots cool, an organic mulch steadily supplies nutrients. Michigan State University notes that a "mulch program has been observed to improve tree performance beyond that of the best herbicide-sod-fertilizer program." So maintain a 2″- to 6″-deep mulch — the looser the material, the greater the depth — of hay, straw, wood chips, leaves, ground corncobs, sawdust, grass clippings, etc. Apply mulches and any fertilizer out to the dripline of the branches, but keep them at least 6″ from the trunk.

Mulches generally supply ample phosphorus, potassium and trace elements, but if new shoot growth is short and weak and the leaves are not large and dark green, more nitrogen may be needed. A ½″ to 1″ layer of well-rotted manure or compost spread under the mulch in spring is a good source, or use ½ pound of bloodmeal, 1 pound of cottonseed meal, or 2 pounds of activated sludge for each year of the plant's age. Use half these amounts for pears and quinces, since too much nitrogen causes succulent growth susceptible to fireblight on these.

Many fruit gardeners recommend fertilizing with a fish or seaweed product or mulching with seaweed if it is available. These are rich sources of minerals, which appear to confer resistance to insects and disease. Potassium also seems to have this effect, as well as increasing sweetness in some fruits; wood ashes are an excellent source. Finally, apples and pears have a very high requirement for calcium and benefit from annual applications of gypsum, or dolomitic limestone may be applied every four or five years.

Thin for Fat Fruit

The size and quality of apples, pears and several other fruits are greatly improved by thinning. These trees tend to produce too much fruit, spreading their nutrient resources thin, overburdening their branches, and reducing their vitality (which can cause every-other-year bearing as well as decreased resistance to pests, disease, drought and winter injury).

So within three to six weeks after blooming, pick off enough fruits to leave the following distances between those that remain: apples and pears, 6″ to 8″; peaches and nectarines, 5″ to 6″; apricots and large plums, 3″ to 4″. Twist off peaches, apricots and nectarines, but leave the stem on the branch for apples, pears and plums.

Be sure to remove all blemished, deformed and undersized fruit, and thin weak branches more than strong ones.

Sometimes a fruit tree will produce luxuriant vegetative growth and little fruit, usually because of too much nitrogen in the soil. Usually "ringing" the plant by cutting away a ring of bark around the trunk or main limbs is advised. This forces carbohydrates manufactured in the leaves to stay in the upper part of the tree rather than moving down to the roots. The practice can be hazardous if the cuts are made too deep — or too wide to heal over in one season.

Much safer is the fruit clamp. Wrap a protective strip of kraft paper around the trunk or limb, then a strip of sheet metal (which can be cut from a tin can), and finally a circular clamp of the type used to hold auto radiator hose. This clamp has a screw to tighten it as much as desired. Applied in autumn, the fruit clamp will result in increased fruit buds on all parts of the tree or branch beyond it. It should not be too tight or left on beyond spring, or the roots will be weakened by lack of carbohydrates.

Pots of Fruit

Dwarf fruit trees of all kinds grow well in containers and will provide beauty anywhere in the garden. The most common container size is 18″ or 24″ wide and deep, and it should have drainage holes and slats on the bottom to raise it off the ground. A soil mix high in compost and peat is recommended, or a soilless mix. As with any container planting, watering must be diligent and thorough, and organic fertilizers applied at the same rates as for ground plantings.

Container trees are best repotted every two years in very early spring. The root ball is trimmed back a quarter to a third, and fresh mix is packed around it when it is set back in the container. This root pruning plus top pruning will produce a high-yielding tree no taller than 4′ to 6′. Since roots will freeze easily in containers, potted trees should be wintered in a garage, cellar or other cool structure.

Where garden drainage is very poor, dwarf trees will thrive in bottomless planter boxes — 3′ square by 2′ high is a good size — set on the ground.

Pest Control Without Pesticides

Even the U.S. Department of Agriculture now recognizes that fruit pests can be controlled without pesticides, provided the gardener is willing to "tolerate a certain amount of insect damage," as it states in the new Home & Garden Bulletin 211, *Control of Insects on*

Deciduous Fruits and Tree Nuts in the Home Orchard Without Insecticides (90¢ from Superintendent of Documents, Washington, DC 20402). Insect injury can be greatly minimized — even totally eliminated, many gardeners say — by these measures:

Practice sanitation to destroy all the places where insects and disease are active, multiply or hide. Promptly pick off damaged fruits and pick up drops, and bury them . . . prune out diseased or damaged branches, and clean and paint wounds and cavities with tree paint or cover them with screening . . . burn diseased prunings and fallen bark and wood . . . keep fruit areas weed-free . . . scrape off the loose bark on apple trees in late winter (codling moth larvae hide there) . . . cut off the black knots that occur on sour cherries and plums, and the cankers on many fruits . . . rub off suckers and watersprouts while they are still very small.

The genetic dwarf fruits, such as the 'Bonanza' peach, grow only a few feet high and are excellent subjects for containers. (*Armstrong Nurseries*)

Aphids and spider mites are often almost completely controlled by their natural enemies such as ladybugs. If mites become a problem, they can be washed off with a spray of soap and water applied under fairly high pressure. The egg masses of tent caterpillars are easily scraped off in fall and winter, but better yet, prevent their formation by banding the trunks with Tanglefoot in spring to cut off the moth's ascent into the tree. A 3″ band of Tanglefoot will also halt ants which carry aphid eggs up the trunks.

A 4″ band of corrugated paper or burlap wrapped around the trunks of apple trees in summer is an excellent trap for codling moth larvae which will hide in its recesses; remove and burn the bands in late fall. Borers can be dug out with a wire probe or knife, and the young trapped with Tanglefoot on the trunks; keep the ground around the trunks clear so birds can find and destroy the eggs and young. Some orchardists tie pieces of soap all around the lower trunk, so that soapy water runs down into the soil whenever it rains to kill borers and other pests overwintering there.

Traps baited with an attractant and coated with a sticky substance inside are now available (Zoecon Corporation, 975 California Avenue, Palo Alto, CA 94304) for such pests as codling moth and Oriental fruit moth. Gardeners also recommend buckets of molasses in solution hung in the trees to capture moths, with a light bulb suspended over them to trap night-flying moths. Plastic apples or oranges from the five-and-dime, coated with Tanglefoot or other sticky material, also work well.

There are also effective "natural" sprays. The 60- or 70-second superior dormant oil, applied to cover every inch of the tree when the temperature is above 45° in late winter before the buds begin to swell, will kill a great many overwintering pests by smothering them. During the growing season, a spray developed at the Indiana Agricultural Experiment Station and very effective on mites consists of 4 cups of wheat flour and ½ cup of buttermilk in 5 gallons of water. Some growers also praise a spray made with liquefied seaweed and onion juice. The plant-derived insecticide ryania (Ryatox, from Bonide Chemical Company, Utica, NY 13502) is widely used against codling moth, aphids, pear sawfly and others.

One of the best ways to grow perfect fruit is to bag it. Simply staple a small plastic or white paper bag (not brown paper — it causes flavor changes in the fruit) over each apple or pear as soon as the fruit is set (immediately after petal fall). In a home fruit planting, this takes less time than one might think, and gives total protection from insects. If paper bags are used, remove them a week or so before picking time to allow the sun to develop color in the fruit.

To prevent birds from raiding the fruit, growers use everything from noisemakers and fluttering pie tins to stuffed owls or hose sections twined around branches to resemble snakes. These vary in effectiveness, but a sure-fire protector is bird netting, sheets of cloth or plastic mesh which are easily cut to size and draped over bushes and small trees.

Rabbits, mice and other small four-footed marauders that feed on the bark of fruit trees can be thwarted by aluminum foil or tarpaper wrap on the trunk, or encircle it loosely with hardware cloth extending from 2″ to 3″ below the soil surface to well above the average depth of snow. Bags of mothballs hung in the trees act as a repellent to deer, liver rubbed thoroughly up and down the trunk is said to repel rabbits, and there is even a repellent that emits the frightening scent of mountain lion (National Scent Co., Box 7, Garden Grove, CA 92640).

Reducing Plans

For the limited-space gardener who wants to reduce the size of fruit trees, dwarfing rootstocks or growing in containers are not the only solutions. A slab of rock or cement for example, placed in the bottom of the planting hole, is recommended by many old-time fruit experts to restrict root growth and thus dwarf the tree.

A newer technique is angle planting. Orchardists have found that standard (full-size) apple and peach trees will grow only "man-high" if they are planted with the trunks at a 45° angle. Vertical branches are allowed to develop from this inclined trunk. In tests at Purdue University, angle-planted peaches produced a high-yielding hedgerow when they were sheared in summer to make a flat, 4′-thick wall of fruiting wood. The trees were planted 4′ apart with the trunks all leaning in the same direction, or for a more decorative effect, 8′ apart with two trees in each hole, inclined at 45° in opposite directions. In Canada, fruit trees are sometimes planted at 45° angles and the branches trained horizontally so that they can be protected in winter with a heavy covering of leaves and snow.

Another unusual method is "looping" the young tree, bending the whip-like trunk into a circle — some growers actually tie the trunk into a knot. This stunts the tree by slowing down the flow of sap to the roots. A three-quarter loop can be made so that the trunk above the loop grows out horizontally for a very low-growing variation of the angle-planted tree.

Doubling Up

Where space is severely limited, plant three dwarf trees in the same hole. "Clump" early, midseason and late varieties of apples or peaches or pears, for example, for a long harvest. Be sure to make a large enough planting hole so the trees can be set about 18″

apart. Prune off most of the roots and branches on the side of each tree that faces the other trees. When the trees are mature, they will need inside pruning each year to insure that sufficient sunlight and air reach the interior of the clump.

Several varieties of a fruit can also be grown on a single tree. Nurseries often sell three-in-one or five-in-one dwarf trees. But since these are rarely superior varieties — or at least they may not be the varieties you want to grow — it will pay to learn to graft your own.

This is an invaluable skill, for even if you have ample space, varieties you especially like may be available only as scions. Grafting can also be used to renew an old tree, or to provide pollination by growing a branch of another variety on a self-sterile tree. It's also useful in special cases: the 'Red Astrachan' apple, for instance, is a biennial bearer, but it has two forms which bear in alternate years — by grafting one onto the other, a tree that bears every year is achieved.

With certain rare exceptions, grafting can be done only within a genus. An apple (*Malus*) can be grafted on an apple, a pear (*Py-*

In cleft grafting, scions cut with long bevels
are wedged into a cleft in the trunk or
branch. (*Organic Gardening and Farming*)

rus) on a pear. Peaches, plums, apricots, nectarines and cherries are all species of *Prunus,* and in most cases are easily grafted to each other. One notable exception to the genus rule is the pear which grafts well onto quince (*Cydonia*) rootstock.

Grafting utilizes a multibudded twig as the scion and is done in early spring as the sap begins to rise. Budding, a variation of grafting, uses a single bud for the scion and is done in mid-summer.

The simplest graft is the cleft graft. The scion, cut from a strong-growing one-year-old shoot, is trimmed on the cut end to a long double bevel. This is wedged tightly into a cleft pried or split open in the cut end of the trunk or branch. The cambium layer of the scion must be aligned carefully with that of the stock. The cambium is the thin layer of growing cells between the bark and wood, and the two cambiums are most easily aligned by matching the inside of the bark of the stock and scion. If there is room, a second scion may be inserted on the opposite side of the cleft in the stock, and the weakest of the two growths is pruned off a year later. The graft is sealed to prevent drying out with grafting wax or tape.

Variations include the side graft, where the scion is wedged into a cleft on the side of the branch or trunk . . . the bark graft, in which the scion end is slipped into a slit cut in the bark . . . and the whip or tongue graft, useful for joining a scion and stock of about equal diameter — both are cut at a slant, with a second cut in the slanting edge of one to form a notch or tongue that matches and locks into a similar notch cut in the other.

In the most common form of budding, a plump hard bud is cut along with a sliver of bark and wood, and slipped into the flaps of a T-cut that goes just through the bark of the stock. The graft is tied or held with rubber bands but not waxed, and if the bud "takes," the portion of the stock beyond it can be cut off the next spring.

Grafting, like all the worthwhile horticultural arts, requires study and practice. A record of 40% to 50% successful grafts is very good. As important as making the graft is the aftercare you give it — cutting away binding materials after growth starts to prevent girdling, sometimes shading the scion until it is established, or splinting it to the stock or staking it so wind will not break it off.

Excellent bulletins on grafting are available from Cooperative Extension Service offices, and nurserymen and garden clubs often give classes on the art. A source of grafting supplies is A. M. Leonard & Son, Inc. (Box 816, Piqua, OH 45356).

---------------------------- Slowing the Season ----------------------------

When late spring frosts threaten tender fruit buds, sprinkling will protect them. Wetting the plants at least once a minute and continuing until rising temperatures melt the ice which forms has protected trellised apples to as low as 23° at Pennsylvania State University.

However, it may be even better to use sprinkling to delay bud development. Utah State University has shown that cooling the trees by sprinkling will delay blossoming until after the danger of frost is past. In an apple orchard, overhead sprinklers were set to go on when the temperature reached 45°, operating on a two-minutes-on, two-minutes-off cycle until the temperature fell below 45°. The sprinkling was begun as soon as the trees had completed their winter rest period, and the sprinkled trees came into bloom 17 days later than unsprinkled trees in the same orchard. At harvest, the sprinkling was found to have delayed fruit maturity by about a week.

Cooling fruits in hot summer weather gives bigger fruit and an earlier harvest, reports North Carolina State University. Overhead sprinklers were activated at 87°, supplying just enough water to match the evaporation rate so as to avoid excessive soil watering. This "evaporative cooling" also results in higher-quality fruit — in apples, it greatly reduced cork spot and bitter pit disorders.

Harvest Hoarding

The old-time cool, moist dirt-floor cellar was an ideal fruit storehouse. In modern hot, dry basements, a separate storage room can serve as well. Build it away from the furnace, of concrete or cinder blocks or stud-board-building paper construction. A tight door is necessary, plus two windows, shaded to keep out light, for ventilation. The ideal storage temperature for most fruits is 32°. Humidity should be 80% to 90%, and occasional sprinkling of the floor will maintain this, most easily if a 3″ layer of gravel is spread over it. The fruit can be stored on shelves or in moistureproof barrels, crocks, galvanized garbage cans, tiles, drums, churns or other containers. If no cellar is available, an insulated garage, shed or porch may provide the proper conditions.

Fruits can also be stored in a container set in the ground and covered with a lid or boards, then a heavy mulch. Or build a "fruit cellar," a pit lined with leaves or straw and covered as for containers. In less extreme climates, a simple method is to lay the fruit on a plastic sheet and cover it with another sheet and several inches of soil.

Plain leaves can be a good storage medium. A gardener writing in *Pomona*, the journal of the North American Fruit Explorers, reports:

> Chestnuts from the East Shore of Chesapeake Bay were found to be twice as sweet when dug out from under leaves and snow than the same chestnuts kept under refrigeration. And this

testing was not by mouth but rather by instrument — the sacrometer. And 'Rome Beauty' apples out of refrigeration are only bakers and not high quality eaters; but edged out from under leaves and snow with the toe, and you have a dessert apple without baking.

Fruitful Sun-Drying

A hot, dry attic, a rack above the kitchen range, or a sunny place outdoors are all suitable for drying fruit. Here's a sun-drying technique used by gardener Al Kulsar:

Mr. Kulsar builds trays 4' to 5' long, with 1" x 4" boards for the sides and wire mesh or plywood for the bottom. The width of each tray is 34", to allow 36" wide cheesecloth to be tacked over the top to protect the fruit from flies. The bottom is lined with clean brown paper.

Clean, ripe fruit — drops are excellent — is gathered on a sunny day and washed. Apricots, nectarines, peaches and pears are cut in half and pitted or cored, then spread cut side up on the trays. Apples should be peeled, cored and sliced, persimmons are simply cut in half, prunes are pricked to allow moisture to escape, and grapes and cherries are dried whole. The tray is positioned in full sun, slanted for maximum exposure. Fruit should be dried chip hard — so that it "rattles when tossed into a cardboard box." It will keep in tight jars for two years, and can be softened for eating by rinsing and placing it while damp in a plastic bag.

For drying in cold or rainy weather, Mr. Kulsar uses mesh-bottomed trays stacked in a raised plywood box, with the top open to vent moisture and a hot plate or other heater below.

Sun-Kissed Preserves

Sunset magazine (Menlo Park, CA 94025) suggests the old-fashioned solar cooking method for making extra-flavorful preserves:

Four cups of halved or quartered apricots or whole strawberries, blueberries, raspberries, gooseberries, currants or boysenberries are mixed with 2 tablespoons of lemon juice and 3 cups of sugar (with sliced peaches or nectarines, use ¼ cup of lemon juice), and allowed to stand 1 hour. Then the mix is brought to a boil with constant stirring, and boiled rapidly without stirring for 4 minutes.

After 30 minutes' cooling, the mix is poured into pans, with no more than ¾" depth of syrup. Each pan is covered with plastic film, with a 1" opening all along one side, and set in bright sun. With hourly stirring and turning of the fruit, the process is complete — depending on the sun's warmth, in from 2 to 10 hours (bring indoors at night if necessary) — when the fruit has become plump and the syrup is as thick as corn syrup.

Shallow trays, cheesecloth and bright sun
are all that is needed to make delicious dried
fruits that will keep as long as two years.
(*Organic Gardening and Farming*)

These preserves will keep a month or more in covered jars in the refrigerator, or they can be frozen, or canned in sterilized canning jars by the water bath method.

Fruit Leather

Organic gardener Frances W. Townley makes the delectable confection known as "fruit leather" from her home-grown apples, apricots, nectarines, peaches, plums and prunes:

To make apple leather, peel and core the apples, grind them in a food chopper, then cook them slowly with 2 to 3 cups of cider per gallon of ground fruit. Add honey to taste if tart apples are used. Spread ¼″ thick on oiled cookie sheets, and allow it to cure for 2 weeks.

Pit fruits are pitted and steamed over low heat (with apricots, add 1½ cups of pineapple juice per gallon of uncooked fruit). Drain off the juice, then sieve the pulp and add 3 teaspoons of almond extract per gallon, plus honey as needed. Spread ¼″ thick on lightly oiled cookie sheets, and when the leather is dry enough to lift, lay it on a cake rack so it can dry on both sides. Or dry in a 120° oven, with the door open to let moisture escape.

When fruit leather has cured to the point where it is no longer sticky, Mrs. Townley says, dust it lightly with cornstarch and stack in layers with waxed paper between. It will keep for a year or more.

More Put-Ups

The intricacies of canning, freezing and other storage methods are detailed in several excellent USDA Home and Garden Bulletins: No. 8, *Home Canning of Fruits and Vegetables* (35¢); No. 10, *Home Freezing of Fruits and Vegetables* (35¢); and No. 56, *How to Make Jellies, Jams and Preserves at Home* (45¢). These may be ordered from the Superintendent of Documents (Washington, DC 20402).

Everyone wants to make their own fruit juices, cider and wine. Fruit presses are becoming widely available; several good ones are made by Rolling River Industries (1 Ranch Rite Road, Yakima, WA 98901; brochure 50¢). The best instruction-and-recipe book we've seen is *Making Your Own Wine, Beer and Soft Drinks*, by Phyllis Hobson (Garden Way Publishing Company, Charlotte, VT 05445; $2.95). Juices and ciders are easily pasteurized in canning jars, or they may be frozen without pasteurization.

Fruitful Resources

American Pomological Society, Dr. L. D. Tukey, Secretary, 103 Tyson Building, University Park, PA 16802

California Rare Fruit Growers, Paul H. Thomson, Star Route, Bonsall, CA 92003

Dwarf Fruit Tree Association, Box 143, Hartford, MI 49057

North American Fruit Explorers, Robert Kurle, Secretary, 10 South 55 Madison, Hinsdale, IL 60521

Southern Fruit Council, R.R. 3, Box 40, Summit, MS 39666

Advances in Fruit Breeding, edited by Jules Janick and James N. Moore (Purdue University Press, West Lafayette, IN 47907; $25)

Dwarfed Fruit Trees, by Harold B. Tukey (Macmillan; $15)

Dwarf Fruit Trees for the Home Gardener, by Lawrence Southwick (Garden Way Publishing, Charlotte, VT 05445; $3.50)

Fruits for the Home Garden, by Ken and Pat Kraft (Morrow; $5.95)

Fruit Trees and Shrubs, Handbook 67, Brooklyn Botanic Garden (Brooklyn, NY 11225; $1.75)

Gardens Are for Eating, by Stanley Schuler (Macmillan; $3.95)

Growing Unusual Fruit, by Alan E. Simmons (Walker; $10)

Grow Your Own Dwarf Fruit Trees, by Ken and Pat Kraft (Walker; $8.95)

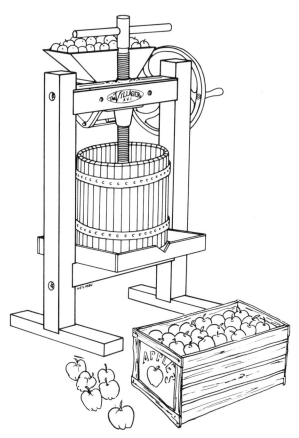

To add to the good spirits of a garden-homestead, get a fruit press and make your own cider and wine. (*Rolling River Industries*)

The Joy of a Home Fruit Garden, by Margaret Tipton Wheatly (Doubleday; $6.95)

Modern Fruit Science, 5th edition, by Norman F. Childers (Rutgers University Press, New Brunswick, NJ 08903; $16.50)

Small Fruit Culture, 4th edition, by James S. Shoemaker (AVI Publishing, Box 670, Westport, CT 06880; $19)

Small Fruits for the Home Garden, by J. H. Clarke (Doubleday; $4.95)

Successful Berry Growing, by Gene Logsdon (Rodale Press, Emmaus, PA 18049; $7.95)

Tree Fruit Production, 2nd edition, by Benjamin J. E. Teskey and James S. Shoemaker (AVI Publishing, Box 670, Westport, CT 06880; $15)

≈ 7 ≈

Exotic, Old and New, Rare and Choice Fruits

———————————— Tree Fruits ————————————

Malus for All

"The most domestic of trees . . . its natural habitat is by the side of man," says Alice A. Martin in *All About Apples* (Houghton Mifflin; $7.95). One of the most ancient plants, the apple (*Malus*) as we know it was brought here by the colonists, and over the years at least 5000 varieties have been named. The breeding and weeding out still goes on, but many old-time as well as the newer apples are "modern" in the sense that they are still popular, preferred and widely available.

Some of the best summer to early fall apples are 'Lodi,' a superior replacement for 'Yellow Transparent' . . . the high-quality new red 'Quinte' . . . 'Red Astrachan,' dating back to 1816 but still regarded by many as one of the finest for pie, sauce, jelly . . . 'Jersey-mac,' a full-flavored, early-ripening 'McIntosh' type . . . the latest 'Jonathan' x 'McIntosh' cross, 'Jonamac,' better than either parent . . . and 'Gravenstein,' an old German origination and the best applesauce apple of all.

Tried-and-true late apples with high ratings for home gardens include the new 'Jonagold,' a 'Jonathan' x 'Delicious' cross often called the finest of the new apples . . . 'Holly,' 'Jonathan' x 'Red Delicious' and an improvement on both . . . 'Macoun,' a 'McIntosh'

Figs are handsome small trees and will produce their incomparably delicious fruit even in the North if given winter protection. (*Organic Gardening and Farming*)

cross distinctly superior in flavor, aroma and texture . . . the large red 'Northern Spy,' an old-time variety still highly acclaimed, and its fine new cross with 'Golden Delicious,' 'Spigold' . . . 'Gallia Beauty,' an improvement on 'Rome Beauty,' the great pie and baking apple . . . the even finer pie apple, 'Rhode Island Greening' — few know it is also good raw when it is "sweetened up" by tree ripening . . . a new 'Golden Delicious' selection from Japan, 'Mutsu,' large and a good keeper . . . the classic 'Newtown Pippin,' a superb cider apple . . . and the new 'Granny Smith' from Australia, very late and long-keeping.

Many other excellent apples are favored regionally, such as 'Wealthy' and 'Haralson' in the Midwest, 'Stayman Winesap' through the South, 'Winter Banana' in southern California. There is even an apple, 'Tropical Beauty' from South Africa, that thrives in Florida and Hawaii. Disease resistance is now a major aim of breeders, and 'Prima,' 'Priscilla' and 'Sir Prize' are the first apples immune to scab, the fungus disease that can necessitate considerable spraying in humid conditions.

The renaissance of the roadside stand is bringing back some of the fine "antique" apples — old-time "good eatin' " varieties that orchardists passed by because they lack commercial qualities. Several nurseries are beginning to offer some of these, while others can be obtained as scions. Connoisseurs can now obtain the spicy 'Esopus Spitzenburg,' tiny red 'Lady' or huge 'Pound Sweet' and 'Twenty Ounce,' snowy-fleshed 'Fameuse,' almost black-skinned 'Black Gilliflower,' the very sweet and long-keeping 'Roxbury Russet,' very hardy Russian 'Duchess of Oldenburg,' and England's unsurpassable 'Cox's Orange Pippin.' Homestead fruit growers specializing in these rare and wonderful apples often find that once customers sample them, they bring advance orders for more than can be produced.

Peerless Pears

The story is much the same for pears — at least 2000 varieties, but only a very small number widely grown. 'Bartlett,' 'Duchess d'Angouleme,' 'Beurre Bosc,' 'Beurre Anjou,' 'Doyenne du Comice,' 'Winter Nelis,' 'Clapp's Favorite,' 'Seckel' and 'Kieffer' are excellent and popular. 'Seckel,' 'Flemish Beauty,' 'Tait Dropmore' and 'Patton' are best choices for the coldest states, while 'Kieffer' resists heat south to the Gulf. The fireblight-resistant older 'Maxine' and new 'Magness' and 'Moonglow' for the North, and 'Orient' for the South, are valuable where this disease is a problem.

'Colette' is an unusual pear from the Midwest, "everbearing" or at least long-season, producing fruit continually from mid-August until frost. Also unusual but rarer is 'Beierschmidt,' very hardy and one of the very few pears that will ripen to perfection on the tree.

Two other especially worthy rare pears are 'Conference,' an old variety with superlative sweet flavor, and an old French variety recently introduced here as 'Atlantic Queen,' bearing huge fruit despite poor soil and summer heat and also apparently immune to fireblight. Pear aficionados would likely extend this list to include such top-quality varieties as the early-ripening 'Dr. Jules Guyot' and 'Bloodgood,' midseason 'Marguerite Marilat,' and late 'Louise Bonne d'Avranche.'

Planting two varieties of pears is advised, as even self-fruitful varieties produce better if cross-pollinated. Nearly all pears should be picked when "mature" rather than "ripe." Pear breeder Vaughn Quackenbush says the best way to check maturity is the "lift-test: lift the pear upward and outward — if it lets go at the point where it is attached to the twig, it is pretty likely to be mature." He states that cold storage, at 30° to 31°, improves most pears, especially the late types, with some requiring several months' storage to attain best quality. They will thereafter ripen in one to three weeks at 65° to 70°. One exception is 'Kieffer,' often criticized as being a poor pear by growers who ripen it at too high a temperature — it will ripen properly only at 55° to 60°.

Splendid Peaches

The climatic range of peaches is constantly being extended. 'Desertgold' is one of several fine new peaches for warm areas, requiring only 350 to 400 hours below 45° to break its rest period. For northern gardens, 'Reliance' has borne fruit after winter temperatures of –25°, while others bud-hardy to –15° or slightly lower include 'Sunapee,' 'Veteran,' 'Prairie Dawn,' 'Madison,' 'Stark Sure-Crop' and 'Stark FrostKing,' plus some new highly praised varieties from Canada's Harrow Research Station in Ontario — 'Harken,' 'Harmony,' 'Harbelle,' 'Harbrite,' etc. 'Madison,' one of the Presidential Series bred by Virginia Polytechnic Institute, has unusual bud resistance to spring frosts.

A great many varieties are suited to areas where winter temperatures do not go below –10°. Widely regarded as the best today in yellow-fleshed peaches are 'Redhaven,' 'Triogem,' 'Garnet,' 'Glohaven,' 'Golden Jubilee,' 'Redskin,' 'Cresthaven,' 'Madison,' 'Jerseyland,' and the Harrow varieties . . . and in white peaches, 'Raritan Rose,' 'Belle of Georgia' (hardy in New England, but must be harvested green to prevent excessive drop), 'George IV' (very high in vitamin C), and the old but still superior 'Champion.' 'Elberta,' long the top favorite yellow freestone peach, is now obtainable in improved cultivars.

The new genetic or natural dwarf peaches, such as 'Bonanza,' 'Golden Treasure' and 'Garden Sun,' grow to only 6′ and can be

New varieties have made it possible to have
home-grown peaches in the Southwestern
desert or in Minnesota's frigid climate.
(*Stark Bro's Nurseries*)

pruned much lower. Although these are bud-hardy to only about
0°, their small size makes them ideal for growing in containers so
they can be moved into cool buildings in winter in colder regions.
The very fine 'Redhaven' peach is now also available in a genetic
dwarf, 'Com-Pact Redhaven,' that grows to 6' to 8'.

Plummery

Until recently, plums were the most neglected fruit in America.
Now there are plums for Minnesota ('Toka,' 'Pipestone,' 'Underwood,' 'Mount Royal,' 'Stanley'), and plums for Hawaii ('Methley'),
plus a host that will thrive between these extremes.

The hardiest plums are generally Japanese or American-Japa-
nese hybrids, but 'Stanley,' the hardiest and most popular of the
prune plums, is European. Prune plums are those that have a
sufficiently high sugar content for drying, but they are also excellent fresh, frozen, canned or for jam. Japanese plums are early,
need two for pollination, and are eaten fresh. Two of the best are
'Shiro' and 'Santa Rosa.' Of the European plums, old 'Golden
Transparent' and other Gage types are all supremely good fresh or
preserved, while the Damsons are considered the standard of ex-
cellence for jellies and jams. At least half a dozen fruit breeding

stations are now concentrating on plums, and nurseries are beginning to list some very superior new ones.

Many ornamental or flowering plums produce cherry-like fruit good for jams and jellies or even eating fresh. 'Thundercloud,' 'Hollywood' and 'Pissardi' are three of the best. And there are cherry-plum hybrids that are well suited to small gardens (see the next section, Bush Fruits).

Prime Apricots

With the development in Minnesota of 'Moongold' and 'Sungold,' both hardy to at least –25°, apricots have become practical garden fruits everywhere except in the Deep South. Unlike most apricots, these two are not self-fruitful, and should be planted together for cross-pollination.

Apricots are exceptionally handsome ornamentals, and their fruit is delicious raw, cooked, canned, frozen and dried — as well as high in minerals and vitamins (apricots are richest in vitamin A of all fruits). Even full-size trees grow to only about 15'. They have just one fault: they bloom very early, so should be planted on north or west exposures to minimize spring frost injury.

Where temperatures rarely go below 0°, 'Moorpark,' 'Blenheim,' 'Tilton,' 'Perfection' and 'Hungarian' are top choices. 'Farmingdale,' 'Alfred,' 'Veecot' and 'Daybreak' are recommended to –15°. 'Goldcot' is an acclaimed new variety from Michigan that has above-average fruit bud hardiness. Many others, both old reliable and superior new varieties, are appearing in nurseries, and extremely hardy apricots are promised by Canadian breeding programs.

A technique for delaying bloom has been developed by fruit hobbyist Al Kulsar. He dehorns his apricot trees — cuts all branches back to stubs near the secondary scaffold limbs. The stubs send up strong 4' to 5' shoots and the following spring bloom two to four weeks later and over a much longer period. His dehorned trees bear abundant crops while similar varieties not dehorned bear none due to frost damage while in bloom.

Peachy Nectarines

To many people, the nectarine or "fuzzless peach" is more richly flavored than any peach, which is perhaps why in the past 15 years nectarines have become almost as popular as peaches both in the garden and commercially.

Nectarines are as variable as peaches, having freestone and cling types and flesh colors from white and yellow through red. Nectarine seed, incidentally, may produce peaches, and vice versa. Even more confusing, nectarines occasionally come true from seed.

Nectarine varieties can be selected to produce fruit over ten weeks. The excellent 'Nectared 1' through '10' series from the New Jersey Agricultural Experiment Station does just this, but there are many other choices. 'Pocahontas,' 'Early Flame' and 'Cherokee' are high-quality early nectarines; 'Redchief,' 'Sunglo,' 'Redgold' and 'Delicious' are midseason; and 'Nectacrest' and 'Lexington' bear in late summer. 'Pocahontas' and 'Cherokee,' new originations from Virginia, are small but have the smooth buttery texture of fine peaches, while many western varieties are larger but more fibrous, and those from New Jersey are intermediate.

Nectarines will grow anywhere that peaches do. A very hardy variety is 'Mericrest' from New Hampshire. 'Diamond Jubilee' is one of the best for warm regions. For very dwarf trees in limited space or containers, plant one of the genetic dwarfs such as 'Nectarina' or 'Garden Delight.'

Cherry Jubilee

Cherries are beautiful trees, and they bear the earliest crops and in great abundance. There has been steady improvement in cherries, and the past two decades have seen the old favorite sweet-sour hybrid Duke cherries supplanted by better varieties of both sweet and sour types.

In sour cherries, the best today are 'North Star,' a genetic dwarf only 6' to 9' tall, hardy in Minnesota and also thriving farther south than other sour cherries . . . also from Minnesota, the high-yielding, semidwarf spur-type 'Meteor,' 10' to 12' . . . and the largest, 'Montmorency,' less hardy but bearing the finest-quality cherries — which can be eaten fresh as well as used for pies and preserves — and available in a semidwarf spur type. Sour cherries are also excellent for juice and cider.

Unlike sour cherries, sweet varieties are self-sterile and need carefully chosen pollinators. Some of the most popular — 'Bing,' 'Emperor Francis,' 'Lambert' — will not pollinate one another, so be sure to check with the nurseryman for pollinizing compatibility when purchasing sweet cherries. 'Early Rivers,' 'Schmidt' and 'Windsor' are considered excellent early, midseason and late varieties, but there are many fine new ones such as 'Vista,' 'Venus,' 'Viva,' 'Sam,' 'Rainier,' 'Vic,' 'Van,' and 'Hudson.' In yellow cherries, 'Stark Gold' is one of the best and hardiest (–30°). Most sweet cherries are hardy to –20°, but they do not like great heat or high humidity.

More dwarf cherries are on the way: England's National Fruit Trials has achieved a 50% reduction in tree size by using gamma radiation to develop dwarfing rootstocks. And a very recent release is 'Compact Stella,' a self-fertile semidwarf sweet cherry of excellent quality, which originated as a mutant through irradiation of dormant scions of the 'Stella' cherry with x rays.

Uncommon and Uncommonly Good

FIG: Fig trees are striking, with big bold deeply lobed leaves, and a glistening sun-warmed fig from one's own tree is a meltingly delectable confection. Figs are hardy only to about 10°, but gardeners in Michigan and Massachusetts produce fine crops by winter "bundling": the plants are cut back to 5' and all the branches tied closely together and wrapped with straw and layers of newspaper or burlap, then tarpaper, and capped with a plastic sheet to keep out moisture. Another method is to grow them in tubs — the "dwarf everbearing" type is best for this — and store them indoors for winter.

Figs can produce two crops a year, one on last year's wood and a second on new wood. In northern areas, 'Brown Turkey' is considered the best variety. Many others — 'Magnolia,' 'Celeste,' 'Mission,' 'Adriatic,' 'Beall' — are also excellent but need a longer growing season to ripen the fruit. Except for 'Smyrna,' grown in California, figs are self-fruitful. They thrive in a fairly heavy and moist soil, and heat and light reflected from a wall or water will increase fruit production.

QUINCE: A wonderful fruit being rediscovered by gardeners is the orchard quince (*Cydonia oblonga*). A pretty, gnarled tree with dense furry foliage and large pinkish flowers, like figs it grows best in a heavy, moist soil. The 3″ or larger pear-shaped fruits have a delicious aroma, and will keep two to three months if not bruised. With a long season as in Mediterranean countries, quince fruits ripen to sweetness on the tree, but here they are harvested too sour and puckery for eating fresh. However, they make wonderful jelly and are also used for jams, marmalade, and quince wine, "butter" and "honey," and may be stewed and canned.

Quinces can be grown in tree or bush form, espaliered or used for hedging, and are hardy to –25°. The variety 'Orange' grows to 10' to 15', others such as 'Champion' reach 20' to 25'. 'Van Demas' and 'Burbank Jumbo' are two favored in the South and West. The orchard quince should not be confused with Japanese flowering quince (*Chaenomeles*), 3' to 6' shrubs which bear small fruits occasionally used for jams and jellies.

PERSIMMON: The Oriental persimmon (*Diospyros kaki*) is the major fruit of the Orient. It is also widely grown here in the South, and as far north as southern Illinois and Pennsylvania. The trees are handsome and have magnificent fall foliage color, and the fruits can be eaten fresh when ripened, or stored, frozen, and used in salads, ice cream, puddings, pies, even made into beer.

The American persimmon is an
undeservedly neglected fruit, and it's hardy
far into the North. (*New York State
Agricultural Experiment Station*)

Northern gardeners can also enjoy persimmons. The American persimmon (*D. virginiana*) grows to 30′ or so, and named varieties such as 'Garretson,' 'Early Golden,' 'Ennis Seedless' and 'Killen' produce fine crops of plump 2″ red-orange fruits where temperatures go down to –20°. The fruits are picked before frost and the astringency is removed by ripening them in a warm dry place. They can be ripened very quickly by putting them in a plastic bag with apples, which give off the "ripening gas" ethylene. Both male and female trees must be planted for pollination.

MULBERRY: It's been said a mulberry tree should be planted only to attract birds away from more valuable fruit. But the best mulberries bear excellent fruit, and the birds can be foiled by netting smaller trees or harvesting daily (by shaking the fruit off onto sheets). Mulberries are fast-growing, round-headed trees that provide fine shade, and the berries may be used raw, in pies, jams and jellies, for wine, or dried like raisins. In parts of Asia, dried white mulberries and almonds form a balanced daily diet.

The black mulberry (*Morus nigra*) is the least hardy and is grown mainly in the South and West. Hardier (–20°) is the native red mulberry (*M. rubra*), generally considered a finer ornamental than a fruit plant, but several named varieties are occasionally offered. Most popular is the white mulberry (*M. alba*), hardy to –20° and available in fine varieties such as 'Wellington' and 'Illinois Everbearing.' Mulberries grow to 20′ to 30′, but a mulberry specialist, Louis Gerardi Nursery, lists dwarfs only 12′ tall.

PAWPAW: The only hardy member of the tropical custard apple family, the native pawpaw or "hardy banana" (*Asimina triloba*) grows to 15′ with multiple trunks, 25′ trained to one trunk. Its large and lustrous leaves turn bright yellow in autumn, and the fragrant 2″ flowers are wine-purple. The 4″ to 6″ fruits, up to 12 ounces each and resembling fat bananas, have a rich banana flavor and texture and are eaten fresh, baked or in pies. The trees are long-lived and will grow in light shade. 'Sunflower,' 'Davis' and 'Taylor' are superior varieties, hardy to –25°.

JUJUBE: Another intriguing small tree, the Chinese jujube (*Zizyphus jujuba*), bears great quantities of 1″ to 2″ round brown fruits that look and taste like dates. Hardy to –20°, the tree is ornamental, with slender prickly branches and small, shining leaves. The fruit, high in vitamin C, may be candied or canned, or dried and kept for years. The jujube fruits best in long hot summers with low humidity.

MEDLAR: The little-known but ancient Persian medlar (*Mespilus germanica*) grows to 20′, is thickly clothed with narrow downy leaves, and bears showy 2″ pinkish flowers. The 2½″ quince-like brown fruits are picked after a light frost to "blet" or mellow. They have a distinct apple-pear flavor and are eaten raw or made into jelly or preserves. The best variety is 'Nottingham,' now available from Southmeadow Fruit Gardens. Medlars are hardy to at least –20°.

CHINESE CHE: Homesteaders interested in trying a really new fruit should consider the Chinese che (*Cudrania tricuspidata*). A 30′ tree with a spreading top, it produces delicious 1″ to 2″ red-fleshed fruits. These ripen in early October in Maryland, and the tree is hardy to at least –10°. Dr. George M. Darrow (Olallie Farm, Glenn Dale, MD 20769), retired head of the USDA Small Fruits Division, is studying the che extensively, and he reports that a mature female tree at the Blandy Experimental Farm (Boyce, VA 22620) bears hundreds of pounds of fruit annually. He notes that che trees may not be totally male or female, the females often bearing enough male flowers to set a good crop.

Fruiting Ornamentals

Finally, don't neglect the fruits many of our best ornamentals produce. 'Dolgo,' 'Cowichan,' 'Gibbs Golden Gage,' 'Redflesh' and 'Hopa' crabapples yield excellent fruit for jelly and eating fresh. "Apples" for jelly and jam are also produced by hawthorns such as *Crataegus mollis* and *C. pinnatifida*, and by the delightful dog-

Sweet, red-fleshed fruit can be harvested by
the hundreds of pounds from a mature
Chinese che tree. (*Dr. George M. Darrow*)

wood known as the Cornelian cherry, *Cornus mas.* Many species
of hackberry (*Celtis*) have sweet edible berries, as does at least one
mountain ash, *Sorbus aucuparia edulis.*

Especially noteworthy for jelly-sauce-pie berries — but also good
fresh and dried — are several serviceberries or shadblows (*Amelanchier*). 'Smoky,' 'Altaglow,' 'Forestburg' and 'Pembina' are
new clones of the saskatoon (*A. alnifolia*) that produce extra-large
"sugar plum" berries (available from Beaverlodge Nursery). This
beautiful shrubby tree that is a cloud of white flowers in spring is
hardy to –40°, and self-fruitful. Saskatoon and other amelanchier
fruits are very high in vitamin C.

Bush Fruits

Blue-Chip Blueberries

High-bush blueberries (*Vaccinium corymbosum*) get top ratings
for ornamental value. Their fragrant white bell flowers, rich green
leathery leaves, masses of frosty blue fruit in summer, and glowing orange to scarlet fall foliage make them ideal for specimen and
foundation plantings as well as informal hedges. They may also
be set 3' to 4' apart for a hedgerow if the gardener is willing to
sacrifice some yield. Blueberry bushes are hardy to at least –20°,

and the best varieties when mature produce 5 to 8 quarts per plant. They grow no taller than 6' and are easily netted to save the crop from the birds.

In addition to full sun and good air circulation, a vital requirement for blueberries is acid soil — pH 4.8 is ideal. If the soil is not naturally this acid, mix in acid peat and/or oak leafmold, sawdust, or woods humus from beneath pines, oaks, firs, etc., to a depth of 12″. A 4″- to 6″-deep mulch of these materials should also be maintained constantly. A highly recommended fertilizer is cottonseed meal, raked into the mulch at the rate of 2 pounds per mature plant in early spring and again six weeks later. The mulch should supply all other nutrient needs, as well as conserve the moisture blueberries need. Prune annually in late winter to maintain eight to ten vigorous canes and remove weak twiggy growth.

With early to late varieties, the blueberry harvest extends a full eight weeks. Some of the best new varieties in order of ripening are 'Earliblue,' 'Collins,' 'Blueray,' 'Bluecrop,' 'Berkeley,' 'Jersey,' 'Herbert' and 'Coville.' In the South, plant the new heat-tolerant "rabbiteye" varieties such as 'Tifblue,' 'Homebell' and 'Menditoo.' Because cross-pollination gives more, earlier and larger berries, several varieties should be planted.

Give the berries at least five days to a week after they turn blue to ripen before picking. Blueberries can be grown in large tubs or halves of barrels or 55-gallon drums, and city gardeners have shown they will thrive in sunny backyards and roof gardens.

Given an acid mulch and fertilizer, a blueberry bush will yield up to 8 quarts of big berries a year. (*Organic Gardening and Farming*)

All-Summer Raspberries

Raspberries (*Rubus*) are one of the easiest fruit crops, and the most rewarding. They can be enjoyed from summer to fall, and the grower even has a choice of fruit colors. Currently the best in summer-crop reds are 'Latham,' 'Taylor,' 'Chief,' 'Boyne,' thornless 'Canby,' and golden 'Amber.' In the everbearing reds, 'Heritage' is widely acclaimed, followed by the early 'Augustred,' 'Southland' for the South, and yellow 'Fallgold' (yellow raspberries derive from sports of red). Of the black raspberries, 'Jewel' and 'Allen' are recommended, plus everbearing 'Black Beauty.' 'Clyde,' everbearing 'Purple Autumn,' and the new 'Lowden Sweet Purple' from Canada are highly rated purples.

Raspberries are planted 3′ apart for a hedgerow, 5′ to 6′ as specimen plants. They do not really need support, but are easier to prune and harvest if plants grown singly are staked, and hedgerow plants are tied to strong wires, 3′ and 5′ from the ground, stretched between posts. Or nail 24″ horizontal crossbars on top of 3′-high posts at each end of the row, and stretch wires between these; the canes are guided up between the wires and will lean on them, making tying unnecessary.

Regular pruning is vital for neat growth and high yields. With the exception of everbearers, red and yellow raspberries should have the canes that have fruited cut to the ground after harvest, and in spring the new canes are cut back to 4′ to 5′ and weak ones removed to leave only three or four canes per foot of row or eight canes for plants grown as single specimens. The more rampant-growing black and purple raspberries are thinned to four to six canes per plant after harvest, and in spring side branches are headed back to 10″; new canes should have their growing tips pinched off in early summer to force branching.

Everbearers produce a fall crop on the tips of new canes, then a crop next summer on the lower parts of the same canes. The tips that fruited in the fall are cut off early the next spring to spur branching, then the entire cane is removed after the summer harvest. However, some growers simply cut all canes to the ground in late fall, which sacrifices the summer crop but eliminates pruning and gives a larger fall crop the next year.

Ever-Better Blackberries

A dead-ripe blackberry (*Rubus*) has the finest, headiest flavor of all berries. There are two types of blackberries, the erect to semi-erect, and the less hardy trailing dewberries. The latter include the boysenberry, loganberry, youngberry and others, some of them species and others crosses with each other or with blackberries or raspberries. Blackberries, incidentally, as well as raspberries, are often grown farther north than is recommended, protected in winter by either bending down the canes and covering them with a mulch or soil, or "bundling" like figs.

'Darrow' is considered the best erect blackberry, hardy to at least –20°, very productive and long-season. 'Humble' and 'Raven' are popular farther south, but the new 'Cherokee' and 'Comanche' are higher-yielding. There are excellent thornless blackberries — 'Smoothstem,' hardy to 0°, the more vigorous 'Thornfree' (–10°), new 'Dirksen Thornless' and 'Black Satin' from Southern Illinois University, and 'Thornless Boysen' for the South.

Blackberries are grown like raspberries. With erect types, weak canes, suckers, and canes that have fruited are pruned out after harvest, then in early spring the side branches are headed back to 12″ to 18″. For trailing varieties, which are trained to a wire trellis, fence or pergola, remove the canes which fruited after harvest, and in spring cut out all but eight to twelve of the strongest canes, heading these back to 5′ and tying them to the supports.

Current Currants and Gooseberries

Currant jelly and gooseberry jam are deservedly prized, and both these vitamin C–rich fruits make excellent pies, too. If dead ripe, they're delicious fresh, and they may also be dried and used like raisins. Fortunately for home fruit growers, areas where growing gooseberries and currants are prohibited (because some are alternate hosts for white pine blister rust) are steadily decreasing — but check with your extension service office before ordering plants.

These are cool-climate plants, thriving best from the Ohio Valley into Canada. They do well in fairly heavy soils and tolerate light shade. A heavy mulch is particularly important in regions of hot, dry summers. They stand windy sites — indeed, a windy location is recommended for European gooseberries to reduce mildew.

Improved American gooseberries are heavy bearers as well as handsome shrubs. (*New York State Agricultural Experiment Station*)

The plants are set 5' apart if grown in rows, and pruning is simple. Gooseberries and currants (*Ribes*) bear mainly on two- and three-year-old canes, so all older canes are removed. Experts advise pruning in late winter and leaving three each of one-, two- and three-year-old canes. In England, gooseberries are often used for espalier or even trained as single-stemmed standards.

'Red Lake,' 'Minnesota 71,' and 'Wilder' are three of the best red currants, while 'White Imperial' is the finest white-fruited variety. Highest rated gooseberries are the American red 'Poorman' and 'Welcome' — the latter is nearly thornless — and green-fruited European 'Fredonia' and 'Chautauqua.' Some fine European gooseberries with berries almost as big as eggs are offered by Southmeadow Fruit Gardens.

Bush Cherries and Cherry-Plums

Of the many bush cherries — some of which have fruit almost as large as the cherries produced on trees — three are especially worth growing. Besides bearing sweet red to purple fruit for eating fresh or making pies and preserves, they are handsome shrubs with glossy foliage and spirea-like white spring blooms.

The native western sand cherry (*Prunus besseyi*) grows to 4' tall, stands considerable drought, and is available now in superior varieties — 'Black Beauty,' 'Brooks,' 'Sioux' and 'Hansen.' Also valuable for specimen planting, shrub borders and hedges is the slightly taller Korean cherry (*P. japonica*), to 6'. The Nanking cherry (*P. tomentosa*) from China grows to 8', and 'Drilea' is an improved form. All are hardy into Canada, and in most cases two varieties should be planted for cross-pollination.

Gardeners are also beginning to grow cherry-plums. These hybrids of the western sand cherry and plums vary from small shrubs to small trees and bear over 1" fruit. All require two varieties or a sand cherry for pollination. 'Opata,' 'Sapalta,' 'Sapa' and 'Compass' are becoming popular. One of the newest is 'Wessex', developed by Percy H. Wright (409 109th Street, Saskatoon, Saskatchewan, Canada), who reports it is hardy to –60°, grows to 8' to 9', and bears red freestone fruit which "hangs on and dries up like a prune, so that it can be eaten with relish up to three weeks after fully ripe."

The Home Vineyard

Grapes (*Vitis*) have become one of the most popular garden fruits. They offer outstanding ornamental value in their handsome foliage, curling tendrils, and rich reds, ambers, greens, blues and blacks of their fruit. The long-lived vines may be grown on trellises, arbors, fences, posts, stumps and the sides of buildings. They take very little ground space and ask only full sun, a not too rich soil and very good drainage. Recent research shows that a high content of organic matter in the soil, plus extra potassium (wood ashes are a good source), are aids to high production.

The gardener's biggest problem is selecting from the ever-growing number of superlative grapes. In the past 20 years, the French hybrids have become prominent. These are crosses of the hardy (–20°) American grapes of the Northeast with the more tender (–5°), drier-climate European or "California" vinifera grapes. Many of these are fine table as well as wine grapes, and most are hardy to about –15°. There is also a fourth type of grape, the muscadine, grown widely in the South where northern "bunch" grapes do not do well. Muscadine vines are strong growers and should be set about 15' apart. They have very few pest or disease problems. Some older varieties are self-sterile, but newer ones such as red-fruited 'Burgaw,' white 'Dearing' and black 'Magoon' can be planted singly or used to pollinate many excellent ones that are not fruitful alone.

In northern grapes, the best blue-black varieties are 'Worden' (even better than the old favorite 'Concord'), 'Buffalo,' 'Alden,' 'Fredonia,' 'Steuben,' 'Sheridan,' and very hardy (–30°) 'Van Buren.' In whites, 'Niagara,' 'Ontario,' 'Portland' and 'Lake Emerald' are tops. Seedless types include white 'Interlaken Seedless,' 'Himrod Seedless,' 'Lakemont' and 'Romulus,' and red 'Suffolk Red,' all hardy to –5° except 'Himrod' (–15°). Best rated in red grapes are 'Urbana' (keeps for three months), 'Catawba' (makes marvelous jelly), 'Red Amber' (hardy in Minnesota), 'Delaware,' 'Yates' and 'Vinered.' Some of the best French hybrids grown primarily for wine are white 'Aurora,' blue-black 'Baco Noir,' 'Cascade' and 'Foch,' and red 'Seibel 9549' ('De Chaunac'). Many other worthy grapes, of course, may be recommended locally.

For most abundant harvests, training is essential. Of the many systems, the four-cane Kniffen and umbrella Kniffen are considered the best. A two-wire trellis is used, the lower wire 36″ above the ground, the top one 65″. Space the vines 8' apart. After planting, prune each young vine to the best single trunk, staking this and allowing only two buds to grow. In late winter or early spring of the second year, prune off all but the strongest cane, leave four to six buds and remove all flower clusters before bloom.

During the third winter, the four canes for the arms can be chosen, cut back to about ten buds and tied to the wires. Four other nearby canes are cut back to two buds to provide the canes for the following year. In subsequent years, retain four one-year canes cut back to 8 to 15 buds (depending on the vigor of the vine) for the arms, and four short "spurs" of two buds each for the development of new canes. Always choose canes that are darkest in color and of at least pencil thickness.

In the umbrella system, the main trunk is tied to the top wire

The huge clusters of vitamin-rich fruit of the
new improved elderberries are excellent for
pies, jelly or wine. (*New York State
Agricultural Experiment Station*)

and two or more canes are bent over this wire and tied to the lower
one. For arbor training, the trunk is pinched when it reaches the
top of the arbor to produce shoots which are trained over the crosspieces. Annual renewal pruning thereafter is the same as for trellised vines.

Domesticated Elderberries

Elderberries (*Sambucus canadensis* and the western *S. caerulea*)
are a newly cultivated fruit crop. Varieties such as 'Adams,'
'Johns,' 'Nova' and 'York' are improvements over wild elderberries, giving higher yields of bigger berries. The 8′ to 10′ shrubs,
hardy to –20°, are quite ornamental, with luxuriant dark green foliage and broad flat clusters of fragrant creamy-white flowers (very
good dipped in batter and fried) in late spring or early summer. A
mature bush will produce at least 15 pounds of purple-black berries, which have a distinctive flavor and make superb jam, jelly,
sauce, pie and wine, and can also be dried like raisins.

Elderberries will stand light shade but must have moist soil.
Plant two varieties for cross-pollination, and be prepared to net the

bushes to protect the crop from birds. To control the spreading growth of elderberries, constantly prune out out-of-bounds suckers. The only other pruning consists of cutting old unproductive canes in early spring and trimming the laterals back to 8″ to 10″ on the older remaining canes.

Fruit of the Rose

Certain roses are a top fruit crop. The "hips" or fruits of some of the very hardy and rugged shrub roses contain sixty times as much vitamin C as oranges. *Rosa rugosa* — called the "sea tomato" in its native Japan — and its varieties and hybrids are handsome, pest-free 4′ to 12′ shrubs with dark green foliage and fragrant rose-pink single flowers all summer. They are ideal for specimen, hedge, foundation and border plantings, and produce hips which are often as large as crabapples. Also very high in vitamin C are the hips of *R. acicularis*, *R. laxa*, *R. cinnamomea* and *R. moyesii*.

Four or five bushes of any of these will supply ample hips for a family for eating raw or stewed or made into a marvelous jelly, jam, sauce or syrup. Recipes are available from the American Rose Society (Box 30,000, Shreveport, LA 71130). Rose hips should be harvested when fully ripe but not overripe — after they turn from orange to red but are not yet dark red.

The Maritime Plum

Fruit gardeners are discovering the merits of the beach plum (*Prunus maritima*). This 5′ to 6′ native of the sand dunes of the Atlantic Coast thrives equally well on heavier soils inland. It stands dry windswept sites and infertile soils, and is hardy to –35°. Masses of white flowers are followed by cherry-like sweet-acid fruits up to 1″ in diameter. These are excellent for jellies and jams when they turn red-purple, and when blue-purple and dead ripe make fine pies. The bushes benefit from pruning to keep them from becoming straggly, and they can be trained as small trees. 'Raritan' and 'Autumn' are new improved varieties.

Fresh Fruits

Several more "new" fruits deserve to be much more widely known and grown. The American highbush cranberry, *Viburnum trilobum,* is a first-rate ornamental, growing to 10′ and hardy to –35°, with showy clusters of white flowers and bright red fall foliage — and it produces large glowing red berries good for jelly and sauce. Four varieties with superior fruit are 'Wentworth,' 'Hahs,' 'Andrews' and the new 'Phillips.' The American species must not be confused with the much similar but bitter-fruited European *V. opulus*.

Very hardy and productive, the American highbush cranberry is one of the best viburnums for garden planting as an edible ornamental. (*New York State Agricultural Experiment Station*)

Equally hardy and handsome are two silvery-leaved buffalo berries, 12' *Shepherdia argentea* and 8' *S. canadensis*. They have boxwood-like foliage, make good windbreaks, and produce great quantities of currant-sized fruits used for jelly, jam and pies, and also dried. Two species of *Elaeagnus* also have fine fruit for jelly or sauce: the silvery-leaved 10' to 15' autumn olive, *E. umbellata*, is now available in a selection, 'Cardinal,' that yields up to 40 pounds of berries, while the 8' cherry elaeagnus, *E. multiflora*, has exceptionally fine-flavored fruit.

A much neglected fruit is the chokecherry, *Prunus virginiana*. Hardy to –50°, it is grown as far south as Georgia and Texas. Dense-growing and useful as a 6' to 20' screen plant, it bears racemes of white flowers and usually dark red to black fruits, but strains with white, yellow or pink fruit have been found. Most chokecherries have astringent fruit useful only for jelly, pie and sauce, but at least one Canadian plantsman reports that sweet-fruited varieties like 'Boughen's Golden' are often eaten fresh from the tree. However, the pits must not be eaten raw, for they contain deadly hydrocyanic acid.

The bower actinidia or tara vine, *Actinidia arguta*, is a handsome deciduous vine, hardy to –30° and bearing white flowers and sweet 1″ greenish-yellow fruits that are eaten fresh or made into jam and sauce. Several other actinidias also have edible fruit, but the best of all is the newly introduced Chinese gooseberry or Kiwi, *A. chinensis*. It bears 2″ furry brown plum-like fruits with delicious ice-green flesh that is very high in vitamin C. Hardy to about 0°, the Kiwi is being grown commercially and by gardeners in California and through the South up to Washington, D.C. Superior varieties include 'Abbott,' 'Bruno,' 'Chico,' 'Hayward' and 'Monty.' Male and female flowers are borne on separate plants.

Stalking Wildlings

Country gardeners know that the wilds can be a source of fine fruits never offered by nurseries. To cite just one example: the brambles (*Rubus*) contain many little-known species such as the creeping cloudberry or baked-apple berry, *R. chamaemorus*, of New England and Newfoundland, which bears delicious gold fruit resembling raspberries, and the 5′ to 8′ salmonberry, *R. spectabilis*, native from California to Alaska, with fine red fruit.

Many other species of *Rubus*, as well as of *Ribes, Vaccinium, Gaylussacia, Gaultheria, Mahonia* and others bear worthy fruit. The best deserve transplanting or propagating for garden use. Books on wild plants — especially the works of Euell Gibbons — provide clues to finding these. And as the North American Fruit Explorers journal, *Pomona*, often notes, superior varieties of many common fruit plants are waiting in the wild to be discovered and disseminated by adventurous gardeners.

Fruitful Sources

Unless otherwise noted, the following offer a wide variety of tree and bush fruits. Many general mail-order nurseries also list a good selection of fruits. With most fruits, it is wise to purchase plants from sources in the same climatic region as your garden.

Adams County Nursery, Aspers, PA 17304

Ahrens & Son Nursery, R.R. 1, Huntingburg, IN 47542 — berries

Alberta Nurseries, Box 20, Bowden, Alberta T0M 0K0, Canada

J. Herbert Alexander, Middleboro, MA 02346 — blueberries

W.F. Allen Company, Box 1577, Salisbury, MD 21801 — berries

Anding Nursery, Route 3, Box 40, Summit, MS 39666 — southern varieties

Armstrong Nurseries, Box 473, Ontario, CA 91764 — genetic dwarfs

Fred L. Ashworth, St. Lawrence Nurseries, Route 2, Heuvelton, NY 13654

Vernon Barnes & Son Nursery, Box 250, McMinnville, TN 37110

Baum's Nursery, R.D. 4, New Fairfield, CT 06815 — old varieties

Beaverlodge Nursery, Box 127, Beaverlodge, Alberta, Canada

Boatman's Nursery, Bainbridge, OH 45612

Bountiful Ridge Nursery, Box 248, Princess Anne, MD 21853

Brittingham Plant Farms, Salisbury, MD 21801 — berries

Buntings' Nurseries, Selbyville, DE 19975

C & O Nursery, Box 116, Wenatchee, WA 98801

California Nursery Company, Box 2278, Fremont, CA 94536

Common Fields Nursery, Town Farm Road, Ipswich, MA 01938 — blueberries

Corwin Davis, Route 1, Bellevue, MI 49021 — pawpaw, berries

Devon Nurseries, 1408 Royal Bank Bldg., Edmonton, Alberta T5J 1W8, Canada

Dutch Mountain Nursery, Augusta, MI 49012; catalog 25¢

Exotica Seed Co., 1416 North Kings Road, Los Angeles, CA 90069 — seed of tropical and subtropical fruits

Dean Foster Nurseries, Hartford, MI 49057

Fruit Haven Nursery, Kaleva, MI 49645

Louis Gerardi Nursery, R.R.1 O'Fallon, IL 62269

Hansen New Plants, Fremont, NE 68025

Hilltop Orchards & Nurseries, Route 2, Hartford, MI 49057 — excellent cultural information in catalog

Kelly Bros. Nurseries, Dansville, NY 14437

Lawson's Nursery, Route 1, Ball Ground, GA 30107 — old apples and pears

Lee's Nursery, Route 2, Box 184-A, McMinnville, TN 37110

Henry Leuthardt Nurseries, East Moriches, NY 11940; catalog 25¢ — espalier specialist; also berries and grapes

Lowden's Nursery, Box 10, Ancaster, Ontario, Canada — berries

Makielski Berry Farm, 7130 Platt Road, Ypsilanti, MI 48197

May Nursery Company, Box 1312, Yakima, WA 98907

Mayo Nurseries, Route 14, Lyons, NY 14489

Mellinger's Inc., 2130 West South Range Road, North Lima, OH 44452

J. E. Miller Nursery, Canandaigua, NY 14424

Walter K. Morss & Son, R.F.D. 3, Bradford, MA 01830 — berries

New York State Fruit Testing Cooperative Association, Geneva, NY 14456 — scions of new and old varieties; membership $4

Owens Muscadine Nursery, Gay, GA 30218 — muscadine grapes

Rayner Brothers, Box 1617, Salisbury, MD 21801

Shiloh Nursery, R. 1, Box 314, Shiloh, OH 44878; catalog $2.25 — grapes

Southmeadow Fruit Gardens, 2363 Tilbury Place, Birmingham, MI 48009

Stanek's Garden Center, East 2929 27th Avenue, Spokane, WA 99203

Stark Bro's Nurseries, Louisiana, MO 63353

Tennessee Nursery Company, Cleveland, TN 37311

Waynesboro Nurseries, Box 987, Waynesboro, VA 22980

Worcester County Horticultural Society, 30 Elm Street, Worcester, MA 01608 — scions of old and new apples

Zilke Brothers Nursery, Baroda, MI 49101

⫷ 8 ⫸

Assorted Nuts

Nut trees have so much to offer — variety, landscape value, and an uncommon crop. To the gardener, until recently their ornamental attributes were perhaps the most important. But today we are likely to think also in terms of a plant's usefulness as a food resource, particularly if the crop is assured for many years and with little effort on our part. Nuts are easy to grow and harvest, store well, and are rich in food value: they are very high in protein and unsaturated fat, rich in calcium and iron, and contain appreciable amounts of some vitamins.

Practically anywhere in the United States and southern Canada, it is possible to find at least one type and variety of nut tree that will bear dependably. While some — the coconut, cashew, macadamia and pistachio — are restricted to the warmest climes, improved forms of butternut, black walnut, hickory and others do well to northern New England and Minnesota. Thus size may be the primary consideration in selecting the best for a given garden situation.

Filberts are good candidates for shrub borders, hedges, or even foundation plantings. Almonds and Chinese and chinkapin chestnuts fall in the apple tree size range. Shagbark hickory, heartnut and butternut rate as medium-sized trees. Pecan and black walnut are majestic and towering. With many, size is a double problem: all except the walnut group (*Juglans*) either require or probably benefit from cross-pollination, and the need for two trees to accomplish this may eliminate some of the larger species where space is limited.

Always buy budded or grafted trees of named cultivars. They bear higher-quality nuts, and bear them earlier, than seedling

Almonds are beautiful small trees, and the
late-blooming 'Halls Hardy' variety will
produce good crops even in the central
states. (*University of California*)

trees. The one exception is the Chinese chestnut when grown in the North, where it often fails at the graft union, making seedlings a better choice. The gardener, of course, may enjoy planting seedlings and grafting desired varieties on these after they are well established.

Kernel Culture

Nut trees need full sun and a deep, fertile soil with good drainage. Frost pockets should be avoided, so plant on a high spot or slope whenever possible. Spring planting is best in the North, fall in milder climates. Add compost or other organic material to the soil, water weekly the first year whenever rainfall is insufficient, and mulch generously out to the dripline of the branches (organic mulches have been shown to result in higher yields than sod around the trees). Nut trees will respond with better crops to feeding early in spring, at the rate of 1 pound of a 10–6–4 or similar formula per 1″ of trunk diameter, beginning a year after planting.

The nuts should be allowed to mature fully and fall naturally from the tree. Gathering them promptly after they fall is especially important for walnuts, to avoid discoloration of the kernels from rotting of the husks on moist ground. Many nuts are most easily husked by tramping on them or putting them through a corn sheller. Wash the nuts and spread them thinly on screens in a well-ventilated place to dry. A hand cracker for walnuts is offered by J. W. Hershey (Downingtown, PA 19335).

Nut trees have few insect or disease problems, but squirrels are notorious thieves of nut crops. An isolated tree, with no nearby trees to offer aerial access, can be protected with a wide metal shield, such as 18″ aluminum flashing (from building suppliers), around the trunk. This should have horizontal slots for the spikes that hold it to the tree, to allow for expansion as the tree grows. To repel squirrels, try bags of mothballs or onions hung in the branches.

Almonds

This member of the rose family, closely related to and in many ways resembling the peach, is a small, pretty, and quite cold-hardy tree. *Prunus amygdalus* reliably produces nuts, however, only in certain areas of California and the Southwest, for it blooms very early and the flowers are destroyed by even light frosts. But there is one variety that will grow and bear wherever peaches thrive. 'Halls Hardy' blooms much later, and unlike other almonds it does not require cross-pollination. A 15′ to 20′ tree that bears masses of delicate pink flowers, it is a fine ornamental for a small garden. Bearing usually begins two or three years after trans-

PRUNUS AMYGDALUS KAPAREIL

New breeding work is producing almonds
that bloom late to escape spring frosts and
that have nuts with sweet kernels.
(*University of California*)

planting. The shell is hard and peach-like, the kernel is slightly
bitter but excellent for cooking and baking.

Chestnuts and Chinkapins

With the loss of the American chestnut (*Castanea dentata*) to a
devastating blight, the Chinese chestnut (*C. mollissima*) has been
discovered by gardeners. This species is blight-resistant, hardy to
at least –20°, and develops into a handsome 35′ round-headed tree.
The nuts are fully as large and flavorful as those of the American
chestnut, and they are encased in a spiny bur that makes them
squirrelproof. The Chinese chestnut does best on a moist but well-
drained, somewhat acid light soil. Its clusters of tiny flowers in
late spring or early summer are quite attractive. A mature tree
should produce well over 100 pounds of nuts per season.

Two native chestnuts are attracting attention. The Allegheny
and Ozark chinkapins (*C. pumila* and *C. ozarkensis*) bear great
quantities of sweet nuts the size of small acorns. Both species
grow as large shrubs or small trees, and are hardy to about –15°.
Two nurseries (Gerardi, Waynesboro) are now offering chinkapins.

They also show promise in breeding: 'Essate-Jap,' a cross of *C.
pumila* and the Japanese chestnut, *C. crenata,* made by the Connecticut Agricultural Experiment Station (New Haven, CT 06504),
is a large, blight-resistant tree with flavorful, early-ripening nuts.
Another result of the breeding program directed by Dr. Richard A.
Jaynes at the Connecticut Station is a cross of the Chinese and
seguin (*C. seguinii*) chestnuts, which has produced a high-yielding, blight-resistant dwarf only 6′ tall.

The development of systemic fungicides, incidentally, may yet make it possible to restore the American chestnut, which has been reduced by the blight to an occasional small tree or clump of sprouts in the woodland. The hope offered by systemics makes it vital to conserve these remnants. Gardeners living or traveling in the natural range of *C. dentata* — Maine to Michigan, south to Mississippi and Florida — are urged to search in the woodlands in early autumn for nuts produced on sprouts, or for chestnut saplings. Single-stem trees are preferable to clumps, as they are more likely to be growing from a nut produced by a tree that had escaped the blight long enough to bear. Taken with a root ball, saplings transplant easily into the garden, or nuts can be planted 3″ deep in rich, light soil, protected from rodents by a wire mesh cage.

Any chestnut tree you discover with a trunk diameter of 8″ or more at breast height should be reported to your county agent — it may have valuable natural resistance to the blight. Two private organizations working to breed American chestnuts with blight resistance are Stronghold (4931 Upton Street, N.W., Washington, DC 20016), and the National Parks and Conservation Association (1701 18th Street, N.W., Washington, DC 20009). Write them for information on their programs and how you can help.

Filberts, Hazels, and Filazels

Of the fifteen known species of filbert and hazelnut — the names are often interchanged, since the botanical differences are minor — several fit easily into small gardens. The European filbert, *Corylus avellana*, grows as a shrub to 15′ or so or can be pruned to a single-stemmed small tree. It is hardy to –20° and bears large nuts, but in cold regions even its best varieties such as 'Barcelona'

One of the best Chinese chestnut hybrids, 'Eaton' bears heavy crops of large, sweet nuts. (*Connecticut Agricultural Experiment Station*)

A handsome, very productive tree, the
Chinese chestnut is being developed in
dwarf forms, and also bred with the
American chestnut to give blight resistance.
(*Connecticut Agricultural Experiment
Station*)

and 'Royal' often produce scant crops because spring frosts injure
the blooms. The smaller (5' to 8') American hazelnut, *C. ameri-
cana*, reliably produces smaller but delicious nuts where temperatures go down to –30°. It is frequently used for a hedge or screen.
'Winkler' and 'Rush' are recommended varieties.

Combining many of the best characteristics are hybrids of the
two species. 'Bixby,' 'Buchanan,' 'Potomac' and 'Reed,' bred by
the New York Agricultural Experiment Station (Geneva, NY
14456), are the finest of these. Mr. J. U. Gellatly (Gellatly Brothers, Westbank, British Columbia, Canada) has crossed the European filbert with the very hardy native beaked hazel, *C. cornuta*,
to produce "filazels" that bear heavy crops of big nuts in areas of
–25° winter lows.

A valuable species that has been neglected is the Turkish filbert
or tree hazel, *C. colurna*. This is a handsome conical tree with
corky bark, 40' to 50' high and hardy to –20°, and bearing small but
high-quality nuts. It is now being made available by the Cole Nursery Co. (30627 Orr Road, Circleville, OH 43113; wholesale —
have your nurseryman order). Mr. Gellatly has interbred the Turkish, Chinese (*C. chinensis*) and Indian (*C. jacquemontii*) tree hazels, achieving several stately, high-yielding hybrids.

Hickories

The pecan (see below) is generally considered to have the finest nuts of all the hickories, but those of the shagbark (*Carya ovata*) are very nearly as flavorful — and the shagbark hickory will ripen its nuts much farther north.

Where there is room for it, the shagbark hickory is one of the most beautiful of all shade trees. It will grow to 100' or more, and has five-leaflet leaves and distinctive bark that sheds in long vertical strips on older trees. It is hardy to –20° and bears thin-shelled sweet nuts. Like all hickories, it has a long taproot so must be transplanted only when young, and it begins bearing at 10 to 15 years of age. Some improved varieties are 'Bridgewater,' 'Glover,' 'Retzer,' 'Weschcke' and 'Wilcox,' but many others have been named and different ones are preferred in different areas.

The shellbark or kingnut hickory, *C. laciniosa,* is also a giant with shaggy bark. Its nuts, however, usually have thick bone-like shells that crack poorly. Some superior selections are 'Keystone,' 'Nieman,' 'Ross' and 'Stephens.' Several other native hickories are also handsome trees — the mockernut (*C. tomentosa*), bitternut (*C. cordiformis*), and pignuts (*C. glabra, C. ovalis*) — but all have either bitter, small or hard-to-crack nuts.

Hickories will do well on poor soils, but it is important to make the planting hole deep enough to accommodate the long taproot, and to firm the soil well.

Pecans and Hicans

The pecan, *Carya illinoensis,* is primarily a southern tree, for it needs a long growing season and sustained summer heat. From Florida to Louisiana, superior cultivars such as 'Mahan,' 'Hastings,' 'Stuart,' and the newer 'Desirable' and 'Harris Super' are widely planted in home landscapes for their great ornamental value and delicious nuts (incidentally, though the nuts have a very high oil content, most of the oil is unsaturated). In the Southwest, cultivars suited to a less humid climate and more alkaline soils, such as 'Apache,' 'Comanche,' 'Sioux' and 'Western,' serve the same purposes.

The USDA Pecan Field Station (Brownwood, TX 76801) is working to breed dwarf varieties of pecan. Most current research, however, is aimed at developing "northern" papershell pecans. Some of the best new varieties which will mature nuts with as few as 150 frost-free days are 'Colby,' 'Fritz,' 'Greenriver,' 'Major,' 'Posey,' 'Starking' and 'Witte.' Their nuts are as flavorful and thin-shelled as those of the southern types and only slightly smaller. Some nurseries also offer seedlings from selected native trees that may extend the pecan range slightly farther north, but the nuts from these are smaller and thick-shelled.

Hicans, crosses of pecans with shagbark and shellbark hickories, are generally as vigorous and ornamental as their parents, and several of these are good to excellent bearers of quality nuts. 'Burton' is one of the most productive. Also highly rated in some areas are 'Bergman,' 'Gerardi,' 'Underwood,' 'Henke' and 'Pixley.'

Pecan and hican trees are as stately and handsome as any hickory, but they appear to have a greater need for good soil — loose and well aerated to considerable depth — if they are to continue to bear well as they grow older. Like hickories, pecans are self-fruitful, but better crops or higher-quality nuts are generally produced by cross-pollination. The flavor of the nuts is improved, say some growers, if they are stored in mesh or burlap bags hung in a dry well-ventilated area for a couple of weeks.

Walnuts, Butternuts and Heartnuts

The black walnut, *Juglans nigra*, is another huge nut tree requiring plenty of room. The species is subject to a number of diseases and pests, and the nuts may be small and hard-shelled, but these faults are overcome to varying extents in improved cultivars like 'Thomas,' 'Myers,' 'Ohio,' 'Sparrow,' 'Stabler' and 'Victoria.' Black walnuts are hardy to –20° and produce great quantities of nuts which are extremely high in protein. The trees' high value for timber has recently been publicized, but their space requirements and the length of time needed to produce marketable logs — about thirty-five years — put this enterprise beyond reach for most gardeners and homesteaders.

Gardeners should be aware of the "allelopathic" qualities of black walnuts: their roots exude a substance toxic to apple trees, tomatoes, potatoes, ericaceous plants and others. The problem is detailed in *Effect of Black Walnut Trees and Their Products on Other Vegetation*, Bulletin 347 of the West Virginia Agricultural Experiment Station (Morgantown, WV 26506).

The Persian or English walnut, *J. regia*, has come into prominence since the introduction of the very hardy Carpathian strain from Poland. The best cultivars are hardy to –30°, bear thin-shelled nuts as delicious as those of the Spanish and French cultivars grown in California and Oregon, and bloom late to escape spring frosts. Often recommended are 'Lake,' 'Metcalfe,' 'Broadview' and 'Burtner,' but many others are available and often locally superior. The Carpathian walnut is a beautiful tree, generally growing no taller than 40' to 50', round-headed, with light gray bark and pleasingly fragrant foliage. The nuts fall free of the husks, which wither before falling and so create a minimum of litter on the lawn. A mature tree should yield up to six bushels of nuts.

The butternut, *J. cinerea*, is as hardy as the Carpathian walnut, and produces a delectable "buttery" high-oil nut that is more delicate in flavor than the black walnut. This native, often called the white walnut, grows from 50' to 75' high and does well on poor soils. However, good fertility and moisture will keep the trees vigorous and less subject to a life-shortening fungus that attacks weakened specimens. The butternut tends to be somewhat brittle in high winds, so it should not be used in exposed locations. Its wood is exceptionally beautiful and favored by wood carvers and makers of fine furniture. Among the best cultivars are 'Craxeasy,' 'Ayers,' 'Van Syckle' and 'Johnson.' Nurseryman Fred L. Ashworth recently introduced 'Chamberlin,' a clone hardy to –50° and producing nuts that crack very easily.

The Japanese or Siebold walnut, *J. sieboldiana,* is a 60', widespreading tree with large and luxuriant compound foliage that makes it look almost tropical, and long strings of nuts. Hardy to –20°, it grows very rapidly and is a handsome ornamental, but its nuts are hard to crack and not particularly tasty. The heartnut, *J. sieboldiana cordiformis,* a sport of the Japanese walnut, has all of its ornamental qualities plus flavorful nuts with smooth, easy-to-crack shells. 'Gellatly,' 'Bates,' 'Fodermaier,' 'Faust' and 'Walters' are some of the finest varieties.

Breeders are producing some worthwhile hybrids between the butternut, heartnut and Persian walnut. Among the most interesting are the heartnut-butternut crosses — called buartnuts or butterjaps — such as 'Dunoka' and 'Fioka,' bred by Mr. J. U. Gellatly.

A method of dwarfing walnut trees is used by nurseryman and nut specialist James Anding (Route 3, Box 40, Summit, MS 39666). Mr. Anding grows English walnut trees as head-high bushes that bear "good crops of the finest walnuts one could wish for."

> We choose a tree about 4' tall and plant it with care, making sure the soil is well drained. At planting time the tree is cut back to about 2' above the ground line. We let four good limbs grow from this stub, one growing upward and the other three going out at wide angles. If necessary, these shoots are pulled down and tied to a brick or horseshoe when they are about 1' long. These shoots are pointed upward about 30°.
>
> Usually no other pruning is needed for two years. If the leader is growing too strongly, it is pruned back to about 1' of new growth each year. This is done when the tree starts into growth in the spring. Each year three or four new side shoots are allowed to grow, others being rubbed off. Beginning the third year all shoots are pruned for fruiting, by pinching out the growing point when the limb has put on seven or eight new leaves. The next year those shoots which were pinched back usually bloom and bear fruit. By gauging the pinching you can

easily grow the tree into a large mound, as wide across as it is high.

With early-bearing kinds, you will eat nuts the fourth year, and the tree should last a lifetime.

Odd Nuts

Quite a few other trees bear edible nuts, though they are seldom grown for this purpose. The ginkgo, *Ginkgo biloba*, bears very sweet ½″ seeds. The Chinese call them "silver nuts" and consider them a delicacy peeled and eaten raw or roasted in boiling fat. But few gardeners have seen these, for the fruiting female tree is rarely grown — the fruit is extremely malodorous.

The American and European beeches, *Fagus grandifolia* and *F. sylvatica*, produce small but unusually delicious nuts. But like the ginkgo, these trees have gained wide attention for their superb ornamental qualities rather than for their cropping possibilities. Two selections of American beech with superior nuts, 'Abundance' and 'Abrams,' were introduced about fifty years ago. More recently, nurseryman Fred L. Ashworth discovered 'Jenner,' which bears regular crops of unusually large nuts.

Many pines bear edible seeds. Well known to nut fanciers are the Colorado pinyon pine, *Pinus cembroides edulis*, found in the Southwest and hardy to –20°, and the Italian stone pine, *P. pinea*, hardy only to about 20° but bearing delicious oil-rich seeds of hazelnut size. Several other "nut pines" are worthy of cultivation: the Mexican, Parry and single-leaf pinyon pines (*P. cembroides*, *P. quadrifolia*, *P. cembroides monophylla*), Korean pine (*P. koraiensis*) and digger pine (*P. sabiniana*). The Korean pine is especially handsome, grows slowly to 50′, is hardy to –35°, and bears great quantities of edible seeds.

The Indians and colonists knew the food value of many acorns. The group generally classified as white oak has acorns with sweet kernels, low in the tannin that makes for bitterness in black oak acorns. In earlier days, the acorns of the white oak, *Quercus alba*, were boiled like chestnuts or roasted for coffee, while others were ground for meal or used in stews. Among the oaks reported to have acorns of good palatability are the live oak (*Q. virginiana*), chestnut oak (*Q. prinus*), bur oak (*Q. macrocarpa*) and chinquapin oak (*Q. muhlenbergii* — not to be confused with the chinkapin chestnut).

New Nuts

Opportunities for improving nut trees through selection and hybridizing, as the reader has probably noted in the discussions of each group, are considerable and greatly needed. This is an exciting project, though necessarily a long-term one. Helpful discussions of objectives and how-to instructions are given in *Breeding Plants for Home and Garden*, Handbook 75 of the Brooklyn Botanic Garden (Brooklyn, NY 11225; $1.75) and in the *Handbook of North American Nut Trees*.

Any gardener who finds or develops a nut tree of unusual hardiness, pest resistance, yield, or size or quality of nut should report it to the Northern Nut Growers Association (4518 Holston Hills Road, Knoxville, TN 37914). The Association publishes a quarterly bulletin and annual report, and can supply the addresses of state and regional nut tree associations. The nurserymen listed below can also be of assistance in suggesting breeding possibilities and evaluating or perhaps testing new trees.

An important point: the nut breeder concerned with producing protein, so badly needed in a hungry world, might concentrate on the walnuts, hickories and pecans, which are the richest in this substance. Chestnuts and filberts are more starchy, high in carbohydrates. Almonds are intermediate, containing both in good proportion.

————————— Nut Guides and Growers —————————

Edible Nut Production, a correspondence course, $6 from Pennsylvania State University (307 Agricultural Administration Building, University Park, PA 16802)

Handbook of North American Nut Trees, edited by Richard A. Jaynes (Northern Nut Growers Association, 4518 Holston Hills Road, Knoxville, TN 37914; $9)

Nut Growing in New York State, Information Bulletin 71; 70¢ from Cornell University (Mailing Room, Building 7, Research Park, Ithaca, NY 14850)

Nuts for the Food Gardener, by Louise Riotte (Garden Way Publishing Co., Charlotte, VT 05445; $4.50)

Fred L. Ashworth, St. Lawrence Nurseries, Route 2, Box 34, Heuvelton, NY 13654

Boatman's Nursery, Bainbridge, OH 45612

Bountiful Ridge Nurseries, Princess Anne, MD 21853

W. Atlee Burpee Co., Warminster, PA 18974; Clinton, IA 52732; Riverside, CA 92502

California Nursery Co., Box 2278, Fremont, CA 94536

Coble's Nut Nursery, Route 1, Aspers, PA 17304

Emlong Nurseries, Stevensville, MI 49127

Earl Ferris Nursery, Hampton, IA 50441
Louis Gerardi Nursery, R.R. 1, O'Fallon, IL 62269
H. G. Hastings Co., Box 4088, Atlanta, GA 30302
Kelly Bros. Nurseries, Dansville, NY 14437
J. E. Miller Nurseries, Canandaigua, NY 14424
Waynesboro Nurseries, Waynesboro, VA 22980

⚘ 9 ⚘

The Indoor Farm

GROWING FOOD INDOORS all winter long is not only possible, it can be as pleasurable and productive (in quality if not in quantity) as the summer food garden. A surprising variety of vegetables, and even some fruits, will thrive on windowsills and porches, under lights, and in all sorts of easy-to-build greenhouses from sunpits to geodesic domes.

In windowsill farming, light is the all-important factor. Fruiting crops like tomatoes must have 8 hours of sun a day, while leaf and root crops need 4 to 6 hours. This means an unobstructed south window for many crops, or supplementing natural light with artificial: fluorescent tubes mounted on the sides or top of a window and lit 16 hours a day can make even a northern exposure capable of growing quite a few vegetables. A glass-enclosed porch or a picture window with an east or west exposure, because of the large expanse of glass, may be as good as a small south-facing window for all but high-light crops. And since most indoor crops will be in fairly small containers, they can be moved around if necessary to follow the light.

Anything from large clay or plastic flower pots to small tubs, trays, window boxes, basins and large cans will serve for containers. Hanging pots and baskets, pillow paks and small moss walls are also as useful indoors as they are in the outdoor container garden. For the potting mix, we like to use soil, sand, peat and vermiculite in equal proportions, plus a sprinkling of dolomitic lime and rock phosphate mixed in well. Liquefied seaweed or fish emulsion applied every two weeks will usually supply ample nutrients for indoor vegetables. When watering, always have the water at room temperature or slightly warmer so as not to cool the roots and retard growth.

This A-frame design of wood framing and Filon Greenhouse Panels is easy to build and inexpensive. (*Filon Corporation*)

'Pixie' is one of the most productive
tomatoes for a sunny window or porch. (*W.
Atlee Burpee Company*)

Be prepared to practice succession cropping with fast-maturing
vegetables. Pop in more seeds of lettuce, radishes, carrots, etc.,
whenever you harvest these. Or have replacement seedlings coming along in other containers — any cool area out of bright light is
fine for starting the seeds.

Fruiting Crops

The new midget tomatoes are the most popular windowsill crop,
and deservedly so. One plant in a 10″ pot will produce several
dozen tomatoes. Stake the plants to grow them upright or let them

trail. 'Tiny Tim,' 'Small Fry,' 'Patio,' 'Pixie' and others are excellent. So are the cherry, plum and pear types, which produce "cocktail-size" fruits for salads, pickling and tomato jam. A new variety bred especially for hanging baskets is 'Tumblin' Tom,' the first true cascading tomato.

Seed of these started in late summer will begin bearing in early winter. You can also dig up a stocky plant from the garden and bring it into a sunny window for winter cropping, or root a branch of a tomato plant by layering it (bend it over, still attached to the plant, and cover a small section with soil, then cut it off and pot it up when roots have formed).

Indoor tomatoes — peppers and peas, too — need your help for pollination. Either shake the plants daily when they are in bloom, or use a small artist's brush to transfer the pollen from flower to flower.

Peppers also do well in 10″ or larger pots or hanging baskets. 'Yolo Wonder,' 'Anaheim Chili' and 'Canape' are good, but try almost any sweet or hot type you fancy. Eggplant should have an even larger and deeper container. Dwarf varieties such as 'Morden Midget' are excellent. Remember that eggplant, like many other indoor crops, is best picked while still small and immature.

With sufficient room and plenty of bright sun, you can try some of the vine crops. The new self-pollinating European cucumbers, very mild in flavor, are easily trained up strings, but a better choice is the new compact 'Patio Pik' — two or three plants of 'Patio Pik' can be accommodated in a 10″ pot. Zucchini and summer crookneck squash are well worth growing if you have the space for bushel-size containers. Even bush snap beans are possible in big tubs, yielding a modest but delicious harvest of tiny beans if given rich soil and lots of sun and water. All of these need quite warm conditions — 75° to 80° during the day — but if you have a cool south window you might want to try peas such as the dwarf 'Mighty Midget' or compact edible-podded 'Little Sweetie' in 12″ pots or tubs.

Winter Greens

Lettuce is one of the easiest of all indoor crops. Leaf and loose-head types are the quickest, yielding harvestable heads in six to eight weeks, and some outer leaves may be picked even earlier. 'Oakleaf,' 'Ruby,' 'Salad Bowl,' 'Summer Bibb,' 'Tom Thumb,' 'Buttercrunch' and 'Grand Rapids Forcing' are a few favorites. Plant lettuce in individual pots or sow in flats or pans and thin to 5″ to 6″ apart. Give lettuce a cool spot nearest the glass.

Endive and escarole are as easy to grow as lettuce. Another tasty green is corn salad, and it can be cropped over many weeks.

Chinese cabbage, especially the loose-leafed 'Pac-Choy,' is fast-growing, and the leaves may be harvested when small for salads or allowed to grow large for use raw or cooked. True cabbage is also a good candidate for a cool window, using small-headed varieties like 'Dwarf Morden,' 'Baby Head' and 'Early Greenball.'

Three salad crops that do well in hot, dry home conditions are chard — 'Red Swiss' is a good choice, 'Rhubarb' is even more ornamental — and the Malabar and New Zealand spinaches. Malabar spinach needs training on strings, New Zealand grows fine in a large pot, and both supply large quantities of young leaves over many weeks. Also very productive is comfrey — plant a root in a 10″ pot and start harvesting the leaves when they are about 8″ long.

Two very fast croppers are garden cress and mustard. Garden or curled cress (not to be confused with upland cress or watercress) will sprout quickly on moist paper towels or a thin layer of soil in a tray and is ready for cutting in 10 days. Mustard is grown the same way but takes a few days longer until harvest. Another prized garnish, watercress, will thrive in a terrarium or in small

Leaf lettuce is a fast grower and needs only bright light and cool conditions. (*Plants Alive*)

pots standing in a tray of water; use a mix of sand and humus material like leafmold. A north window is fine for all of these.

Root Crops

Carrots, radishes and beets lead the list of easy root vegetables. Plant the succulent little "baby" carrot varieties like 'Baby Finger Nantes,' 'Sucram' or 'Short 'n Sweet' in sandy soil in a container 5″ deep, or larger types in deeper pots. Thin the small varieties to 1½″ and harvest them when they are little-finger size, the bigger kinds while they are still far from full size. Succession sowings made every three weeks will give a continuous supply.

Radishes are fast growers and almost any except the giant types are suitable. 'Cherry Belle,' 'Sparkler,' 'Scarlet Globe Forcing' and 'Icicle' are some of the best. If you like mild rather than peppery radishes, keep the soil moist. Two good beets are 'Little Egypt' and 'Early Red Ball.' Sow them frequently and pick the tops for greens, or harvest the whole plant when it is about 4″ high and use it raw in salads. Turnips also supply good tops as well as roots, and 'Tokyo Cross' will grow rapidly in an 8″ or 10″ pot.

Start onions from seed and use the thinnings for scallions, or plant onion sets, garlic cloves or shallots in a large flower pot to supply tangy leaves for salads all winter. And if you really want to be adventurous, grow a potato plant in a 12″ pot or tub. The vine is pretty, and in three to four months you should garner a harvest of small new potatoes.

Spicy Garnishes

Many herbs can be grown in pots, tubs or hanging baskets, but remember that nearly all herbs need full sun. Even in a south window they will benefit from supplementary artificial light, which will help prevent them from becoming straggly and unproductive. A few 4″ or 5″ pots should give an ample supply of seasoning herbs for the family. Or grow several kinds in a small strawberry jar, which you can transfer to the table at mealtimes for an unusual edible centerpiece.

All can be grown from seed, but to save time clumps of parsley, chives and thyme may be dug up from the garden, trimmed back and potted up. Basil is sown anytime, chervil should be sown frequently for salads and garnishes, salad burnet has graceful trailing stems so is good in baskets. Mint and winter savory do best in a cool spot. Tarragon does not come true from seed, but stem cuttings are easy to root.

Most herbs thrive best indoors when somewhat potbound. It's also important not to overwater them, and to fertilize very sparingly if at all.

Some Satisfying Fruits

Despite glowing advertisements that appear regularly in gardening magazines, indoor fruit trees are more of a decorative asset than a productive one. Given a great deal of sun, several dwarf citrus trees which have beautiful glossy foliage and creamy fragrant flowers will yield an appreciable number of small fruits good in drinks or for marmalade — if you remember to hand-pollinate the flowers.

The Otaheite and Calamondin oranges are the most popular and bear as many as a dozen fruits at a time, each one-quarter the size of a regular orange. Another favorite is the Meyer lemon, but larger fruit — up to 5″ — is produced by the Ponderosa lemon. Several other varieties of dwarf oranges and lemons are occasionally sold, as well as dwarf tangerines and a dwarf Persian lime. Another interesting subject is the kumquat, a citrus relative which bears 1″ orange-yellow fruits which are eaten raw, skin and all, or pickled. All of these need full sun and considerable moisture and fertilizer.

We've heard of pineapples, bananas, date palms and other tropicals being fruited successfully in the home, but even a small degree of success is rare with any except the citrus group. These are candidates for the greenhouse, where there is more light and more room and controlled conditions of temperature and humidity.

Vegetables by Lamplight

If you have a fluorescent light setup for starting seedlings for the garden, keep it working all winter growing vegetables. The usual arrangement of two 40-watt tubes in a reflector, lit 16 hours a day, will do a good job of raising lettuce, radishes and possibly a few other crops. But for most vegetables, more light is necessary.

Four 40-watt tubes make a much more efficient setup. Reflector units containing this many tubes are available, or as a less costly alternative, you can mount four or more single commercial strip fixtures on a board painted white for reflectivity. The tubes should be no more than 4″ apart. For tall plants, tubes mounted on the sides of the growing area are also helpful. The ballasts on fluorescent lamps produce heat, but they can be detached and mounted away from the growing area if this is a problem (if you're growing in a cold basement, it may be an asset).

There are tubes with internal reflectors that increase the light substantially, and also high-output fluorescents which supply almost one-third greater light intensity. General Electric's Cool White Panel Fluorescent, 80 watts but only 12″ square, is another solution, giving a concentrated high-light growing area of any size

A sophisticated high-intensity light garden, the Cornell Automated Plant Grower has six trays that move around a vertical bank of fluorescent tubes. (Plans are given in Information Bulletin 40, 35¢ from Mailing Room, Research Park, Cornell University, Ithaca, New York 14850.) (*Cornell University*)

when mounted in banks. Also consider the 80-watt 8'-long fluorescent tubes, which in effect more than double the length of the growing area since the light falls off at the ends of fluorescents and the longer tubes have a longer middle section.

Two mail-order sources offering a wide selection of light gardening equipment are the Floralite Company (4124 East Oakwood Road, South Milwaukee, WI 53172) and the Shoplite Company (650 Franklin Avenue, Nutley, NJ 07110; catalog 50¢). A ready-made 8' multitube unit is available from Famco, Inc. (300 Lake Road, Medina, OH 44256). The new Verilux TruBloom lamps (Verilux, Inc., 35 Mason Street, Greenwich, CT 06830), incidentally, are being hailed by light gardeners as the most efficient fluorescents yet produced, emitting light that is very close to natural daylight.

Watering and fertilizing must be watched carefully under lights, since the constant intensity and greater duration (compared to winter daylight) may increase the need for moisture and nutrients. If the area is not naturally humid, frequent misting, a cool-vapor humidifier, or enclosing the light garden with plastic sheeting will increase the humidity and benefit the plants.

The cost of lighting equipment and electricity does not make cropping by artificial light a money-saving proposition. But when adequate natural light is lacking, it is a way to grow a variety of salad crops and some root and fruiting ones. And the technology of light gardening is advancing rapidly.

The new bulb-type high-pressure sodium and metal halide lamps supply as much as 1000 watts. In Alaska, these HID (High Intensity Discharge) lamps are already being used to grow salad crops year-round on a large scale, and greenhouse growers in many northern states are using them for supplementary lighting in winter to improve plant quality and yields (more on this later). Much research remains to be done on these new types of lamps, but someday they may make it possible to grow even corn and melons entirely under lights. The first high-intensity unit for the home gardener is already on the market — Nitegro, in 400- and 1000-watt models to light areas up to 4' x 10' (JD-21 Lighting Systems, 1840 130th N.E., Bellevue, WA 98005).

Mushrooms in the Dark

A specialty crop that deserves to be a staple of the indoor garden is mushrooms. They're exceptionally nutritious, low in calories but high in protein, vitamins and minerals, and fun to grow.

The preplanted kits offered in many seed catalogs are the easiest way to grow mushrooms. These are simply watered and kept in a shaded spot at 50° to 70°, with high humidity but good ventilation. They will produce a crop in about a month, followed by successive "flushes" over several weeks.

For growing on a larger scale in a basement or outbuilding, however, it is much more economical to prepare your own compost and plant spawn, which is a pure culture of the microscopic spores of the mushroom fungus. Spawn is available from sources such as W. Atlee Burpee Co. (Warminster, PA 18974; Clinton, IA 52732; Riverside, CA 92502). Many materials are suitable for mushroom compost — commerical growers formerly relied on strawy horse manure, but today corncobs, hay and poultry manure or dried brewers' grains are commonly used. A good recipe is 100 pounds each of ground corncobs and straw and 20 pounds each of tankage

With preplanted kits, mushrooms are an
easy indoor crop. (*Organic Gardening and
Farming*)

or similar organic fertilizer, leafmold, whole grains and either
greensand or granite dust. These are mixed and moistened thoroughly and the pile is turned twice at 5- or 6-day intervals, then the
compost is put in the beds about a week later.

The beds are filled with 5″ of compost, and when it has cooled to
80° the spawn is planted. Spawn generally comes in brick form,
and pieces a little smaller than a golf ball are broken off and
planted 1″ deep, about 10″ apart each way in staggered rows. In
two to three weeks, the blue-gray threads of the mycelium will be
seen spread through the compost. The bed is then "cased" or covered with 1″ of loam soil. A temperature of 60° to 65° is best, and
humidity should be maintained at no less than 80%. When the
pinheads begin to appear, keep the bed moistened with a gentle
spray or sprinkling.

Harvest the mushrooms when the caps have begun to expand
and expose the gills. Pick by grasping the stems and twisting
slightly. About 4 pounds per square foot is considered a good crop.
The beds will alternately rest and produce flushes over a long period. As each flush is completely picked, clean out the remaining
mushroom tissue and fill the hole with fresh soil. When the last
flush peters out, the compost is taken to the garden for soil building, and the bed is scrubbed and dried in the sun before refilling it
with fresh compost.

For intensive cropping in small space, build the beds in tiers, allowing 12″ between the surface of the compost in one bed and the bottom boards of the bed above it. Mushrooms don't need absolute darkness, so any area where there is dim light and temperature and humidity conditions can be controlled is suitable.

To dry mushrooms, string them in a chain with a needle and thread and hang them in a warm, dry place for two weeks. Use mushrooms raw in salads (try them with raw spinach and a garlic–red wine vinegar–oil dressing). Mushrooms can be frozen after blanching in boiling water for one minute.

Sprout Farming

An even more nutritious — and much faster-producing — staple specialty is sprouted seeds. When the seeds of vegetables and grains sprout, their food value increases amazingly: vitamin C, niacin and riboflavin quadruple, some of the B vitamins increase as much as 13-fold, other nutritional elements rise up to 20 times. Seeds are also generally low in fat, and many are good sources of vegetable protein. They can be sprouted anywhere, anytime, with the simplest equipment and without sunlight.

A great many seeds will sprout well — not only the mung beans, which the Chinese have sprouted for food for 5000 years, but also alfalfa, barley, corn, peas, soybeans, lentils, rye, millet, garbanzos, fenugreek, sunflowers and others. Seed sold for garden use should not be used, since these may have been treated with chemicals. Supermarkets sell many suitable grains and legumes, so do Oriental and health food stores. A mail-order source of organically grown untreated seed for sprouting is the nonprofit Green Valley Seeds (11565 East Zayante, Felton, CA 95018; send self-addressed stamped envelope for catalog).

Wide-mouth jars, shallow flower pots or saucers, bowls, foil pans, colanders and many other containers are suitable for sprouting seeds. A 7″ bulb pan, for example, will supply daily servings of mung bean sprouts for a family of four for a week. The seeds are soaked overnight, then drained (the water can be used in cooking or to water other indoor crops). Discard any broken or imperfect seeds, then put the others in the container and cover it with a double layer of cheesecloth held on with rubber bands.

Put the container in a warm spot — minimum 60°, maximum 80° — and rinse the seeds three times a day. The hulls will usually separate from the seeds during the rinsing and are easily skimmed off. In 3 to 5 days the sprouts will be 1″ to 3″ long, plump and crisp and ready for harvest. If you like green sprouts, which have a sweeter flavor, remove the cheesecloth a day before harvest and put the container in bright light so chlorophyll can develop.

Several variations on this basic method have been worked out.

One that provides concentrated cropping consists of a series of shallow trays mounted on top of each other, with small holes drilled in their bases. Water is simply poured into the top tray and drains down to rinse the seeds in the lower trays. An automated, self-powered system that rinses the seeds every two hours, speeding up growth to produce 4″ sprouts in 5 days, has been developed by the Rodale Research and Development Group (directions for building your own are $1 from Sprouter Plans, OG Readers Service, Rodale Press, 33 East Minor Street, Emmaus, PA 18049).

Another method used by old-time Chinese sprout farmers produces an even greater increase in vitamin content. "Earth box" sprouts are grown by placing the soaked seeds on soil or compost in a shallow tray or box, then covering them with a ¼″ layer of fine soil. The soil both holds the moisture necessary for sprouting (eliminating the need to moisten the seed several times a day) and provides additional nutrients that raise the sprouts' food values. Laboratory tests of mung bean sprouts grown in earth boxes showed they had 19 milligrams of vitamin C per 100 grams, compared to 10 milligrams for sprouts grown in water. Calcium was also significantly higher.

Sprouts will keep for several days in the refrigerator in plastic bags. Use them liberally in salads and sandwich fillings, or steam them over low heat in a tiny bit of water in a covered pan for about 10 minutes. Add sprouts to soups, stews, casseroles and Oriental dishes, and use them with eggs, rice — even in making bread. Many sprouts can be roasted, too. A good book of techniques and recipes is *Sprouts to Grow and Eat,* by Esther Munroe (Stephen Greene Press, Box 1000, Brattleboro, VT 05301; $4.50).

In-House Greenhouses

Extending the growing area within the home by using existing openings to light or creating new ones is a way to increase winter food production considerably. With the many new materials and devices for making enclosed environments for plants, ways of doing this have become almost legion. Costs can vary from a few dollars to several thousand.

A window greenhouse is the simplest permanent extension, adding extra illumination through its sides and roof, plus more shelf area, to the window. Prefabricated aluminum-and-glass units are available from several manufacturers, as well as molded plastic "bubble" window greenhouses. The prefabs can be fitted together and built in to cover the full length of a house wall.

Homemade units, however, are often more versatile and can be handsome, even striking, in design. Usually they are made of wood and may be glazed with plastic or glass. Plans for a window

An inexpensive window greenhouse adds a
surprising amount of plant-growing space.
(*Lord & Burnham*)

greenhouse are obtainable free from Swingline Inc. (32–00 Skill-
man Avenue, Long Island City, NY 11101), and several of the
books listed at the end of this chapter contain plans and building
instructions. The only extra equipment needed may be a small
heater in cold climes, where heat from the house may not be sufficient in frigid weather.

Basement window wells and cellarways can make good greenhouses. The window well can be enlarged if desired, then enclosed
with wood framing and glass or plastic sheets. The "roof" or main
glazed panel should be slanted at a 45° angle to catch maximum
sun, and be sure to make provision for opening a panel for ventilation on warm days. A cellarway may be simply covered over with
glazed panels, or a standard greenhouse structure can be constructed over it. If the basement is heated, the open cellar door
may supply enough heat on cold nights. For unusual window well
and cellarway greenhouse conversions, there are acrylic bubbles,
in 40″ to 14′ widths, by Dilworth Manufacturing (Box 21, Edge-
mont, PA 19028).

If you're building a new home, by the way, or remodeling an old one, consider adding a sunporch. It will give you a year-round growing area and more pleasure than a patio, which is useful only in the warmer seasons. The roof of a sunporch as well as its sides can be glazed, or a skylight might be built into it (Holgenol Sky Windows, 310 Green Street, Havre de Grace, MD 21078, makes acrylic skylights that are easily installed in any roof).

Another idea — actually an ancient one which is being revived — is the atrium. This interior court, popular with the Greeks and Romans, is being included more and more in public buildings and private homes. The modern version, however, is roofed over with glass or plastic, making it an inside-the-house greenhouse.

A final note on the newest technique, the transparent wall. Picture windows are commonplace, but a house we saw recently in New England has south, east and west walls of clear plastic. The designer used two sheets of polyvinyl chloride (PVC) plastic with an air space between. This has excellent insulating value, as good as Thermopane glass but costing only one-tenth as much. The house has a shed roof that rises to the south, giving a tall transparent south wall through which the sun penetrates far into the house in winter. Thus the whole house is in effect a greenhouse, and plants thrive in it.

The Nature Bubble (Feather Hill Industries, Box 41, Zenda, WI 53195) is a one-piece molded plastic window greenhouse. (*Feather Hill Industries*)

Moving to the outdoors, the coldframe and its more versatile counterpart, the hotbed, are very useful as season extenders or even winter food producers. In the coldest climes, salad crops sown in late summer can be harvested into quite severe winter weather in a coldframe or hotbed, all winter long where the climate is mild.

Both are identical as far as the box-like frame and transparent cover or lid are concerned. Concrete blocks are sometimes used, but usually the frame is made of wood, about 2″ x 10″ planking. Fir painted with linseed oil or other protective material should last at least ten years. The frame should be set 4″ into the ground and should extend above it about 12″ in front, 18″ in the rear. The lid must slope toward the south, and there must be no trees or buildings to obstruct the sun. If possible, locate the structure where a building or plantings will shield it from winter winds.

Because standard coldframe and hotbed sash is 3′ x 6′, the width of the structure is usually 6′ while the length is a multiple of 3′ — two sashes will cover a 6′ x 6′ frame, three are needed for a 9′ x 6′, etc. But if you can get secondhand window sash, which varies in size, simply adjust the size of your frame to fit. Or custom make your own sash, of flexible plastic stapled on both sides of wooden framing, or of rigid plastic sheets.

The sash will need propping open on bright sunny days to avoid

A hotbed heated by light bulbs, manure or a heating cable will grow winter salad crops at very low cost. (*Robert Mann*)

A coldframe is triple-purpose: it can shelter
tender crops in the fall, supply winter
vegetables, and start seedlings for the
garden in spring. (*Organic Gardening and
Farming*)

excessive heat build-up. On cold nights, insulating mats of burlap
bags filled with leaves, fiberglass matting or any handy blanketing
material will hold in warmth. Leaves or soil banked up against
the sides of the frame are also helpful.

By adding heat, you make your coldframe into a hotbed and increase its usefulness. Electric light bulbs are sometimes used for
heating, but manure or soil heating cables are surer and more
carefree. The manure method uses a 12″ depth of strawy horse
manure which is covered with 6″ of soil when the heat from the
decomposition of the manure has dropped to about 100°. Thermostatically controlled electric soil heating cables, however, provide
the steadiest, most even heating. The cable is laid out on a 2″ layer

of sand or vermiculite, then a 1″ layer of soil or sand is spread, covered with a sheet of hardware cloth or other narrow-mesh wire to protect the cable from being damaged by planting tools. Put 4″ of fertile soil over this.

Seedlings of lettuce, endive, etc., sown in the garden or in flats are transplanted into the frame just before hard frosts, and you will be able to harvest greens unharmed by the cold for many weeks. In spring, of course, a coldframe or hotbed is indispensable for starting or hardening off seedlings for the garden. In summer, the sash can be replaced with lath and the frame used for propagating plants from cuttings.

Vegetables from Pits

For all-winter vegetable production with very low initial and maintenance costs, the sun-pit greenhouse is ideal.

Basically a sun-pit is a big deep coldframe, glazed on the south roof but otherwise of solid insulated construction. Sun heat coming through the glazing is stored in the structure to maintain above-freezing temperatures, aided by covers applied over the glass at night and in dark weather. Supplementary heating — which may be as little as a few light bulbs — should be necessary only in extended periods of frigid weather, or if plants needing warmer temperatures are grown.

Sun-pits can be dug into the side of a south-facing bank or built on flat ground with a conventional peaked roof, the south side of which is glazed and the north of solid insulated construction. Sash is often used for the transparent section, but fiberglass, rigid plastics and plastic sheeting on wood framing is also practical. The foundation and sides may be of wood (we've seen railroad ties used for this), rocks, cement blocks, concrete or stabilized earth. The floor should be of dirt or dark gravel to absorb heat, and if the interior walls can be painted, use flat black to increase their heat absorbency. If possible, locate the steps and door into the greenhouse on the side away from prevailing winter winds.

Architect Ken Kern (Sierra Route, Oakhurst, CA 93644) has designed some unusual sun-pits. In his Kern-Form pits, he uses pipe frames or precast cantilevered units that combine framing and benches, and a rounded roof of fiberglass on the south, concrete insulated with earth on the north. With a few basic carpentry tools, an 8′ x 21′ Kern-Form pit can be home-built for around $300.

Lettuce, parsley, kale, chives, chard, radishes, onions and other cool-season crops will thrive even without extra heat almost anywhere. A Maine gardener reports that although the temperatures in his pit often go below freezing, the vegetables survive and revive perfectly well. Very little watering is needed in a sun-pit, and opening the door or a sash slightly will provide adequate ventilation when needed. A sun-pit will also keep tender plants like tomatoes, brought into it from the garden before frost, growing and bearing into winter, and it is great for starting seedlings for the garden. A hotbed, made by installing a soil heating cable in a bench and covering the bench with a plastic tent, will give warm-season crops a fine start.

Some gardeners build a sun-pit as a lean-to greenhouse on the south side of the home, using open basement windows as a source of supplementary heat. A Pennsylvania homesteader has gone even further than this: he uses a sun-pit to help heat his home. His lean-to pit has a fiberglass south wall that slants up steeply for maximum collection of solar radiation. Under the upper two-thirds of this wall he has placed homemade black-painted aluminum heat absorbers. The heat these collect is circulated through ducts into the house by a fan. The lower third of the wall is unobstructed fiberglass to admit sunlight that enables him to grow vegetables all winter.

Super Structures

In aboveground greenhouses, the variety of designs and materials available today is amazing. Ready-made units, in addition to the standard even-span type (the kind that looks like a house), include

Built as a lean-to, this sun-pit gets warmth from the cellar at night to supplement the heat it stores up in its walls and floor. (*Organic Gardening and Farming*)

Geodesic domes are extremely strong,
provide maximum interior space, and allow
greatest light transmission. (*Redwood
Domes*)

arch, dome, A-frame, circular and gazebo styles. If you want to build your own greenhouse, the choice is much wider. You can have a Gothic arch or a geodesic dome as good as any manufactured one, or go to a far-out design like multibarrel vault or a hyperbolic-paraboloid.

Each of these has its advantages, and the only way to choose wisely is to check out all of them. Get the bulletins, plans and catalogs listed at the end of this chapter, and evaluate each design in terms of cost, appearance, permanence, ease of maintenance, availability of materials if you're building your own, etc.

Aluminum or galvanized steel makes the most permanent, maintenance-free framing. Wood is less expensive but can be quite durable, and laminated or pressure-treated fir or pine is adequate for both plastic and glass houses. Galvanized pipe is being used often today (Kee Klamps, 79 Benbro Drive, Buffalo, NY 14225, has galvanized slip-on fittings that make putting together framing, benches and racks easy). Another new idea is framing with thin-wall electrical conduit (described in literature on Copolymer greenhouses by the DBB Company, Drawer 8, Dayton, OH 45401).

Glass is still the most popular glazing, but it may not be for long. Top-grade clear fiberglass-reinforced plastic (FRP) gives as good or better plant growth than glass, it is four times as efficient as glass in keeping heat in the house, and if coated with a special laminated film called Tedlar, it will need refinishing only every 15 to 20 years. Fiberglass is hailproof, and comes in rolls and corrugated panes. There are also several types of glass-like rigid plastics, of which acrylic (Plexiglas) is the best known. It has excellent light transmission and greater impact strength than glass, but costs as much or more than glass.

Plastic films are the least permanent coverings. Standard polyethylene lasts only months, but is an easily applied covering for a greenhouse used for winter vegetable production. A simple greenhouse of this type with a space heater can grow tomatoes, for example, which need 60° at night, in fall and spring, with lettuce and root crops at 40° night temperature in the winter.

It's the ultraviolet rays of sunlight that break down polyethylene, but ultraviolet-inhibited copolymer films like Monsanto 602 will last two years or more. These films are proportionally more expensive than polyethylene. Even longer-lasting and thus more costly are the weatherable vinyl films, such as Eskay-Lite and Amerex UV, which are good for as long as four to six years.

Thermodynamics

Since heating is the biggest single operating expense in a greenhouse, manufacturers and growers have been making heat conservation a major objective.

With plastic houses, a double layer of film with a 1″ to 2″ air space between can reduce heating costs by as much as 40%. Usu-

The Gothic arch greenhouse is handsome, easily constructed, and may be covered with plastic film or permanent fiberglass. (*Peter Reimuller*)

ally wood strips are used to separate the layers, but a new wrinkle is to apply the sheets together, the bottom one attached tightly to the frame, the top one left loose. A small squirrel-cage blower is used to maintain an air space between the two layers. The newest idea of all is the totally air–supported "bubble" house, which has no foundation or superstructure. It is held up only by air pressure from a fan, and has an air-lock door to allow entry. Sometimes bubble houses are made with double layers of film to conserve heat, with a small fan to hold the layers apart.

The double-wall principle is employed in a ready-made greenhouse designed especially for vegetable production. The Vegetable Factory (100 Court Street, Copiague, NY 11726) has unique twin-

This planting scheme gave 650 pounds of vegetables in an 8' x 12' Vegetable Factory greenhouse for a total annual operating cost of $136 in the New York metropolitan area. (*Vegetable Factory, Inc.*)

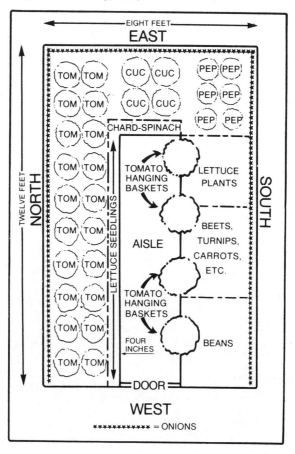

AirCap bubble plastic sheeting is an
excellent greenhouse insulator, easily
applied by pressing it to the glass while wet.
(*Sealed Air Corporation*)

pane walls of ice-clear fiberglass-reinforced acrylic bonded to an aluminum core. Heating costs are very low. A laboratory report states that the 8′ x 12′ free-standing model will produce 650 pounds of vegetables a year in the New York metropolitan area at an average cost of 19¢ per pound including all operating expenses.

A layer of film attached on the inside of any greenhouse has good insulating value, but often it is hard to affix. Commercial growers are using "tents" of film, cloth or paper hung over wires and report that this reduces nightly heat requirements by 50%, but setting up the tent at night and taking it down in the morning can be a laborious job. However, there is an easily applied, very effective insulator — a packaging material called AirCap (available from greenhouse supplier E. C. Geiger, Box 285, Harleysville, PA 19438). This is a transparent bubble plastic made of two layers of polyethylene, with one layer flat and the other shaped like a muffin tin so that air is trapped between them in a continuous array of bubbles. It is applied by simply wetting the glass and pressing the bubble side against it. Incidentally, in areas of heavy snow, it may be wise to insulate only the sides and ends of a greenhouse, since snow could pile up on an insulated roof and cause it to collapse.

The science of collecting and storing solar heat is still in its infancy, but greenhouse growers have developed several good ideas. A simple one uses metal cans or drums, painted black and filled with water, placed in the greenhouse where the sun will strike them. The water absorbs heat rapidly and releases it slowly at night. Another, developed for sunny southern areas, employs a big polyethylene bag connected by poly tubes to an indoor storage pit containing rocks. A fan brings air, sun-heated in the bag, to the rocks which hold the heat for use as needed. A variation uses water in the bags, circulated by a pump and stored in a tank.

The Ohio Agricultural Research and Development Center is testing a pond filled with salt water to collect and store solar energy during the summer to heat a greenhouse in winter. Agricultural engineers expect water temperature in the bottom of the 12′ deep pond to approach the boiling point. At the University of Delaware's new Energy Conversion Unit (Newark, DE 19711), Dr. Maria Telkes captures solar heat in salt hydrates contained in plastic tubing. These compounds melt under the sun's heat, then slowly solidify to release the heat at night.

Many firms are beginning to produce solar collector panels and storage units, and the efficiency of these is increasing while costs are decreasing. One of the first companies to enter the field, Enclosures Inc. (Moreland, GA 30259), is already delivering complete solar collection–storage–distribution systems to commercial greenhouses. These systems are reportedly very low in initial and operating costs, and have proved successful as the main source of heat all winter as far north as North Dakota.

Where you locate your greenhouse, incidentally, can influence its heating requirements. Fuel bills are reduced by a hill, wall or plant windbreak on the side of prevailing winds. Avoid low-lying spots where air as well as water drainage may be poor, for frost pockets add to heating costs. An insulated foundation wall will also lower fuel use — Microfoam (Specialty Markets Division, Du Pont Company, Wilmington, DE 19898) is a light-reflecting insulating material for this purpose — or build a second wall a foot or so outside the foundation, filling the space between with soil to make a planter box.

─────────────── Operating Systems ───────────────

Heating methods vary from small room heaters to complex automated heating-ventilating systems that also provide carbon dioxide to stimulate growth. For a small greenhouse, many kinds of thermostatically controlled space heaters are available (but be sure to note their venting requirements, since some fuels produce gases that will injure plants). If you have a large greenhouse, the fan-jet tube system that combines heating and ventilating may be the best choice. This mixes heated air with fresh air from outdoors and circulates it through a perforated plastic convection tube. A vegetable grower reports that installing the convection tube at ground level, so the jets of warm air strike the plants and soil, kept his crops free of fungus diseases and gave a 34% increase in tomato and cucumber yields.

Drip irrigation has made watering a simple task. A drip system is as easily installed and works as efficiently on ground beds and soil-filled benches as in the garden. For pot plants, combine drip irrigation with a capillary watering mat. The latter is a porous fiber or fiberglass mat that is laid down on the bench and kept constantly moist by the drip hose. The moisture is transmitted from the mat by capillary action through the pots to the roots of the plants.

The newest technique you may want to explore is artificial lighting. At a recent greenhouse management seminar in Seattle, experts reported that supplementing natural light in dull weather by means of the new high-intensity discharge (HID) lamps make it possible to grow "summer quality" plants all winter.

Three of these bulb-type HID lamps are now being used by commercial growers: the high-pressure sodium Lucalox and metal halide Multi-Vapor by General Electric Company (Nela Park, Cleveland, OH 44112), and the metal halide Metalarc by GTE Sylvania (730 Third Avenue, New York, NY 10017). These are made in 400-, 750- and 1000-watt sizes, and can more than double the light in northern greenhouses in winter. The lamps can be triggered by photoelectric controls to turn on whenever natural light falls below a certain level. While HID fixtures are more expensive than fluorescent fixtures, operating costs are lower, and the fixtures are smaller, thus causing less shading of natural light.

Picking Winter Winners

Theoretically, almost any vegetable can be grown in a greenhouse, but some require more space than you may be willing to give them, and others, like watermelons, that do not do well under low light and short days, should not be attempted as a winter crop without supplementary lighting.

This still leaves a great variety that will grow and produce in a greenhouse without special equipment. The only limiting factor is the temperature range you provide: cool-season lettuce, for example, can thrive at 55° during the day and 45° at night, but tomatoes, cucumbers, beans and other warm-season crops require 70° days and 60° nights. If you want to grow both types, the higher temperature range must be provided, and all will do well.

Ted Marston, publisher of the excellent indoor gardening magazine *Plants Alive* (5509 1st Avenue South, Seattle, WA 98108), reports fine success with the following in his home greenhouse:

Cool-season salad crops yield big harvests in
small space and at minimum fuel cost.
(*Vegetable Factory, Inc.*)

'Romano' Italian pole beans and 'Prizetaker' pole limas, 'Amstel
Forcing' carrots, 'Fertila' and 'Victory' gynoecious cucumbers,
'Early Beauty Hybrid' eggplant, 'Green Curled' endive, 'Broad Lon-
don' leek, 'Buttercrunch,' 'Grand Rapids' and 'Paris White Cos' let-
tuce, Malabar spinach, 'Southport White Globe' onions, 'Green
Shaft' and edible-podded 'Oregon Sugarpod' peas, 'Ace' and 'Can-
ape' peppers, 'Cherry Belle' radish, 'America' spinach, and 'Patio,'
'Pixie,' 'Kirdford Cross' and 'Michigan-Ohio Forcing' tomatoes.

Walter F. Nicke, who gardens in Hudson, New York, says, "I
guess you can grow just about any vegetable indoors. Miniature
corn was fun in my greenhouse but not very productive. Potatoes
do well — I grow them in a plastic can of about 9″ size. Strawberries are decorative and give a nice clean crop. I grow the variety
'Suwanee' in 4″ pots (5″ might be better), and the harvest is a very
good one."

Many other varieties and crops are good greenhouse subjects —
try those recommended earlier in this chapter for the windowsill
farm, plus others you find suggested in seed catalogs. Use ground
beds, benches and the many kinds of containers recommended at

the beginning of this chapter. All the practices of outdoor vegetable growing — soil enrichment, fertilizing, pest control, succession cropping, interplanting and so on — should be followed as carefully in the greenhouse as in the garden. With almost all greenhouse crops, starting them in flats or peat pots and transplanting them to their permanent places gives better results than direct seeding.

Two of the most popular greenhouse crops, tomatoes and cucumbers, deserve special mention. For full-size tomatoes (in contrast to the small-fruited "cherry" and similar kinds), special short-day greenhouse varieties must be grown. 'Tuckcross,' 'Vendor,' 'Michigan-Ohio Forcing' and 'Tropic VF' are some of these. Usually seed is sown in early July in the North for a fall-winter crop, in early November for a spring crop. Don't forget that indoor tomatoes must be hand-pollinated — shake or tap each flower cluster, or touch a vibrating electric toothbrush to it, several times a week as long as there are open flowers.

With tomatoes, the 60° night temperature requirement can be circumvented by growing a variety like 'Tuckqueen' which will set fruit well at lower temperatures, or by burying a heating cable in the soil. Tests in England showed normal growth and fruiting of the variety 'Eurocross BB' when the root zone was maintained at

Strawberries in pots produce an excellent crop and do not need high night temperatures. (*Walter F. Nicke*)

'Slobolt' looseleaf lettuce is one of the best
for a warm greenhouse, since it does well at
higher temperatures than other varieties.
(*Robert Mann*)

70° or higher and the night air temperature was allowed to go as
low as 45°.

A useful bulletin is *Growing Greenhouse Tomatoes,* Circular
276, from the College of Agriculture, Washington State University
(Pullman, WA 99163). A method of growing high yields of tomatoes in bottomless cylinders set on a bed of soilless medium is described in *Production of Greenhouse Tomatoes in Ring Culture
and in Troughs,* Cornell Vegetable Crops Mimeo 149, from the De-

partment of Vegetable Crops, Cornell University (Ithaca, NY 14850).

The long, thin-skinned self-pollinating European cucumbers are extremely productive, but they must have a night temperature no lower than 65°. They are rapid growers and heavy feeders and need lots of moisture. Grow them on a trellis and follow the pruning and training system outlined in Chapter 4. Allowing too many fruits to set will reduce both yield and quality. Some of the best varieties are 'Toska 70,' 'Femland,' 'La Reine,' 'Rocket' and 'Brilliant.' Excellent cultural directions are supplied with seed ordered from Stokes Seeds (Box 548, Buffalo, NY 14240).

What about fruits in the greenhouse? The citrus and citrus relatives suggested for growing in south windows in the home will do well along with vegetables in a greenhouse, but others which come from more tropical regions need more heat and humidity. Bananas, mangoes, pineapples and the like are subjects for hot, steaming jungle-like conditions. They will not be successful in the same greenhouse with vegetables unless a section is partitioned off and their special needs are met there.

Pound for pound, the self-pollinating gynoecious cucumbers give higher yields than any other crop. (*Plants Alive*)

Recommended Reading

The Apartment Farmer, by Duane Newcomb (J. P. Tarcher, 9110 Sunset Boulevard, Los Angeles, CA 90069; $7.95 hardcover, $4.95 paperback)

Build Your Own Greenhouse, by Prof. Charles D. Neal (Chilton Book Co., Radnor, PA 19087; $9.95)

Home Greenhouses, Circular 879 (Agricultural Information Office, 112 Mumford Hall, University of Illinois, Urbana, IL 61801; free)

The Indoor Light Gardening Book, by George A. Elbert (Crown; $10.95)

Organic Gardening Under Glass, by George "Doc" and Katy Abraham (Rodale; $8.95)

Greenhouse Plans

A-Frame Home Greenhouse, Filon Corporation, 12333 South Van Ness Avenue, Hawthorne, CA 90250

A Gothic Greenhouse for Town and Country Homes, Circular 892, Virginia Polytechnic Institute, Blacksburg, VA 24060

Experimental Greenhouses: Dome, Plan 822-350; *Gable*, 822-352; *Multibarrel Vault*, 822-356; *Gothic Arch*, 822-358; *Quonset*, 822-360; *and two Hyperbolic-Paraboloid*, 822-354 and 822-362, $1 per plan, Extension Agricultural Engineer, Pennsylvania State University, University Park, PA 16802

The Cornell Twenty-One Plastic Greenhouse, $2, Department of Vegetable Crops, Cornell University, Ithaca, NY 14850

(The Cooperative Extension Service in most states has plans for home and commercial greenhouses, and also helpful bulletins)

Greenhouse Manufacturers and Suppliers

Aluminum Greenhouses, Inc., 14615 Lorain Avenue, Cleveland, OH 44111

Brighton By-Products Co., Box 23, New Brighton, PA 15066

Environmental Dynamics, Box 966, Sunnymead, CA 92388

E. C. Geiger, Box 285, Harleysville, PA 19438

Gothic Arch Greenhouses, Box 1564, Mobile, AL 36601

Greenhouse Specialties Co., 9849 Kimker Lane, St. Louis, MO 63127

Janco Greenhouses, 10788 Tucker Street, Beltsville, MD 20705

Lord & Burnham, Irvington, NY 10533

Maco Products, Box 3312, Salem, OR 97302

National Greenhouse Co., Box 100, Pana, IL 62557

Redfern's Prefab Greenhouses, Mt. Hermon Road, Scott's Valley, CA 95060

Redwood Domes, Box 666, Aptos, CA 95003

Peter Reimuller, Greenhouseman, Box 2666, Santa Cruz, CA 95060

Semispheres, Box 26273, Richmond, VA 23260

X. S. Smith, Red Bank, NJ 07701

Space Age Industries, 15820 Lake Michigan Drive, West Olive, MI 49460

Sturdi-Built Mfg. Co., 11304 S.W. Boones Ferry Road, Portland, OR 97219

Texas Greenhouse Co., 2717 St. Louis Avenue, Fort Worth, TX 76110

Turner Greenhouses, Box 1620, Goldsboro, NC 27530

Waterworks Gardenhouses, Box 905, El Cerrito, CA 94530

⚸ 10 ⚸

How to Succeed on the New Frontier

THE REWARDS OF GROWING even a small portion of one's own food are so great that almost anyone who tries it wants to reap these rewards on a larger scale. Just how far you go in staking your claim to a better life through growing-your-own depends on many things. If you dream of getting back to the land on a large scale, of seeking new economic and personal freedom on 1, 5 or 50 acres, you'll have to be hardheaded in facing a multitude of practical considerations.

It's possible to achieve a high degree of independence, even total self-sufficiency, almost anywhere in these United States. People are doing it on Vermont's stony acres as well as in California's much more beneficent clime. The Vermonters are generally younger and work much harder, and they can't afford to make many mistakes. But those who have done it successfully anywhere have certain things in common — the most important of which is that they realized the need for a lot of tough thinking, evaluation and planning before they made their move.

Going All-Out?

First and most vital, are you truly suited to what could amount to a completely new lifestyle? If you've always been a city dweller, are you seeing rural life as it actually is, or looking at it through rose-colored glasses that show only the vine-covered cottage and a garden overflowing with delectable crops? There's a certain amount

Sheep are easy to care for and mild-mannered, and they produce meat and wool at low cost. (*Organic Gardening and Farming*)

of loneliness and isolation, too, and long, often monotonous work, and you need enthusiasm for the labor as much as for the result. Plenty of capital and even above-average intelligence can't substitute for the right mental attitude. Be sure your spouse has the same enthusiasm and sense of purpose — the majority of successful homesteaders are closely knit family units in which every member is pulling for the same goal.

Do you have the physical stamina to clear land of trees and brush, dig planting holes, haul and spread organic matter, perhaps even build a barn? This is not as important as attitude, for strength will increase with better food and exercise, but any physical incapacities should certainly be taken into account. Many disabilities need not be insurmountable handicaps, however. We know a 78-year-old man who is unable to bend or stoop but who raises enough vegetables to have a surplus for sale by growing them in beds raised to waist level. (Read *Gardening for the Elderly and Handicapped*, by Leslie Snook; $1.50 from Walter F. Nicke, Box 71, Hudson, NY 12534; catalog 25¢.)

The third factor, and the harshest reality many new homesteaders must face, is money. Good land is no longer cheap anywhere. The only general rule that can be given these days is that the farther you go from a metropolitan center, the cheaper the land will be, with the exception of resort areas. But even in the hinterlands you may have to look long and hard, and remember that while mortgage costs are fixed, taxes will go up with land values if the area becomes popular.

A hasty purchase of a property that is unsuitable in any important aspect, just because it is a bargain, can end in long regrets. To avoid financial disaster or unnecessary hardship, go slow. If it's at all possible, rent first in the locale you're interested in, and get to know the area, its facilities and people. Then evaluate each prospective purchase for the hundred-and-one details that are important to your goal and that could strain your resources if they go wrong.

The single biggest action you can take to insure success is to draw up a checklist, covering your wants in detail and everything that can affect their accomplishment. It should include the factors any wise prospective homeowner investigates, from the size and soundness of the house and capacity of the water supply to schools for the children and the condition of access roads in all kinds of weather. Add to these your own special considerations. You'll want to investigate, for example, zoning and building codes, since these might restrict you in building a greenhouse or selling produce. Topography, soil depth and fertility, drainage, the uses to which the land has been put, what crops can be grown well and sold in the immediate area — all of these should be on your checklist.

How much land do you need? You can build up your soil to produce bumper crops, but if you live in a harsh northern climate the shortness of the growing season will limit the kind and number of crops you grow. With high fertility and intensive methods, a family of four should be able to raise all the vegetables and fruits they can use on a total area of one-quarter to one-half acre, including a greenhouse for winter food production. If you plan to have goats or chickens or rabbits, figure on a minimum of one-half acre for housing and producing the feed for a small number of any one of these.

You can save a good bit of your "start-up" money, incidentally, by locating sources of soil-building materials before you even take possession of your new home. A farmer who has piles of rotted manure or spoiled hay, a sawmill with sawdust or wood shavings for the taking or a highway department that will deliver truckloads of leaves, can keep your first-year food production expenses down to the cost of seeds and plants. If you move in in the fall and your soil is below par, having specific sources of free or nearly-free soil-improving materials that can be obtained and applied immediately will help you to get your land in shape for good production the following year.

Last but far from least, every successful homesteader agrees on one point: it is essential to have a steady, dependable source of income that can be continued through the early years of developing your garden-homestead. Taxes, utilities, repairs, clothing and all the other day-to-day costs of living must be met with cash that won't, at least for some time, be forthcoming from the productive capacity of your homestead.

This may mean obtaining work locally, but steady jobs that pay fairly well are few and far between in exurban and rural areas. So you will likely need a skill, craft or trade, and it should be one that you have already proved can produce sufficient income. If you re a photographer, carpenter, writer, weaver, machinist or mechanic, you will have an adequate measure of security — provided your skills can be profitably marketed locally or by mail.

You'll find countless opportunities, of course, as we'll see later, to develop new income-producing skills and products once you've established your land. But until that happy time when everything is built or rebuilt and functioning properly, an outside source of income is vital. Don't count on finding it after you've made your move — plan for it as you plan every other step of the way.

Taken in one dose, in the space of the above few paragraphs, all these cautions may seem discouraging. But they're simply asking the family seeking the highest degree of independence and security to put patience and planning first. Appraise your strengths and weaknesses as realistically as you appraise those of the land you're thinking of buying, and you'll greatly increase your chances of achieving all that you want from your garden-homestead. Take the time to research and study every angle. A tremendous amount of information is becoming available on all aspects of modern homesteading — you'll find much of it in the Appendix.

──────────────── Output for Income ────────────────

The ideal garden-homestead pays for itself, and for you too. The land can yield more than wholesome food at low cost. It can produce part or all of your cash income. Just how much depends to a large extent on the size of your property, of course, but it can also depend on your ingenuity.

There are many ways of making money from food plants, from growing a wide variety of vegetables and fruits and selling them at a roadside stand, to raising high-value specialty crops. If you choose the first method, you simply grow more of the crops you're growing for your own consumption. To get good prices and steady customers for your produce, however, takes a bit of marketing savvy. Too many roadside stands are merely structures stocked with produce. If the structure is attractive and the landscaping around it is well designed and grown, so much the better. But most important of all are the signs that tell the customer what you have for sale.

Start with a large, easily seen and read sign that gives the name of your stand (tests show that including your own name, such as "Smith's Home-Grown Vegetables," inspires more customer confidence than the usual "Fresh Vegetables"). This sign can also state that your produce is naturally grown on organically enriched soil and without pesticides.

Then make the sign on each display say something about the value of the produce: "New European Cucumbers — Eat 'Em Skin and All," "Fingerling Potatoes, for the finest Potato Salad," etc. Where nutritional value is exceptional, say so: "Jerusalem Artichokes, More Vitamins and Minerals than Potatoes — and No Starch." Tempt customers to try a fruit or vegetable with which they may be unfamiliar by giving simple directions for preparing it. Remember that you are selling value rather than price, so the price should be in letters no larger than those used to describe the produce. Experiment with colored cards and various colors of ink to make signs that will look attractive against the fruit or vegetable they're promoting.

Always offer only your best produce, the straightest carrots and most perfect cabbages, keeping any blemished specimens for your own use. Put larger-than-usual signs on delicacies such as baby beets or carrots, early peas or vine-ripened melons.

Some growers take the produce to the customer. They build up a route and several times a week take around a selection of their

Low overhead and low prices equal good
profits for the family that sells its surplus
produce at a farmers' market. (*Organic
Gardening and Farming*)

best vegetables and fruits for steady customers to choose from, and
often take advance orders for crops that are nearing maturity.

A third method is the farmers' market. This venerable institu-
tion is being revived — there's even one now in the heart of Manhattan — where growers assemble with their produce and home-
processed foods once or twice a week and sell from stalls or directly
from their trucks. Customers come from far and near to get fresh
produce at below-supermarket prices. Usually the growers pay a
flat rental fee and/or a percentage of gross sales to the owner of the
land where the market is held. The organization of a farmers'
market can be quite simple, with just a few growers getting together to sell in concert, or it can be huge and involve a rented

building, regular advertising and even incorporation as a nonprofit business.

For information on setting up a farmers' market, send a self-addressed stamped #10 envelope to Farmers' Market, Evanston Chamber of Commerce (807 Davis Street, Evanston, IL 60201); $1 to Hunger Action Center, Evergreen State College (Olympia, WA 98505) for its *Farmers' Market Organizing Handbook;* $2 to Natural Organic Farmers Association (R.F.D. 1, Box 247, Plainfield, VT 05667) for its *Organizing Farmers' Markets* manual.

High-Cash Crops

Specialty cropping is a somewhat different proposition. Raising a large amount of only one or two crops concentrates the time and work involved, but the crop or crops must be chosen carefully and the market assured. If you already have a sizable roadside stand or route clientele, you can market your specialty through these outlets and gain a reputation as the grower of the finest asparagus or strawberries or whatever the specialty may be. You can also sell direct to local vegetable and fruit markets, but contract with them first for your output and try to get them to promote the crop with signs extolling its special virtues. For some crops, direct sales to restaurants may be possible. With others, a "pick-your-own" operation is the most profitable.

Choose crops that are not being shipped in or grown by anyone else in your area, or that you can grow better or earlier. Raspberries are very good, so are fine dessert strawberries like 'Fairfax' that don't ship well. Butter-and-sugar varieties of sweet corn, popcorn, leeks, uncommon beans, baby beets, pears and many others bring high returns. Mushrooms grown in your cellar and bean sprouts from the kitchen may make worthwhile cash crops if you can produce them in volume.

Consider processing some crops, too, or encouraging customers to put up their own. Ground and bottled horseradish is a good seller, and a gardener we know sells dill along with her cucumbers to people who like to make their own dill pickles. Dried herbs, rose hip and beach plum jams and jellies, relishes, fruit butters and fruit leather and many other specialties can make you well known and bring premium prices.

Any crop that can be forced can give very profitable first-on-the-market sales. Strawberries, for example, can be produced three weeks early by planting cold-stored plants (a source is Bunting's Nurseries, Selbyville, DE 19975) of varieties such as 'Pocahontas,' 'Florida 90,' 'Sequoia,' 'Fresno' and 'Tioga' in July. These are mulched to control weeds, and blossoms and runners are removed as they appear to produce a plant that has two or three branches of the crown when growth stops in the fall. Ten to twelve weeks before the fruit would normally ripen, a polyethylene tunnel or cloche is set over the plants. All that remains to be done is to water when necessary and roll up the cover on sunny days to provide ventilation and access for pollinating insects.

Any unusual crop can also be extremely profitable, provided you educate your customers to its value. The catalog of Nichols Garden Nursery (1190 North Pacific Highway, Albany, OR 97321; 25¢) is a treasure of such unusuals, especially European and Oriental vegetables.

If you have the special conditions they require and can develop a market for them, two very unusual and profitable crops are wild rice and cattails. Wild rice currently retails for about $5 to $6 a pound, and growers harvest several hundred pounds per acre. This highly nutritious grain grows well in the northern three quarters of the country in ponds and streams. A naturally low, wet spot is easily made suitable by erecting soil dikes to maintain a 6″ to 12″ depth of water. The seed is sown in midspring, and the crop is harvested in late summer. A source of seed is Game Food Nurseries (Omro, WI 54963; catalog $1). Cultural information is available from the Cooperative Extension Service, University of Minnesota (St. Paul, MN 55101).

You don't need waterfront land to raise the highest priced farm crop, wild rice — it can be grown on a small scale in gardens over much of the country. (*U.S. Department of Agriculture*)

Cattails, also known as reed mace, flags, bulrushes and Cossack asparagus, have been called America's greatest native food plant. The young stalks in early spring can be used in salads, boiled, creamed or added to soups and stews. Later in spring, the ripe golden male flower is delicious cooked like corn on the cob, or if allowed to ripen, its protein-rich pollen can be gathered in a bag as "pollen flour" for cakes and pancakes. But it is the rhizome, which is harvested from the mud with a potato rake from October to April, that is the great food producer. The sprouts growing from it are a wonderful "winter asparagus," and the core of the rhizome is used like potatoes or better yet, dried and ground to make a flour that is higher in protein than corn flour and higher in minerals than corn, wheat or rice flour.

Cattails will yield up to 30 tons of flour per acre. Although they grow naturally in marshes and wetlands, they are a good farm and garden crop, easily grown on any low, wet site or on upland sites with irrigation, says Professor L. C. Marsh of Oswego State College (Oswego, NY 13126). Cattails are a perennial crop, for no matter how efficiently the rhizomes are harvested, enough always remain in the soil to produce an excellent crop the next year.

Another potential source of income are wild plants that can be domesticated. Some weeds actually make good garden and farm crops. Why not be the first in your area to offer postelein, a spinach-like vegetable popular in European markets — it's nothing more or less than our common weed purslane. Like the dandelion, it thrives in dry, sunny plantings. Equally easy to grow is the edible variety of burdock, called "gobo" in Japan. The young shoots of lamb's-quarters are delicious in salads, steamed or creamed. Many people relish the young shoots of pokeweed, too (but the older shoots, leaves and roots should not be harvested as they contain a poisonous alkaloid). Milkweed's pink-tipped early shoots are a treat cooked like asparagus, and the young pods are used like okra.

Many less well known wild plants are worthy of domestication. Dr. William G. Dore of Canada's Plant Research Station (Ottawa, Ontario), for example, recommends the ground-bean, a weedy native vine that bears underground "beans" which are delicious raw, cooked or dried. An organization recently formed to investigate the food potential of all plants is the International Association for Education, Development and Distribution of Lesser Known Food Plants and Trees (Box 599, Lynwood, CA 90262).

------------------------------ Sidelining ------------------------------

A greenhouse, if it's large enough, presents several opportunities for cash income. Besides greens, tomatoes, some of the root crops and others which are easily grown for winter vegetable sales, a valuable line is vegetable seedlings and bedding plants for gardeners who want to get an early start in spring. Tomato and pepper plants rank highest in demand in vegetables, while petunias, impatiens, begonias, marigolds and geraniums are the top sellers in flowers. But don't restrict your production to these — try others in small numbers and see how they sell. Always grow the best (which aren't necessarily the very newest) varieties, and advertise their advantages as persuasively as you do the crops on your summer stand. In flowers, incidentally, you might want to consider some biennials and perennials, which are started in midsummer and wintered over in a coldframe for spring sales.

If you decide to go into this kind of project in a big way, perhaps even erecting temporary plastic greenhouses and marketing to a garden center or other outlet, get the best handbook on the subject, the 516-page second edition of *Bedding Plants: A Manual on the Culture of Bedding Plants as a Greenhouse Crop*, edited by John W. Mastalerz (Pennsylvania Flower Growers, 103 Tyson Building, University Park, PA 16802; $8).

Another "growing" opportunity is the small nursery. Demand for trees and shrubs for home and public landscaping has never been higher. Growing them from seed takes very little work and time, and woody plants double in value every two years or less. Here again, investigate the demand first, grow only the best varieties, and test one or two species not commonly grown in your area but outstanding in some way. If you have expert knowledge of a certain group of plants, it may pay you to specialize and sell by mail. Gardeners have built sizable businesses growing rare dwarf conifers, fine varieties of fruit trees or grapevines, lilacs, rhododendrons and others.

An extension of this idea is selecting or breeding improved plants. There's a great need for new and better plants for both food and landscaping. In your own garden and wherever you go, be on the lookout for plants that are superior in any way, that are untouched by a pest that attacks other plants of the same species, or that have larger flowers or fruits, unusual foliage coloration, greater hardiness or any other valuable trait.

Breeding superior characteristics into a species is an even more fascinating avocation, but it requires good knowledge of the plant and of the hybridizing work that has already been done with it — plus a great deal of patience in the case of woody plants. But the financial rewards can be high. The Plant Variety Protection Act gives a "plant inventor" the exclusive right to reproduce his discovery for 17 years. He can market it himself, sell the patent rights to others, or license the rights on a royalty basis. A booklet, *Questions and Answers Concerning Plant Patents*, is obtainable from the Commissioner of Patents (Washington, DC 20231). Also useful is *Breeding Plants for Home and Garden*, Handbook 75 of the Brooklyn Botanic Garden (Brooklyn, NY 11225; $1.75).

If you have a sizable area of woodland on your property, the timber may be of value, but it will take careful management and harvesting. Consult your state forester, and get Farmer's Bulletin 2187, *Managing the Family Forest*, 30¢ from Superintendent of Documents (Washington, DC 20402). A small woodlot may supply surplus firewood for sale, or white birch logs that people like for decorating their fireplaces, or bittersweet, bayberry, holly and mistletoe for holiday wreaths and swags.

Late winter is sugaring time, and many
trees besides the sugar maple have sweet
sap that can be boiled down to make syrup.
(*Sugar Bush Supplies Company*)

Maple sugaring is big business over much of the northern part of the country, but this profitable late-winter occupation need not be confined to its traditional areas nor to the traditional sugar maple. Norway, silver, red, Oregon and other maples also yield sweet sap, and so do birches, black walnut and butternut. Most hardy hardwoods, in fact, reputedly produce sap that makes syrup with distinctive flavors, so it's worth experimenting. Tapping does not harm the trees.

Only simple equipment is needed. A ⅜″ hole is drilled 2″ to 2½″ deep, slanting slightly upward. Any rigid tube can serve as the spout or "spile" — an elderberry or sumac stem with the pith pushed out is fine. The sap is collected in a jar, can or pail. Several spiles and large containers are needed for big trees, which can yield several gallons of sap a day. Boil it down over an outdoor fire if possible, since it takes about 40 gallons of sap to make 1 gallon of syrup, and the other 39 gallons of moisture could peel the paint and wallpaper from your kitchen. Use shallow pans, and when a candy thermometer registers 219°, the syrup has the right consistency. To make sugar, continue boiling until it reaches 236°, then beat until it starts to thicken, and pour into molds. A supplier of professional equipment is the Sugar Bush Supplies Co. (Box 1107, Lansing, MI 48904).

A "sweetening" crop that can be grown in the garden, incidentally, is sweet sorghum or sorgho. A small patch of this sugarcane-like plant will yield enough sorghum molasses for a family, a quarter acre will give plenty for sale. Sorghum is easily grown in rows like corn, and many varieties are available — one of the best for the North is 'Sugar Drip' (R. H. Shumway, Rockford, IL 61101). To make the syrup, the stalks are chopped, with the leaves removed, by hand or in a shredder-grinder, then squeezed in a cider press. The liquid is boiled down like maple syrup, skimming off the nonsugar materials that float to the top. The seeds in the big tassels at the tops of the stalks can be threshed out and ground into flour. Homesteader Gene Logsdon recommends sorghum flour, mixed 2 parts to 1 part of regular flour, for pancakes, cookies and bread.

For most garden-homesteaders, bees are the most practical source of sweets for the family and for sales. Keeping bees is fun, with the proper equipment there is little danger of being stung, and honey is a more delicious and nutritionally better sweetener than refined sugar. Beekeeping does not require a large investment, and takes only eight hours work a year per hive. Excellent information is found in *Beekeeping for Beginners,* Bulletin G-158, 30¢ from the Superintendent of Documents (Washington, DC 20402) and in the catalogs of suppliers such as the A. I. Root Co. (Medina, OH 44256), Dadant & Sons (Hamilton, IL 62341) and Walter T. Kelley Co. (Clarkson, KY 42726).

With very little human help, bees make
nature's finest sweetener — a premium
product for your table or to sell. (*Dadant &
Sons, Inc.*)

A few more ideas for earning extra money: collecting organic
matter and making compost for sale to gardeners . . . raising earthworms for fishing and soil improvement . . . renting garden plots,
with the soil prepared for planting, to people who don't have space
to grow their own vegetables . . . producing seed of unusual crops
and selling them by mail . . . if you have a large pond, stocking it
with fish and letting people catch all they want at a flat rate per
pound . . . tool sharpening, or repairing garden machinery . . . and
tilling gardens for others.

Products and services, of course, don't always have to be exchanged for money. The old-time barter system that was so important in the last century works very well today, too. Surplus crops
and your time and labor can be exchanged with neighbors on an
as-available basis or arranged in advance. Cooperative purchasing of machinery and supplies is another good idea — it can save
money, make possible the purchase of otherwise unaffordable
equipment, and keep machinery from standing around idle.

Cottage Crafts

Many crafts fit in beautifully with food production activities.
Often the raw materials are a by-product of these activities, and

usually craft work can be done in the winter when the garden demands little time.

A couple in Kentucky raises Angora rabbits, spins yarn from their fur and dyes it with dyes they make from plants, and sells the yarn at $3 an ounce, handmade garments at $50 to $150 — and the rabbits produce valuable manure for the garden and meat for the table. Even dyeing purchased yarn can be profitable (read *Natural Plant Dyeing,* Handbook 72, Brooklyn Botanic Garden, Brooklyn, NY 11225; $1.75).

Another homesteader makes unusually handsome birdhouses from home-grown gourds. Custom-made basketry fences woven of birch and willow whips from the woodland are an Ohioan's specialty. Beautiful furniture and carvings are made from old fruit and nut trees by a homesteader who collects apple, pear, cherry, plum and walnut logs and branches and seasons them in a dark, dry cellar for up to a year (Albert Constantine and Son, 2052 Eastchester Avenue, Bronx, NY 10461, sells many woodworking tools and books). A gardener who loves herbs has a thriving business making sachets, pomanders, catnip-filled toys for cats, and giant

The Soil Conservation Service and state fisheries provide assistance in stocking and managing ponds to produce large crops of fish. (*Soil Conservation Service*)

"tea bags" of mixed herbs for herbal baths, which she sells both wholesale and retail.

Sometimes a craft can become big business. For many years, the hobby of Jafie Brannin (3535 St. Germaine Court, St. Matthews, KY 40207) was trying to make improved garden tools. Recently he patented his Vegetender, a sort of angled knife blade on the end of a hoe handle. It weeds better and easier than a hoe, and is also ideal for digging, edging and many other uses. A major manufacturer of garden products is now putting the Vegetender on the market.

Cottage industries are appearing everywhere. Once traditional in New England, Appalachia and parts of the Midwest, they're now springing up in every state. Generally they are based on handicrafts such as pottery, weaving, rug-making and woodworking, but the same approach is working well with many types of light industry. There's a new trend toward group- or community-owned sawmills, chick hatcheries, smokehouses, grist mills and refrigerator lockers, and small factories that make anything from tool handles to toys from local raw materials are being seen more and more.

Every person has at least several talents, and putting them to work in an individual or group enterprise produces greater satisfaction and security than can be found in working for a big and impersonal corporation. The consumer benefits, too, for the smaller the business, the higher the quality of its product.

In setting up a communal cottage industry, remember that while its organization can be quite flexible, it's important to have definite rules covering investment, working hours, overall authority and so on, to keep it operating smoothly.

—— Getting Your Goat (Or Chickens, Rabbits, Etc.) ——

To many of us, being able to produce our own pure eggs, milk and meat is one of the best reasons for getting back to the land. In commercial production, livestock and poultry are raised at high speed with stimulating chemicals, hormones and antibiotics, none of which add to the quality or wholesomeness of the product. For a small expenditure of time, you can have a finer product, and at considerable savings. The only drawback to keeping animals and poultry is that it ties you down. They need daily attention, and family vacations are out unless you can work a cooperative arrangement with another homesteader.

The details of raising all kinds of home livestock are given in many of the excellent manuals noted in the Appendix, so we'll just mention a few points here that may be helpful in deciding what you want to raise.

For most people, goats are a better choice than a cow. Goat milk is more nutritious, and goats need less pasture, hay and grain. A small shed is adequate for housing them (but they need stronger and higher fencing than a cow). Their milk production is less, about 4 to 7 quarts daily for two goats compared to 10 to 15 quarts from a cow, but this should be adequate for the average family's milk, butter and cheese consumption. Goat manure is a very rich fertilizer-soil conditioner, much higher in nitrogen than cow manure. Goat meat, called chevon, is considered a delicacy by many people.

A dozen laying hens will give you plenty of eggs, and if you choose an all-purpose breed like the Rhode Island Red or Plymouth Rock, you'll have broilers and fryers as well. It's generally best to start with day-old chicks, for which you'll need a brooder (which can be as simple as an inverted box with a small heater). Housing can consist of any windowed structure that is not drafty or damp and that allows 4 to 5 square feet of floor area per bird. Nests, roosts, food hoppers and waterers are not expensive, and if you can grow some greens and grains the cost of a dozen eggs or a pound of chicken will be at least 50% below store prices.

A goat is easier to feed, house and handle than a cow, and its milk is actually more healthful. (*Organic Gardening and Farming*)

For a few minutes' work a day, a small flock
of an all-purpose breed of chickens will
supply both eggs and meat. (*Organic
Gardening and Farming*)

Ducks, geese and quail are three more birds ideally suited to the
small property. Pekin and Muscovy ducks are excellent for meat;
Khaki Campbell and Indian Runner produce eggs as efficiently as
chickens. Their housing needs are about the same as those of
chickens, and a pond isn't necessary; a sunken basin or trough in
the yard is ample. Geese take even less care than ducks, requiring
only rudimentary shelter in the worst winter weather and subsist-
ing on grass and weeds most of the year. A flock is easily started
by buying fertile eggs and letting a hen hatch them.

If you'd like to raise a more exotic bird, consider quail. The
Pharaoh D-1 is a top producer of eggs and meat in captivity (information and birds are obtainable from Marsh Farms, 14232 Brook-
hurst, Garden Grove, CA 92643). You may even decide to go in for
squabs, guinea hens or pheasants — but above all, stay away from
turkeys, which are probably the dumbest, most temperamental
and disease-prone birds on earth.

Rabbits are often called the ideal meat source, and for good reason. Two does and a buck will produce from 40 to 50 rabbits a
year, and they can be eaten as fryers at 10 to 12 weeks of age or
allowed to grow larger for eating at 7 or 8 months. Some breeds,
such as Flemish Giant and New Zealand, grow up to 20 pounds
and are best suited to a large family's table. Rabbits need only a

simple cage or hutch with some heat in the coldest weather. Good quality hay, greens, root crops and fresh vegetable residues like corn husks and pea shells make up their diet. Rabbits are very inexpensive to feed, making them the most profitable meat you can produce. Rabbit tastes something like chicken, and is low in fats and calories. *Domestic Rabbit Production,* by George S. Templeton (Countryside Publications, Route 1, Box 239, Waterloo, WI 53594; $7.95) is the best manual available.

The modern pig is the most efficient feed-to-food-and-manure converter ever bred. Garden wastes, root crops and kitchen scraps, plus grain and a mineral supplement, will bring an eight-week-old pig bought in April up to 200 pounds by December. This is the easiest way to produce a supply of pork for a family of four. Buy from a reputable breeder, selecting a long, lean, short-legged piglet to get an animal that will make high-quality meat and not too much lard. An open-front shed is all that is needed for shelter.

A few sheep are worthwhile if you have a good pasture — an acre will carry two ewes and their lambs — and can supply or procure clover, alfalfa or soybean hay for the winter. They will fatten well on only 100 pounds of grain per sheep per year. Shelter needs are the same as for pigs. If you choose a so-called medium-wool breed, which produces both good meat and good wool, you can spin yarn and dye it with plant dyes for bonus income.

The New Life-Support Systems

The most exciting idea to come to fruition in the last quarter of this century will be the "ecological house." A number of new-old and brand new technologies are coming together to make the self-sufficient, nonpolluting home a reality.

All or much of the home's heat and hot water will be supplied by solar panels. A windmill and solar cells will produce its electricity. Water will come from a well and a roof collection system. An attached greenhouse will help to heat the house and may be used for hydroponic culture of vegetables. The crops will be fed with liquid nutrients from the eco-house's waste digestion plant, which employs digestors and algae tanks to produce both fertilizer solution and methane gas for cooking.

These concepts are not only practical, they're already being put to use. Such a house has been built in a suburb of London. Homes using some or all of these principles have been constructed in California, Massachusetts, Arizona and several other states. A gardener in West Virginia has built a four-bedroom home that derives 80% of its power and heating from solar, wind and methane production systems. In Millbrook, New York, the Research and Administration Building of the New York Botanical Garden's Cary

Arboretum uses solar energy for most of its heating, cooling and hot water needs. Grassy Brook Village, a 43-acre cluster development of 20 condominiums being built in Brookline, Vermont, will employ solar heating, wind power for generation of electricity and such energy-saving devices as roof gardens for extra insulation.

Hundreds of companies are tooling up to produce hardware for closed eco-systems that use energy supplied by the sun, wind and wastes. The leading American research organization in the field, the New Alchemy Institute (Box 432, Woods Hole, MA 02543), is developing technology that will enable a family to sustain itself in a suburban home with a small yard. The Institute has food production and solar and wind energy projects in Massachusetts, California, Prince Edward Island, Costa Rica and India. Its annual report, published as *The Journal of the New Alchemists,* describes new discoveries in low-technology life-support systems for small-scale use, systems that use a minimum of nonrenewable resources and do a minimum of harm to the environment.

Windmills, for example, are becoming practical through new rotor designs that tremendously increase their efficiency. Solar energy is tapped in many ways, most advantageously in geodesic dome greenhouses that grow both plants and fish. A pool in the New Alchemists' dome is stocked with an edible fast-multiplying African fish called tilapia. The water is circulated by a windmill and heated when necessary by a small solar heater. The fish live

A home-built methane digester will produce gas for cooking and heating from garden and household wastes. (*Organic Gardening and Farming*)

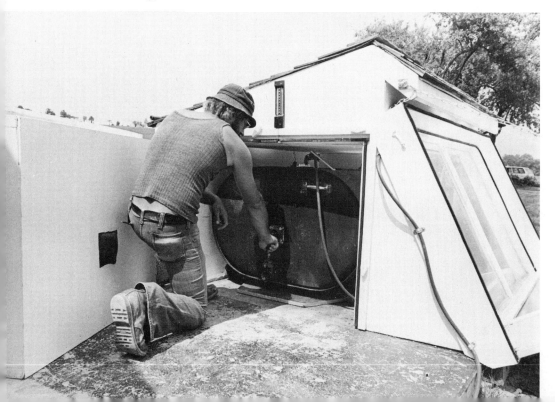

on algae which in turn are nourished by the wastes from the fish. These wastes are also used to fertilize the winter vegetables in the greenhouse, and up to 100% increases in yields have resulted.

The Institute has also perfected "solar fish ponds," clear plastic cylinders 5′ high and up to 5′ wide, that operate in any sunny indoor area. Algae grow abundantly in the light coming through the walls, and the system produces fish at the incredible rate of one for each gallon of water in the tank. High-yielding aquaculture has thus been made possible in the home.

Home production of methane gas is also being given much attention. Methane or "marsh gas" is produced in nature by the anaerobic (airless) decomposition of plants and animal wastes. Simple family-size methane digesters — a fancy name is bio-gas units — are easily fabricated from metal tanks or other containers. These are fed with animal and human manures, garbage and garden wastes, and the methane is piped into holding tanks for use in heating and cooking. The digested solids are removed periodically and applied to the garden as compost. Designs for digesters are found in *Methane Digesters,* Newsletter No. 3 of the New Alchemy Institute West (15 West Anapamu Street, Santa Barbara, CA 93101; $3).

Composting toilets that make compost from human wastes are already on the market. Developed in Sweden, some of these units also handle kitchen wastes. The process is anaerobic and totally odorless, and produces 60 pounds per person of high-analysis fertilizer–soil conditioner per year. This is easily removed from a storage tank. The best-known unit, the Clivis Multrum (Clivis Multrum, Inc., 14 Eliot Street, Cambridge, MA 02138), also saves the average family up to 40,000 gallons of water a year since it uses only one-half cup per flush.

An old-time appliance being brought up-to-date is the wood-burning stove. Wood is plentiful except in some of the central and western states, and highly efficient wood stoves are excellent for heating and cooking. A combination of a solar heating system and a wood stove often can supply the entire heating needs of a home even in the far North. The most efficient stoves are made of heavy gauge sheet metal, steel plate or cast iron, and are completely airtight and thermostatically controlled for top fuel economy. But even metal drums can be made into barrel stoves (kits are offered by Markade-Winnwood, Box 11382, Knoxville, TN 37919). The U.S. Forest Service's Northeast Experiment Station (6816 Market Street, Upper Darby, PA 19082) has free plans for a sawdust-burning stove, and also a booklet, *Enjoy Your Fireplace,* which gives the heat values of many woods.

A growing number of organizations are providing publications and courses on integrating all these new techniques and equipment into home systems. The Farallones Institute (15290 Coleman Valley Road, Occidental, CA 95465) maintains an Integral Urban Homestead and offers courses in Whole Life Systems. The widely acclaimed work of the Community Environmental Council (109 East de la Guerra Street, Santa Barbara, CA 93101) includes demonstration and educational activities on its Mesa Project, a polycultural farm and alternative energy research center. Many other such projects are described in *Self-Reliance*, the newsletter of the Institute for Local Self-Reliance (1717 18th Street, N.W., Washington, DC 20009), which serves as an invaluable clearinghouse of information as well as conducting its own research.

Three important how-to books on the new technologies are *Other Homes and Garbage*, by Leckie, Masters, Whitehouse & Young (Sierra Club Books, 530 Bush Street, San Francisco, CA 94108; $9.95) . . . *The Owner-Built Home*, by Ken Kern (Scribner's; $12.95 hardcover, $6.95 paperback) . . . and *The Owner-Built Homestead*, by Ken Kern (Owner-Builder Publications, Box 550, Oakhurst, CA 93644; $5).

--------------------------------- Free Enterprise ---------------------------------

Becoming a producer instead of a consumer is the theme of this book. This, of course, is going against the current of modern industrial society, but recent developments have made it apparent that the intricate and fragmented technology of an impersonal market economy has neither satisfied people's inner needs nor proved capable of dealing with global problems such as energy, food supply and the aspirations of emerging nations.

Some of the best minds of our age are saying that to survive we must forge a new structure, combining the best of the old with appropriate new low-energy technology. This new post-industrial society will be far more decentralized, with much less of the production, marketing and management concentrations that waste resources and frustrate the true needs of people.

The beginnings of this new society are already apparent. More and more individuals and families are starting to practice some form or aspect of the concept we call garden-homesteading. These are not dropouts from society, but rather people who have perceived that emphasis on consumption, on possessions and status, limits the quality of life. Their message is getting across to many others. Organic gardeners and farmers, environmental activists, recyclers, naturalists and the owner of a solar home are no longer regarded as cranks but as people who perhaps hold a clue to the creation of a more livable world.

If you believe that it's getting late, that disappearing resources, higher and higher energy costs and more and more waste and pollution are indications of disaster ahead, you're in good company. And you'll agree that it's time to make a move toward independence, toward making ourselves more food and energy self-sufficient. It's time to start fulfilling some of our basic needs directly instead of working ever harder to pay ever-increasing amounts of cash for food and goods produced in far-off places.

Doing it yourself, growing and building your own to whatever extent you can, is the truest form of free enterprise. The sense of satisfaction and the very real security it confers may well be the most vital elements of a happier life.

☙ Appendix ☙
Sources and Resources

THERE ARE SEVERAL outstanding sources of information and help on growing-your-own and garden-homesteading: the U.S. Department of Agriculture, four periodicals, three publishers and specialist book dealers, and a number of old and new books which are or will become classics. You'll find each and every one of these, at one time or another, indispensable for general learning or specific guidance.

——————— The U.S. Department of Agriculture ———————

The national and local offices of the USDA and its agencies such as the Soil Conservation Service are a basic, constantly available resource. The *List of Available Publications of the USDA*, 45¢ from the Superintendent of Documents (Washington, DC 20402), describes bulletins on everything from growing asparagus to building a barn. More specific information for local conditions is found in the publications of the Cooperative Extension Service in each state.

The County Extension Agent, headquartered in the Cooperative Extension Service office in each county, can assist with almost any agricultural or horticultural problem you have. If he doesn't know the answer, he will refer your query to other experts at the office or to state or national USDA services. For lists of state publications, the address of the County CES office, etc., write your state Cooperative Extension Service at the following addresses:

Alabama: Auburn University, Auburn, Al 36830

Alaska: University of Alaska, Fairbanks, AK 99701

Arizona: University of Arizona, Tucson, AZ 85721

Arkansas: University of Arkansas, Little Rock, AR 72203

California: University of California, Berkeley, CA 94720

Colorado: Colorado State University, Fort Collins, CO 80521

Connecticut: University of Connecticut, Storrs, CT 06268

Delaware: University of Delaware, Newark, DE 19711

Florida: University of Florida, Gainesville, FL 32601

Georgia: University of Georgia, Athens, GA 30601

Hawaii: University of Hawaii, Honolulu, HI 96822

Idaho: University of Idaho, Moscow, ID 83843

Illinois: University of Illinois, Urbana, IL 61801

Indiana: Purdue University, Lafayette, IN 47907

Iowa: Iowa State University, Ames, IA 50010

Kansas: Kansas State University, Manhattan, KS 66502

Kentucky: University of Kentucky, Lexington, KY 40506

Louisiana: Louisiana State University, Baton Rouge, LA 70803

Maine: University of Maine, Orono, ME 04473

Maryland: University of Maryland, College Park, MD 20742

Massachusetts: University of Massachusetts, Amherst, MA 01002

Michigan: Michigan State University, East Lansing, MI 48823

Minnesota: University of Minnesota, St. Paul, MN 55101

Mississippi: Mississippi State University, State College, MS 39762

Missouri: University of Missouri, Columbia, MO 65201

Montana: Montana State University, Bozeman, MT 59715

Nebraska: University of Nebraska, Lincoln, NE 68503

Nevada: University of Nevada, Reno, NV 89507

New Hampshire: University of New Hampshire, Durham, NH 03824

New Jersey: Rutgers University, New Brunswick, NJ 08903

New Mexico: New Mexico State University, Las Cruces, NM 88001

New York: Cornell University, Ithaca, NY 14850

North Carolina: North Carolina State University, Raleigh, NC 27607

North Dakota: North Dakota State University, Fargo, ND 58102

Ohio: Ohio State University, Columbus, OH 43210

Oklahoma: Oklahoma State University, Stillwater, OK 74074

Oregon: Oregon State University, Corvallis, OR 97331

Pennsylvania: Pennsylvania State University, University Park, PA 16802

Rhode Island: University of Rhode Island, Kingston, RI 02881

South Carolina: Clemson University, Clemson, SC 29631

South Dakota: South Dakota State University, Brookings, SD 57006

Tennessee: University of Tennessee, Knoxville, TN 37901

Texas: Texas A&M University, College Station, TX 77843

Utah: Utah State University, Logan, UT 84321
Vermont: University of Vermont, Burlington, VT 05401
Virginia: Virginia Polytechnic Institute, Blacksburg, VA 24061
Washington: Washington State University, Pullman, WA 99163
West Virginia: West Virginia University, Morgantown, WV 26506
Wisconsin: University of Wisconsin, Madison, WI 53706
Wyoming: University of Wyoming, Laramie, WY 82070

Periodicals

The Avant Gardener, Box 489, New York, NY 10028; twice-monthly, $10 a year

Country Journal, 139 Main Street, Brattleboro, VT 05301; monthly, $12 a year

Mother Earth News, Box 70, Hendersonville, NC 28739; bi-monthly, $10 a year

Organic Gardening and Farming, Emmaus, PA 18049; monthly, $7.85 a year

Publishers and Booksellers

Garden Way Publishing, Charlotte, VT 05445 — a wide range of books on growing, building, energy sources, etc., and its Classic Reprint Series includes the famous Country Bookstore Bulletins by Ed and Carolyn Robinson, creators of the "Have-More Plan," and also the *Starting Right* series on homestead livestock.

Mother's Bookshelf, Box 70, Hendersonville, NC 28739 — a dealer offering a great variety (about 500 titles) of the latest self-sufficiency books, plus classics such as Smith's *Tree Crops: A Permanent Agriculture* and Aldo Leopold's *A Sand County Almanac*.

Rodale Press, Emmaus, PA 18049 — currently the largest publisher of new books on all aspects of natural gardening, homesteading and health. Some of its best books are *The Encyclopedia of Organic Gardening; Organic Plant Protection; Homesteading; Stocking Up; Low-Cost, Energy-Efficient Shelter* and *The City People's Book of Raising Food*.

Books

Buying Country Property, by Herb Moral (Garden Way Publishing; $3)

Cloudburst: A Handbook of Rural Skills and Technology, edited by Vic Marks (Cloudburst Press, Box 79, Brackendale, B.C., Canada; $4.50)

The Compleat Farmer, compiled from fifty years of *The American Agriculturist* (Universe Books, 381 Park Avenue South, New York, NY 10016; $6.95)

The Complete Homesteading Book, by David E. Robinson (Garden Way Publishing; $5.95)

Country Comforts: The New Homesteader's Handbook, by Christine Bruyere and Robert Inwood (Drake Publishers, 381 Park Avenue South, New York, NY 10016; $6.95)

Country Women: A Handbook for the New Farmer, by Jeanne Tetrault and Sherilyn Thomas (Doubleday; $6.95)

Farming for Self-Sufficiency, by John and Sally Seymour (Schocken Books, 200 Madison Avenue, New York, NY 10016; $7.50)

First-Time Farmer's Guide, by William Kaysing (Straight Arrow Books, 625 Third Street, San Francisco, CA 94107; $7.95)

Five Acres and Independence, by M. G. Kains (Dover Publications, 180 Varick Street, New York, NY 10014; $2.50)

Flight From The City, by Ralph Borsodi (Harper & Row; $1.95)

Grow It!, by Richard W. Langer (Avon; $3.95)

Homesteading: A Practical Guide to Living Off the Land, by Patricia Crawford (Macmillan; $3.95)

Living The Good Life, by Helen and Scott Nearing (Schocken Books, 200 Madison Avenue, New York, NY 10016; $4.95)

One Acre and Security, by Bradford Angier (Random House; $2.45)

The Up-Dated Whole Earth Catalog, edited by Stewart Brand (Random House; $6)

Two Acre Eden, by Gene Logsdon (Doubleday; $5.95)

❧ Index ❧